THE NEW TOTALITARIAN TEMPTATION

TODD HUIZINGA

THE NEW TOTALITARIAN TEMPTATION

GLOBAL GOVERNANCE AND THE CRISIS OF DEMOCRACY IN EUROPE

ENCOUNTER BOOKS

NEW YORK · LONDON

CONTENTS

For Vici, Philip, Nicholas and Sarah

INTRODUCTION:
UNDERSTANDING THE EU

This is a book about the European Union, an organization that is exceedingly opaque, dauntingly complex and full of mutually opposing currents and interests. It is not surprising that the EU is poorly understood. But a grasp of the EU is necessary in order to understand international affairs, the global economy and the world's most important alliance – the transatlantic alliance between North America and Europe. This book is not an "EU for Dummies;" nor is it a handbook that would explain the bureaucratic machinery of the EU institutions, or the technicalities of the EU treaties. Rather, it is a sketch of the EU's essence: what kind of organization the EU is, how it is understood by those who are committed to the European idea, what its reason for being is.

Current events have made it more crucial than ever to understand what makes the EU tick. What are the ideological roots of the eurozone crisis? Why do so many EU leaders seem willing to risk exposing their people to more jihadist terror and to invite a potentially unmanageable de-Westernization of Europe by opening the floodgates to immigrants from a burning Middle East? And finally, what does all of this imply for the United States and Europe, the transatlantic alliance, and the world at large?

In dealing with these questions, this book is meant to sound an alarm. It is written out of great admiration for Europe, in the hope that Europe's postwar democracies and the Western idea of self-government rooted in truth will not be lost to a new ideology – the soft-utopian ideology of global governance that has become the EU's driving force.

THE SOFT UTOPIA OF GLOBAL GOVERNANCE

The European Union, rising from the ruins of two devastating world wars, embodies a longing for a world of peace, prosperity and stability. It is more than just a free-trade area, a customs union or an international organization through which the member states pursue their national interests. It is meant to be the harbinger of a new era, in which a cosmopolitan and harmonious Europe provides the model for a worldwide system of supranational governance. In this new world order, power is to be wielded not primarily by national governments on behalf of national electorates, but by an ever-thickening web of international organizations administering a growing body of international law and regulation, purportedly in the interests of a global citizenry.

The EU is, in effect, a "soft utopia," engendered in the birthplace of the "hard utopias," the antihuman ideologies that led to immense misery, death and ruin in the twentieth century. Unlike the hard utopias of communism and fascism, the EU has no political prisons or secret police. Despite its own deficiency of democratic legitimacy, it has helped foster the worldwide spread of democracy, free markets and the rule of law since its inception. Like communism and fascism, however, it is in essence a utopia – a political construct that seeks humankind's ultimate purpose in a better-than-possible world created by politics. It puts politics before people, as it seeks to remake human beings in the service of its political project rather than to adapt the project to human beings as they are.

But the EU does not seek to realize its dream by force; it is too comfortable and too relativistic for that. The European idea itself remains amorphous, and its underlying ideology vague. There is nothing jagged or sharp-edged about the EU.

Despite the soft edges and vagueness, it is not impossible to delineate the EU and describe the essence of its soft utopia. The first thing to understand is that the EU cannot be defined in familiar categories, in the way that one could define the United States as a nation-state with a constitutional liberal democracy, for example, or the United Nations as a global international organization functioning as a forum for cooperation among its member states. The EU is *sui generis*. It is far more powerful than a traditional international organization, and its members are far more politically and economically integrated, but neither is it a European superstate. It is like nothing that has come before it, and, more than sixty years after the establishment of its first predecessor, the European Coal and Steel Community, the EU is still evolving, still in the process of becoming. And no one really has a particular end state in mind.

In fact, the EU has been in the process of becoming for so long that many believe the very essence of the EU is process – constant motion and change. Many commentators have said that the EU is "postmodern," not only in the sense that it heralds a new, peaceful world beyond the modern world of nation-states and balance-of-power politics, but also in the way it exemplifies process rather than outcome, diversity rather than singularity, dialogue and open-endedness rather than conclusion, becoming rather than being. If nothing else, the EU is a fascinating and quintessentially European mind game.

But when all the vagaries, blurred distinctions and fuzzy edges are stripped away, the EU is essentially the following: a constantly evolving union of twenty-eight Western and Central European nation-states in which the governing and intellectual elites, in the interest of realizing an unprecedented degree of peace, stability and prosperity, are pooling, and thus relinquishing, significant elements of the member states' national sovereignty, and doing so over the heads of their national electorates. The EU aspires to function as a model of global governance on a continental scale. Thereby, the most ambitious among the EU elites and acolytes aim to lead the way into a new world order in which wars will be unthinkable, or at least very rare.

Preventing war has been the noble obsession of the EU and its predecessor institutions from the beginning, since the European Coal and Steel Community (ECSC) was launched in 1952. Its members were Germany, France, Italy, Belgium, the Netherlands and Luxembourg. The essence of the ECSC was its supranational character. By vesting the ECSC with substantial authority over the coal and steel industries of its member states, the founders hoped to bind those states' economic interests together and thus foreclose the possibility of yet another war arising out of national rivalries, especially between France and Germany. The ECSC was also an elitist project. The general citizenry was not consulted.

The ECSC was supported and fostered by the United States, which had lost hundreds of thousands of young men fighting two brutal wars on the European continent, and which, as the postwar guarantor of the free world's cohesion, wanted to be sure that Germany and France would never go to war again. In fact, Americans were very active in pushing sometimes reluctant Europeans to support the ECSC. The United States would continue to be a significant engine promoting European integration, although the Americans, like the peoples of Europe itself, never understood exactly what it was they were supporting.

The ECSC was the first milestone on the long institutional road to the EU, which did not officially come into being until 1993. The immediate successor of the ECSC, the European Economic Community (EEC), was established in the Treaty of Rome in 1957. The treaty's preamble begins by expressing the signatories' determination "to lay the foundations of an ever closer union among the peoples of Europe."[1] The concept of "ever closer union" has been the primary motivating force of the EU ever since, and its careful formulation exemplifies three key characteristics of the EU: it is visionary and purposeful, but also vaguely defined.

With few exceptions, the most ideologically committed EU policymakers have always been visionaries. They have acted upon a vision of a Europe that would rise above the Europe of nation-states. Whether those nation-states would disappear into a European superstate, or continue to exist but be united through their common membership in a pan-European sovereign entity, the vision has always involved bringing about a radically new European order.

The vision is connected to a purpose. The EU's objective is to establish a permanent peace and preclude the possibility of war on the European continent. Thereby, the EU aims to function as a

model for – and thus help bring about – a global order of peace,
justice and stability.

Beyond the desire for peace and amity, the EU's vision and purpose are unclear. Just as the phrase "ever closer union" is vague and open-ended, the means of achieving this ever closer union and what it will look like when achieved are ill-defined, while the motives and the driving ideology remain amorphous. But this vagueness is strategic: it has served to maintain relatively constant forward movement toward realizing the vision, and has done so in a twofold way: (1) by bringing in governments and elites of diverse views and visions, while placating everyday citizens who would not accept a vision that gave a subordinate place to the nations and cultures to which they naturally rendered their primary allegiances; and (2) by preserving the EU's room to maneuver and evolve, even while no one really knew exactly what it was becoming.

The crucial importance to the soft utopia of remaining ill-defined can hardly be overstated. European elites themselves are engaged in a perennial debate that can be summarized as: What is the EU, and what do we want it to become? To dismiss this ongoing debate as merely European navel-gazing is fundamentally to misunderstand the EU.

The basic disagreement goes roughly as follows: Is the EU essentially a customs union, a single market and a forum to enhance political cooperation among sovereign nation-states, or is it something that will ultimately subsume within itself the bulk of the sovereignty and independence of its member states, thereby prefiguring a true system of global governance? This disagreement often plays out along national lines, because of the different histories, interests and cultural values of the various EU member states. Take the three largest member states as examples: Germany, France and the United Kingdom.

In Germany, the vision of a unified Europe transcending the Europe of nation-states has always exerted a strong attraction. The Germans, admirably, have been wrestling with their nation's history as the cradle of Nazism and the homeland of the perpetrators of the Holocaust for almost seventy years now. Patriotism has a bad name. It means something different to Germans than it does for perhaps any other nationality in the world. Even the general population of Germany – despite habitual grumbling about Brussels and a great unwillingness to be the payors of Greece and other eurozone members threatened with insolvency – is reflexively in favor of the European Union, and of giving up a significant degree of national sovereignty to the EU. In Germany, being a good person means being pro-EU, because being pro-EU is widely assumed to be synonymous with being pro-European and antinationalistic. Such a person has learned the moral lesson from Germany's horrible past. He shares in the passionate determination that war should never again arise from German soil.

The French have a different view of the EU. For many it is a vehicle to increase French influence in Europe and the world, to minimize the American footprint in Europe, and to give outlet, in the spirit of the French Revolution, to the ideals of liberty, equality and fraternity. The French also stand to benefit from the EU in a way that is ironically reminiscent of the old balance-of-power politics of nineteenth-century Europe: the EU binds their rival Germany, and serves as an instrument for France to bend Germany to its will. Thus, whereas the French sometimes seem almost as committed to the ideal of supranationality as the Germans, French culture and history and France's traditional rivalry with Germany militate for supranationality as a means to promote French interests and French national grandeur. In contrast, the Germans' dedication to supranationality functions as a renunciation of any and all attachment to German national greatness.

The typical British attitude toward the EU differs greatly from that of either the French or the Germans. The English value their singularity and their national sovereignty, based partly on geographic isolation from the daily affairs of the European continent. They take pride in their history as the oldest continuous democracy in the world, and in the achievements of the British Empire. With this history coloring their perspective, the British are generally more attuned than other Europeans to the EU's lack of democratic accountability, and they are more protective of their national sovereignty against encroachments from Brussels.

SUBORDINATING DEMOCRACY AND BENDING REALITY

In this book, we will engage in case studies that illustrate the EU's nature as a soft utopia. We will see how, in the dogged pursuit of a more integrated Europe, EU leaders have overridden the will of the voters, rewritten history in their own image, and subordinated the merits of fundamental policy decisions to the far-off and ill-defined goal of achieving the European dream.

First, we will look at five instances of voters rejecting comprehensive new EU agreements in referenda. The salient fact is not that the voters rejected these agreements, but how the EU responded to these votes. In three cases, in Ireland twice and in Denmark once, the EU refused to accept the will of the voters. Instead, it forced second votes and applied massive pressure so that the voters would "get it right" and vote yes. In the other two instances, the failed referenda in the Netherlands and France in 2005 on whether to accept the "European Constitution," the EU did not demand second referenda – because French and Dutch leaders had made unequivocal political commitments to accept the results, and because these votes occurred in larger and older member states with more weight in the EU. What the EU did to overcome the will of Dutch and French voters was simply make some cosmetic changes to the rejected agreement, rename it and get it passed as a treaty, which unlike a "European Constitution" did not require the approval of voters in most member states.

Second, the debate about whether to include a reference to Europe's Christian heritage in the EU constitution grew out of an attempt to rewrite Europe's history in the secularist image of the majority of EU enthusiasts. The attempt was successful – the draft constitution contained only a severely watered-down reference to Europe's "religious" roots.

Third, European monetary union, the introduction of the euro, is the most momentous example of a policy decision made not on its own merits, but in pursuit of the utopia of a politically integrated Europe. It defied basic economics to introduce a common currency to countries with radically varying levels of productivity and economic development. But the decision was taken, in the words of some of its most enthusiastic supporters, explicitly because they believed a common currency would prove unsustainable without political integration. Thus, it would ultimately force Europeans to accept a politically integrated EU. But that didn't happen. And with the 2008 global financial crisis that began in the United States and the ensuing sovereign debt crisis in the eurozone, economic reality asserted itself. Massive bailouts were necessary to avert sovereign default in Greece especially, but also in

Ireland, Portugal, Spain and Cyprus. As of this writing, the survival of the eurozone is by no means certain, regardless of encouraging words emanating from Frankfurt and Brussels.

Beyond the specific issues of a common currency and repeating referenda, the EU's utopian ideology affects all areas of policy and practice. The EU's approach to human rights is perhaps most emblematic in that, like the ideology of global governance, it is transformative and liberationist. The global governance movement seeks to transform the world by liberating peoples from their traditional primary allegiances to local communities and nation-states with a common history, culture, language and values. Likewise, the primary objective of the globalists' human rights advocacy is to liberate individuals from the mediating institutions, such as family and church, that are associated with traditional, community-based, locally rooted life and that imply an objective moral code based on an essentially unchanging human nature. In the globalists' view, human nature is malleable, and individuals should therefore be free to transform themselves, to define and redefine themselves as they wish, unfettered by community, tradition or inherited values.

The belief in the liberationist and transformative right to define oneself and to determine for oneself what it means to be human is especially apparent in the areas of LGBT rights, women's rights and children's rights.* The EU's approach to each of these priority areas kicks against the traces of traditional views on human nature and on the importance to the individual of deference to family and church and other time-honored institutions – especially those institutions that imply a commitment to an authoritative moral code revealed by God or transmitted through religious tradition, an acceptance of the limits of human knowledge and capability, and skepticism toward transformative globalist ideologies.

Neither the global governance movement nor the human rights movement associated with it accepts, in principle, any limits handed down by tradition or by the human experience of reality. Just as global governance, heralded by the EU, can bring about a

---

* "LGBT" is the abbreviation for "Lesbian, Gay, Bisexual and Transsexual." But the terminology in this arena is fluid. Sometimes, the term is expanded to "LGBTI" to include intersex people.

utopia of peace and prosperity for the human collective, so can
unlimited choice and absolute autonomy for individuals allow
every person to remake and redefine him- or herself at will. This
belief has clear implications for the classical rights, such as freedom of religion, which are based on an anthropology that is less
fluid and much more compatible with the idea of objective truth.
Thus, we will also examine the state of religious freedom and the
threats to it in today's European Union, especially the growing use
of antidiscrimination and hate-speech laws to suppress faith-
based views or practices that conflict with the EU's conception of
human rights.

THE TROUBLED WATERS OF TRANSATLANTIC RELATIONS

Unfortunately for the transatlantic alliance, and for the worldwide
spread of democracy and prosperity that the partners in the transatlantic alliance have worked so hard to realize, the EU's soft utopianism has profound implications for its relations with the United
States. In the short-to-medium term, appearances can be deceiv-
ingly placid. After all, the Europeans are our best friends in the
world. We are bound together by history and by commonalities in
our culture and values. But the Europeans can also be our most
tenacious antagonists. Anti-Americanism is an inevitable outgrowth
of the European idea. As the world's most powerful nation-state
and one that jealously guards its national sovereignty, the United
States by its very existence stands in the way of the EU vision of a
world that has evolved beyond the nation-state. The same goes for
Israel, which suffers unrelenting EU hostility largely because the
existence of a democratic and proud nation-state, and moreover a
country grounded in an essentially ethnoreligious view of nationhood, flies in the face of the EU's supranational, postreligious and
postethnic vision for the world. The fact that Israel dares to be
fundamentally Western and yet rejects much of the EU's perspective on the world inflames EU ire.

Naturally, fissures and imbalances are developing constantly
in the complex U.S.-Europe relationship. What has often gone
unnoticed is that many of the more serious tensions have resulted
from the fundamental contradiction between the United States' concern to safeguard its national sovereignty and the EU's advocacy of

global governance. This has been the key point of friction in the U.S.-EU dispute over the International Criminal Court. Even the near break between the United States and many EU member states over Iraq during the George W. Bush years had much more to do with this fundamental difference in worldview than most observers realize. Throughout the war on terror that began on September 11, 2001, many in Europe have opposed U.S. policy primarily on global governance grounds – they opposed the U.S. decisions to open the Guantanamo prison and to invade Iraq without a UN mandate, and they continue to oppose unilateral anti-terror actions by the Obama administration. Even as the civil war in Syria spreads to Europe in the form of an uncontrollable refugee influx and deadly terror attacks on European soil, a robust military involvement of EU forces other than the French in Syria appears unlikely to most and unthinkable to many.

Another enduring source of transatlantic tension is that the United States remains deeply shaped by traditionalist Christian faith, while secularism pervades Europe. Global governance and secularism are more closely connected than is immediately apparent, and this book will delve into the connection.

After pondering these aspects of soft utopia in the EU's past and present, we will turn to the EU's future. Today the EU is at a crossroads, having been shaken to its core by the eurozone crisis. Will the policy response meet with success? If so, it could prove to be a Great Leap Forward toward the soft utopian European dream. The policy response is now shaping up to be a transfer of an unprecedented level of sovereignty from the member states to the EU in the areas of banking policy and regulation, budgetary and fiscal policy, and economic governance. What does this mean for the European idea on the one hand, and for the EU's already considerable democratic deficit on the other hand?

Or will the policy response prove unfeasible? Will EU leaders continue to talk European unification, but inevitably, out of the nature of things, act in their own national interests? Currently, the UK is acquiescing to the EU's policy response to the eurozone crisis while declining to participate itself, being a nonmember of the eurozone. The British are talking seriously of repatriating powers that have previously been ceded to the EU, and might even withdraw from the organization. Could this mean that the EU will essentially break up, with the UK and perhaps others in its wake either limiting their participation in the EU to certain policy areas or leaving altogether?

In addition, there are portentous questions related to demography and migration, brought into stark relief by the migration crisis of 2015 and the terrorist attack on Paris in November. Will postwar European social democracy prove unsustainable given the demographic trends in Europe today? How will the EU cope with the unprecedented influx of migrants from a Middle East that is collapsing into chaos? Was the savage ISIS-inspired massacre of 130 innocent people in Paris only a foretaste of how a growing, strongly anti-Western Muslim population will change Europe? What are the implications of all this for the transatlantic alliance? Despite Europe's manifest problems, are the EU and its soft utopia winning the war of ideas even in the United States? These are the questions we will examine in our appraisal of the EU's future.

FILLING THE VOID

A final, crucial point about the European Union: the EU's global governance ideology grew partly as an answer to the devastation of European wars, but also in response to a spiritual void. In essence, it is post-Christian. The loss of a religious sense of purpose has left a hole in the European soul, which is being filled for many by a belief in the vision of supranational governance. In today's atheistic Europe, to put one's faith in global governance and a united Europe is often a subconscious attempt to recover the hope for redemption from this vale of tears, from the world as it is, without appealing to God. The soft utopia that is the EU might be considered the natural, almost inevitable face of Christendom gone apostate.

The resort to unrealistic secular dreams in the absence of religious purpose is doing tremendous damage to democracy and the rule of law. But it's not too late. With persistence and determination, the EU can be reformed. A democratic Europe of sovereign nation-states can be restored, and the United States and Europe together can renew the West's commitment to self-government.

PART ONE

DEFINING THE SOFT UTOPIA

CHAPTER 1:
SOMETHING COMPLETELY DIFFERENT

If you spend any time at all in Brussels, the de facto capital city of the European Union, you are bound to hear that the EU is *sui generis,* Latin for "the only one of its kind." The EU is unlike anything that came before it, and most definitely not to be understood as anything like an international organization in the usual sense of the term.

The uniqueness of the EU lies primarily in the degree of supranationalism it exhibits.* In fact, supranationalism has been

---

* It is important to distinguish the terms "international," "transnational" and "supranational." To quote John Fonte, "The term international is used mainly to denote relations among sovereign nation-states.... On the other hand, transnational means 'across' or 'beyond' nations ... the term signifies legal action and authority beyond national laws, constitutions, and officials. Transnational politics is activity directed at the internal political affairs of nation-states, undertaken by both foreign and domestic non-state actors and by foreign states.... Supranational means 'above' or 'over' the nation-state. While advocates of transnational law are sometimes ambiguous about respect for national sovereignty, those who champion supranational law are more explicit about their aim to transfer decision-making authority (sovereign self-government) from the nation-state to global institutions, superior to any national institution." Fonte, *Sovereignty or Submission: Will Americans Rule Themselves or Be Ruled by Others?* (New York: Encounter Books, 2011), xxiii–xxiv. The EU could its primary distinguishing feature and the overriding ideal of its acolytes ever since the creation of the EU's first direct institutional forerunner, the European Coal and Steel Community. In their joint declaration upon signing the Treaty of Paris to establish the ECSC on April 18, 1951, the six signatory ministers said:

> In signing the Treaty establishing the European Coal and Steel Pool… the Contracting Parties have given proof of their determination to set up the first supra-national institution and thus to lay the real foundations of an organized Europe.
>
> All European countries are free to participate in such an organized Europe. We sincerely hope that other nations will associate themselves with our efforts.[1]

WHAT THE EU IS NOT

The EU's uniqueness comes out in sharp relief when one compares it with other international organizations that might seem at first glance to be similar. What sets the EU apart is the ceding of significant sovereign powers of the member states to the EU itself, as embodied in its institutions.

Take the Organization of American States (OAS), for example. Like the EU, the OAS is a regional organization. Its member states span the Americas, from Chile and Argentina in the south to Canada in the north. Similarly, the EU's member states span most of Europe, from Spain and Cyprus in the south to Sweden and Finland in the north. The EU boasts twenty-eight member states and the OAS includes thirty-five member states. Both have common institutions, and the OAS member states, like the EU member states, make declarations and cooperate on economic and political affairs.

But after that, the differences begin to outweigh the similarities. The OAS is an international organization of sovereign member states, in which national governments of the Western Hemisphere come together to discuss issues and solve problems in their mutual

---

be characterized as either a transnational or a supranational organization, depending on the context. The vision of the global governance advocates in the EU is a supranational future for the EU and the world.

national interests. OAS members do not give up any sovereignty when they join. In fact, Article 1 of the OAS Charter explicitly stresses the member states' sovereignty and expressly forbids the organization from intervening in their internal affairs.[2] Of course, there are inevitable attempts to hijack the OAS in the service of political agendas that cannot be achieved in the member states by democratic means, notably having to do with LGBT rights and "sexual and reproductive health,"[3] but this does not change the basic nature of the OAS as an international organization of sovereign member states, rather than a supranational organization like the EU in which member states pool their sovereignty.

Many people think of the EU as essentially an economic entity based on a free-trade agreement, perhaps like the United States, Canada and Mexico under the North American Free Trade Agreement (NAFTA). This impression may derive from the name of the predecessor organization of the EU, the European Economic Community (EEC), or from concepts such as the single market and the European Monetary Union, which gave birth to the euro.

Certainly the EU is, in part, an economic entity. Like NAFTA, it is a free-trade bloc. But it is much more than that. The EU is also a customs union. And this entails closer, more restrictive ties than free trade, as Daniel Hannan, a British Conservative member of the European Parliament, explains: "A customs union involves internal free trade, but also a common external tariff. Its members surrender their separate commercial policies, and give up the right to sign trade agreements. Instead, trade negotiations are conducted, and treaties signed, by the bloc as a whole."[4]

Beyond this, most of the EU member states are united by a common currency. Nineteen of the twenty-eight member states share the euro. Most of the other nine member states aspire to have it in the future, but they do not yet meet the qualifications for the eurozone. These are mostly countries that were communist satellites of the Soviet Union, with planned economies. They are still developing as free markets and are expected to join the eurozone when they qualify. The only countries in the EU that qualify for the euro but freely choose (for now) not to join are the United Kingdom, Denmark and Sweden.

The EU, as we have seen, differs from international organizations such as the OAS and from free-trade areas such as NAFTA mainly in that the member states of the EU have relinquished substantial aspects of their sovereign powers to the EU institutions. In this respect, the EU is not just an economic entity but also a profoundly political one. It is better described not as an international organization, but as a *supranational* or at least a *transnational* organization, with "managing" institutions to which the member states have transferred considerable powers. The principal five EU institutions are the European Commission, the Council of the European Union, the European Parliament, the European Council and the European Court of Justice.

The European Commission is the executive arm of the EU. It administers EU law and policy and enforces its implementation in the member states. It also possesses formidable legislative power, known as the "right of initiative." Under the EU treaties only the Commission can initiate legislation, other than under certain exceptional conditions.

The Council of the European Union is an institution in which the governments of the member states are represented by cabinet-level ministers, so it is also known as the Council of Ministers. The Council meets in multiple configurations, depending on the issue area. For example, the foreign ministers of EU member states meet once per month as the Foreign Affairs Council; environment ministers meet as the Environmental Affairs Council; economic and finance ministers meet as the ECOFIN Council; and so on. All in all, the Council of Ministers has ten configurations. Thus, while it is referred to in the singular, it is not really *one* council, but *ten* councils – a phenomenon that only the impenetrably complex EU could pull off. And although it is made up of ministerial-level officials of the executive branches of the member states, it primarily serves a quasi-legislative function within the European Union. In conjunction with the European Parliament, it reviews, amends and passes EU legislation as drafted by the Commission.

The European Parliament (EP) is a supranational legislature made up of 751 members who are elected by voters in their respective member states. The members of the European Parliament (MEPs) generally belong to a national political party in their respective member states. These parties join forces in EU-wide "political groups." For example, the center-right political group, the European People's Party, is made up of national Christian Democratic and Conservative parties from the member states. The center-left political group, the Progressive Alliance of Socialists and Democrats, is composed of Social Democratic and Socialist parties from the member states. There are similar political groups of Green parties, liberal parties, Euroskeptic conservative parties, and others. The European Parliament does not draft legislation; that is the sole prerogative of the European Commission. The EP does not have the power to levy taxes. Neither does the EP have MEPs belonging to a governing coalition and other MEPs representing the opposition, as in the parliaments of the member states, because there is no elected EU government and thus no opposition. So what does the European Parliament do? It amends legislation, along with the Council of Ministers, and its approval of legislation, along with the Council's, is necessary in most policy areas in order for it to become law. Importantly for the United States, the EP's assent is needed too for most international agreements that the EU wants to enter into. The EP also helps shape EU policies in areas such as foreign affairs and human rights, by writing reports, issuing declarations and resolutions, and carefully scrutinizing other EU actors' words and actions on those issues.

The European Council, not to be confused with the Council of the European Union described above nor with the Council of Europe (an organization that is separate and distinct from the European Union), is made up of the presidents and prime ministers of the EU member states. Headed by a president who is appointed by the member states and not a part of any member-state government, the European Council is the top decision-making body in the EU. It meets at least four times per year and sets EU policy at the highest level.

The European Council is the only EU institution that was established in practice rather than in a treaty.[5] Its beginning can be traced back to the Yom Kippur War of 1973 and the ensuing global energy crisis. In October 1973 a coalition of Arab states invaded territories that had been occupied by Israel since the 1967 Arab-Israeli war, thus igniting the Yom Kippur War. In quick succession came the war itself, Soviet threats of intervention, an American-brokered ceasefire, and the reduction of oil deliveries to the West by Arab oil-exporting nations, precipitating a global energy crisis. All of this happened with nary a peep from Europe. Acutely unsettled by their own insignificance, the leaders of the European Economic Community member states decided to meet more often so that Europe "could speak with one voice on important global issues."[6] Approximately a year later, in 1974, the new French president, Valéry Giscard d'Estaing, succeeded in establishing the European Council as a regular meeting of heads of state and government to decide authoritatively on the most important matters of foreign policy and European integration. Since then, the European Council has become the most important embodiment of what Luuk van Middelaar, an EU analyst and philosopher, calls the "in-between sphere."[7] In the European Council, leaders of EU member states do not represent just their own governments nor the EU itself, but become actors "in between" the two.

A final very important EU institution is the Court of Justice of the European Union (CJEU). Actually consisting of three distinct courts, the CJEU resembles the U.S. judiciary in that it functions like an independent branch of government, with the highest of its courts, the European Court of Justice (ECJ), analogous to the U.S. Supreme Court. It provides the final interpretation of the treaties and can declare EU legislation or actions in line with the treaties, thus clearing the way for their entry into effect, or out of line with the treaties, thus rendering them null and void. The judiciary has been a true motor of European integration, in having declared EU law to supersede the national law of the member states, and in having introduced the doctrine of direct effect, meaning that citizens of EU member states – since they are directly affected by EU legislation – can, as individuals, dispute the validity of a national law of their member state if they can show that it impinges on their rights under EU legislation. This was a game-changing step in the development of the EU into an organization whose decisions take precedence over member-state policy and law.[8]

THE EU'S MEMBER STATES

The EU has undergone a series of enlargements ever since the European Coal and Steel Community was established in 1952 with six founding members: Germany, France, Italy, the Netherlands,

Belgium and Luxembourg. Now it is easier to name the European countries that are *not* members of the EU. In Western Europe, the only nonmembers are Norway, Iceland and Switzerland, along with microstates such as Liechtenstein, Monaco and Andorra. In Central and Eastern Europe, west of the former Soviet Union, the only nonmembers are Albania and some of the countries that emerged out of Yugoslavia: Serbia, Kosovo, Macedonia, Bosnia-Herzegovina, Montenegro. These countries all desire to join, a desire that is shared by the EU but will not be realized for several years, perhaps decades. The former Yugoslav republic of Croatia is the newest member state, having joined on July 1, 2013. All of the former satellite states of the Soviet Union (which constituted the Warsaw Pact) are now EU members. Even three of the countries that used to be part of the Soviet Union itself are now in the EU, namely the Baltic states – Latvia, Lithuania, Estonia. EU membership is a distant possibility for other former Soviet republics – Ukraine, Moldova, Belarus; and perhaps even a possibility for Georgia, Armenia and Azerbaijan. Turkey is a unique case. It has officially enjoyed the prospect of membership since 1963, but the political and cultural barriers to membership posed by its authoritarian government and its largely Muslim population have so far been insuperable.

The process of joining the EU further illustrates its unique supranationality. In order to accede to the EU, a country must fulfill all of the requirements of the *acquis communautaire*, a French term roughly translatable as "that which the community has agreed upon." The *acquis* contains thirty-five chapters of EU regulation covering subjects as wide-ranging as taxation, education and culture, environmental policy, freedom of movement within the EU of goods, workers, services and capital, and many more. According to an estimate of the think tank Open Europe, the *acquis communautaire*, which it aptly defines as "the body of EU legislation which European companies, charities and individuals have to comply with," is more than 170,000 pages long.[9]

The long negotiations in which agreement is reached on how the aspiring EU member will fulfill all of the *acquis's* stipulations are very intrusive. The process involves EU monitoring of whether a country is actually implementing all of the *acquis*-mandated changes. Only upon unanimous agreement of the member states, and with the support of the European Commission, the European

Parliament and the Council of Ministers, is the way cleared for a candidate country to join. In the final steps, the candidate country and all of the EU member states sign and ratify the accession treaty. Clearly, any country that wants to join the EU pays a high price in national sovereignty. In order to be a part of the EU, each member state must fit the EU mold in terms of democracy, the economy, the rule of law, efficiency, and – it must be stressed – values and ideology.

WHAT IS THE EU?

The EU is not like the OAS or NAFTA, or any other international organization. It is a supranational organization exercising significant sovereign powers of its own that often trump the powers of the member states. EU law supersedes member-state national law, for example, and EU edicts and regulation affect everyday life in every member state.

Is the EU therefore comparable to a federal nation-state, such as the United States, with its members roughly equivalent to the fifty states? Some would say so, but the comparison is false. Unlike the United States, the EU cannot claim to have a citizenry with a common understanding of its national history and a sense of belonging to the same nation. "Europeans" persist in thinking of themselves first in national terms – as Italians, Dutchmen, Spaniards, Greeks, etc. – before they think of themselves as Europeans.[10] And this is not surprising. There is no European demos. Although ethnicities and languages do not track exactly with national borders, each European nation-state has its own long history, culture and self-understanding. There is no unifying language. The EU has twenty-four official languages. English is now the lingua franca, having replaced French at the latest in 2004, when ten new member states joined, mainly from Eastern Europe, where the second language of elites was generally English.

So what is the EU? To repeat what I said earlier, here is the best definition I can think of: the EU is a constantly evolving union of twenty-eight Western and Central European nation-states in which the governing and intellectual elites, in the interest of realizing an unprecedented degree of global peace, stability and prosperity, are pooling, and thus relinquishing, significant elements of the member states' national sovereignty, and doing so over the heads of their national electorates.

But as we will see in the following chapter, to try to define the EU is to go out on a limb and risk being sawed off. There is a caveat to everything one could attempt to say about the EU. On the one hand, the essence of the EU is supranationalism. But what does it mean to be supranational in an organization in which the member states jealously but inconsistently and confusedly – sometimes in deed but not in word and sometimes in word but not in deed – guard their national prerogatives? Because of this unresolved conflict, and as a tactical response to it, the essence of the EU is also to have no definable essence: to exist in the "in-between-ness" described earlier. The constant change, uncertainty and flux of postmodernity are integral features of the EU.

To paraphrase Gertrude Stein, the EU is the EU is the EU. It must be understood on its own terms. After you have finished this book, you will know the EU as well as it can be known, and you will understand how the fate of democracy in the EU will affect the transatlantic alliance and the future of liberal democracy in the world.

CHAPTER 2:
POSTMODERN: THE EU AS
AN UNANSWERED QUESTION

In late 1951, in the heady days when the postwar dream of peace through European integration was in the air, Alcide De Gasperi, prime minister of Italy and a founding father of European integration, mused about what steps Europe should take toward a more harmonious future: "Which road are we to choose," he asked, "if we are to preserve all that is noble and humane within these national forces, while co-ordinating them to build a supranational civilisation which can give them balance, absorb them, and harmonise them in one irresistible drive towards progress?"[1]

This query captures the great unanswered question of the European Union – the foundational uncertainty that has stymied so many attempts to understand what the EU really is. Is it a group of states that work very closely together in almost every realm but nevertheless retain their national sovereignty, or is it a supranational entity that absorbs and digests the member states? And this foundational uncertainty, in turn, arises out of a disagreement so profound that it encompasses both means and ends. De Gasperi directly asked, "Which road must we take?" He assumed agreement on the ultimate end: the building of a "supranational civilization." But there is no agreement there, either – no consensus among EU

elites on the question "What do we want to achieve?" Both of these
basic questions – which road must we take and where do we want to
end up – are still very much subjects of heated disagreement.

CLASHING VISIONS

Selected pronouncements from some of the greatest European
statesmen suffice to illustrate the clash of visions for the EU.
Almost all of these competing visions cluster around one of two
paradigms: the intergovernmental, sovereigntist paradigm, or the
supranational, integrationist paradigm. The first sees the EU as an
organization of sovereign member states whose power supersedes
that of the EU. The second envisions the EU as a supranational
governing entity distinct from the EU member states and exercising significant sovereign powers over them.

On the sovereigntist side, Charles de Gaulle, president of
France, called for a strong "Europe of nations" in which the various countries of Europe would collectively form an effective coun-
terweight to the United States on the one hand and the Soviet
Union on the other.[2]

Margaret Thatcher, the British prime minister from 1979 to
1990, was perhaps the most forceful advocate of the sovereigntist
vision of the European Union (at the time, the European Community) as an organization promoting cooperation among independent
and distinct member states. She elaborated on this view in her
famous speech at the College of Europe in Bruges, Belgium, in 1988:

> My first guiding principle is this: willing and active cooper-
> ation between independent sovereign states is the best way
> to build a successful European Community. To try to sup-
> press nationhood and concentrate power at the centre of a
> European conglomerate would be highly damaging and
> would jeopardise the objectives we seek to achieve. Europe
> will be stronger precisely because it has France as France,
> Spain as Spain, Britain as Britain, each with its own cus-
> toms, traditions and identity. It would be folly to try to fit
> them into some sort of identikit European personality....
> We have not successfully rolled back the frontiers of the
> state in Britain, only to see them re-imposed at a European

level with a European super-state exercising a new dominance from Brussels. Certainly we want to see Europe more
united and with a greater sense of common purpose. But it
must be in a way which preserves the different traditions,
parliamentary powers and sense of national pride in one's
own country; for these have been the source of Europe's
vitality through the centuries.[3]

A prominent voice on the integrationist side was Helmut Kohl,
the chancellor of Germany from 1982 to 1998 and a tireless advocate
of a united Europe. In April 1992, shortly after the signing of the
Maastricht Treaty, which would turn the European Community
into the European Union, Kohl said, "The Treaty on European
Union marks a new, decisive step in the process of European integration that in a few years will lead to the creation of what the
founding fathers of modern Europe dreamt of after the last war:
a United States of Europe."[4]

José Manuel Barroso, the president of the European Commission from 2004 to 2014, also laid out a strongly integrationist
vision. He talked of political union and supranational democracy:
"Regarding the need to perfect our political union and enhance
the democratic legitimacy that should underpin what I call Europe
3.0, it should be based on the Community method as the system of
checks, balances and equity between the institutions and the
Member States that offers the best starting point for further supranational democracy."[5] The "community method" is a way of making policy that gives prominent roles to EU-level institutions, as
opposed to the "intergovernmental method," in which the governments of the member states play the leading part. Barroso's use of
the term "community method" underscores his view of the EU as
a "supranational democracy," a "political union" of the EU member states under the umbrella of the EU institutions.

Tony Blair, the British prime minister from 1997 to 2007, was
one of many representatives of the intermediate position. As a
Labourite, Blair was relatively pro-EU in comparison with his
Conservative Party compatriots, but he wanted the elected heads
of member-state governments to rein in the unelected European
Commission. He called for the European Council, representing
the heads of government, "to set out a clear, focused and strong
platform of change for Europe. I mean a proper programme –

almost like a manifesto for change – that is sufficiently precise that afterwards the commission knows exactly what it is supposed to do and has the full support of the council in executing it."[6]

So there has always been serious divergence of opinion – even diametric opposition – regarding what the EU should be trying to achieve, as well as what path it should take to reach its goal. Charles de Gaulle wanted a Europe of sovereign nations coming together to form a bloc large enough to fend off the Soviet Union on the one hand and counter the domination of the United States on the other. Margaret Thatcher wanted willing cooperation between sovereign member states in order to advance prosperity and liberty in a Europe of related but distinct peoples. Helmut Kohl wanted a United States of Europe and set about trying to achieve it as one of the principal architects of the Maastricht Treaty on European Union. José Manuel Barroso wanted a "perfected political union," a supranational democracy with the community method somehow functioning to provide checks and balances between the member states and the EU institutions. Tony Blair wanted an efficient European Commission carrying out the agenda given to it by the member states. These widely differing visions explain why a serious observer of the EU has to admit that it is impossible to establish with certainty what the EU is.

The disagreement on the question "What do we want the EU to be?" renders unanswerable the next question, "How do we achieve what we want to achieve?" How, then, has the EU been so successful in maintaining its seemingly inexorable forward movement toward a supranational dream? How has it escaped the paralysis that typically comes with uncertainty and division over goals?

One of the answers is that the EU – despite the well-known fact that it sometimes does seem nearly paralyzed in its slowness – can be exceedingly pragmatic. If the question "What do we want to achieve?" pertains to an easily identifiable and relatively urgent short-term or medium-term goal, the EU often does well. An EU statement, policy paper, even EU treaties can go forward without consensus among the parties through the pragmatic use of constructive ambiguity – by phrasing the controversial parts in such a way that each party can interpret them according to individual preference. When it comes to policy implementation, skillful, persistent pragmatism has led to many successes. The EU has accomplished major things – for example, developing an EU-wide single market, promoting trade, introducing the euro, and growing from six to twenty-eight member states – via pragmatic pursuit of specific ends.

At the same time, these specific accomplishments through short-term pragmatism cannot occur without somehow affecting the overall trajectory of the EU toward either the supranational or the sovereigntist pole. And here, the cards are stacked against the sovereigntists. With each agreement on a short-term goal, the sovereigntists lose a bit more ground to the supranationalists. In fact, the supranationalists have already rigged the game. Within the supranational institutional context of the EU, pragmatic cooperation – whenever it occurs and regardless of the short-term end – can be sold to the public as visionary. The integrationists can claim each accomplishment achieved by means of cooperation among member states, within the institutionally supranational EU, as proof of the validity of the supranational vision. With each example of cooperation, the achievement of the vision appears closer and becomes more plausible.

THE EU ENIGMA

Here again is Alcide De Gasperi's opaque question: "Which road are we to choose if we are to preserve all that is noble and humane within these national forces, while co-ordinating them to build a supranational civilisation which can give them balance, absorb them, and harmonise them in one irresistible drive towards progress?" He gave an answer, of sorts:

> This can only be done by infusing new life into the separate national forces, through the common ideals of our history, and offering them the field of action of the varied and magnificent experiences of our common European civilisation. It can only be done by establishing a meeting-point where those experiences can assemble, unite by affinity, and thus engender new forms of solidarity based on increased freedom and greater social justice. It is within an association of national sovereignties based on democratic, constitutional organisations that these new forms can flourish.[7]

What does this mean? What is an "association of national sovereignties?" It is unclear. In answering his own question, De Gasperi in reality left it unanswered. At any rate, one somehow gets the sense that a clearly defined forum for cooperation of sovereign nation-states is not what he had in mind. A garden-variety international organization just does not seem to encompass his grandiose vision of world-historical change, emanating from Europe. Yet De Gasperi does not seem to have been advocating the abolition of the European nations and the formation of a single European nation-state, a United States of Europe. He wanted it both ways.

If one observes the European Union today, it appears that De Gasperi got his wish. And that is a key to unlock the meaning of the European Union: it is two different things. It is a group of distinct and independent states that work together yet retain their national sovereignty; and it is a supranational entity that absorbs and integrates the member states. It *can't* be both, but it *is* both. And it maintains a certain balance, remaining enough of everything to enough of everybody to keep the momentum going toward the soft utopia of supranationalist governance.

Even practitioners, not just out-of-touch philosophical dreamers, often refer to this "bothness" of the EU. Wolfgang Schäuble, currently the German minister of finance and long an establishment figure in the supposedly staid, gray-suited German center-right, writes of his vision for the future of the EU:

> To describe it technically, Europe would be something like a "multi-level democracy," not a federal state whose focus would be centered in a body politic that was basically like a nation-state. At the same time, though, it would be much more than a federation of independent states whose connecting element would remain tenuous and weak. No, Europe would be a mutually complementing, intermeshing system of democracies of varied scope and jurisdiction: a "national-European double democracy."[8]

A "national-European double democracy" built from "mutually complementing, intermeshing democracies of varied scope and jurisdiction"? Schäuble may be a practitioner rather than an abstract philosopher, but you can tell he was reared in a culture that lives and breathes the impenetrable "thought-edifices" of philosophers such as Kant, Hegel, Heidegger and Habermas. In the original German, moreover, the entire quotation is in the subjunctive mood, which usually expresses something counterfactual – and which here betrays the unreality that surrounds so much of the foundational thinking about the EU.

Maybe, then, the great unanswered question is *unanswerable*. Maybe the EU really is best understood as a postmodern, quintessentially European mind game. And maybe its inscrutability is the key to the EU's success. Never answering the most basic question – while hiding what one is doing behind a smokescreen of unintelligibility – may be what makes the EU a largely unnoticed and thus acceptably soft utopia, rather than a blatantly oppressive and unacceptably hard utopia. In an interview with the German weekly *Der Spiegel* in 1999 (when he was prime minister of Luxembourg), Jean-Claude Juncker, now the president of the European Commission, spoke of how European integration was being pushed forward by the governing elites: "We decide something, and then we just throw it out there and wait awhile to see what happens. If there are no big howls of protest and no uprisings, because most people don't even understand what was decided, then we just go on – step by step, until there is no turning back."[9]

In other words, the EU is process. It is constantly evolving into something new – something that no one clearly understands; something about which every point of view is right, and wrong. As Juncker revealed in his statement to *Der Spiegel*, the EU's impenetrability is also intentional. Subterfuge is a central component of its modus operandi. Being unknowable has always been an aspect of the EU. That attribute might be good in a poem or a work of art, but not in a polity, which cannot be democratically accountable to its citizens unless they understand it.

By the process of developing an undefinable supranationality, De Gasperi and the other founding fathers of the European project – like Barroso and Juncker in our own day – wanted to achieve a soft utopia that would be a regional model for what we now call global governance. In the next chapter, we will examine the utopian ideology of global governance and how it grounds the EU.

CHAPTER 3:
THE UTOPIAN DREAM OF WORLD PEACE

The European dream of a supranational paradise of peace, prosperity and amity has gone global. As we have seen, the founding fathers of European integration already had this idea in mind. The opening words of the Schuman Declaration, proposing the establishment of the European Coal and Steel Community in 1950, were not limited to Europe. Summing up the purpose of the first truly supranational undertaking in modern history, Robert Schuman, the French foreign minister and probably the primary founder of the European Union, declared: "World peace cannot be safeguarded without the making of creative efforts proportionate to the dangers which threaten it."[1] Jean Monnet, the principal intellectual architect of the European project and Schuman's close associate, also revealed his global perspective early in the process of European integration: "The sovereign nations of the past can no longer provide a framework for the resolution of our present problems. And the European Community itself is no more than a step toward the organizational forms of tomorrow's world."[2]

With the end of the Cold War, the vague aspirations of the EU's first-generation fathers have become a full-fledged ideology of global governance, although still an amorphous one, both strategically and intellectually.

Among high-level EU officials, Pascal Lamy is one of the more articulate advocates of global governance. A Frenchman, he served as the European commissioner for trade from 1999 to 2004, and as secretary general of the World Trade Organization from 2005 to 2013. In a speech on the twentieth anniversary of the fall of the Berlin Wall, Lamy said that the Cold War's ending had "caught everyone by surprise," suddenly presenting the world with new challenges that hadn't been prepared for: "A new world order was being born. And yet there was not enough thinking and discussion about its governance structures.... Global challenges need global solutions and these can only come with the right global governance . . . ."[3]

The statement "global challenges need global solutions" is key. The global governancers base their entire case on the assertion that a globalized world requires a globalized form of governance. The German philosopher Jürgen Habermas, a leading proponent of global supranational governance, puts the argument as well as anyone, with a dash of Germanic fogginess. The processes of globalization, he writes,

> enmesh nation-states in the dependencies of an increasingly interconnected world society whose functional differentiation effortlessly bypasses territorial boundaries.... Nation-states can no longer secure the boundaries of their own territories, the vital necessities of their populations, and the material preconditions for the reproduction of their societies by their own efforts.... Hence, states cannot escape the need for regulation and coordination in the expanding horizon of a world society . . . .[4]

The EU, according to Habermas, "already represents a form of 'government beyond the nation-state' that could serve as an example to be emulated in the postnational constellation."[5]

Habermas and Lamy both exemplify the foundational consensus of European elites that the EU is the model for the governance of a future world in which unrestricted national sovereignty will have become a thing of the past. In the speech quoted above, Lamy purports to establish the post–Cold War need for global governance and then goes on to tout the European Union as the prototype, "the most ambitious experiment to date in supranational governance. It is the story of a desired, defined and organized interdependence between its member states." The EU is "the laboratory of international governance – the place where the new technological frontier of international governance is being tested."[6]

Another longtime member of the EU governing elite, the previously cited German finance minister Wolfgang Schäuble, also illustrates how the view of the EU as a model for global governance is shared across nations and along the political spectrum. A center-right establishment figure, Schäuble agrees with Lamy, a mainstay of the French center-left, in the belief that people beyond Europe could take inspiration from "a national-and-European 'double-democracy' as a model for global governance in the twenty-first century."[7]

What exactly *is* global governance, then? There is a plethora of definitions, including several helpful ones on the Wikipedia page for the term. They range from the purely descriptive and technical, to characterizations that give more sense of both the ideological purposes and the real-world implications of the global governance movement.

To start with the technical, Adil Najam, dean of the Pardee School of Global Studies at Boston University, defines global governance very broadly as "the management of global processes in the absence of global government."[8] Another technocratic definition comes from Thomas G. Weiss, director of the Ralph Bunche Institute for International Studies at the Graduate Center, CUNY: "'Global governance' – which can be good, bad, or indifferent – refers to concrete cooperative problem-solving arrangements, many of which increasingly involve not only the United Nations of states but also 'other UNs,' namely international secretariats and other non-state actors."[9] In *The UN and Global Governance: An Idea and Its Prospects*, Weiss and his co-author, Ramesh Thakur, offer a slightly more elaborate definition: "the complex of formal and informal institutions, mechanisms, relationships, and processes between and among states, markets, citizens and organizations, both inter- and non-governmental, through which collective interests on the global plane are articulated, duties, obligations and privileges are established, and differences are mediated through educated professionals."[10] Notice who is doing this very comprehensive governancing, so comprehensive that it sounds like *governing* the world: "educated professionals," not elected officials.

A shorter definition that captures the central idea is this: "Global governance or world governance is a movement towards political integration of transnational actors aimed at negotiating responses to problems that affect more than one state or region."[11] The key words here are "political integration of transnational actors." But the chief merit of this definition is that it describes global governance accurately as a "movement," rather than focusing, misleadingly, on the innocuous-sounding mechanics of "cooperative problem-solving arrangements."

GLOBAL GOVERNANCE IS *SUI GENERIS* – JUST LIKE THE EU

As the definitions above imply, global governance does *not* mean world government to the great majority of its advocates. For instance, Habermas writes, "The democratic federal state writ large – the global state of nations or world republic – is the wrong model."[12] Rather, he envisions a "politically constituted global society that reserves institutions and procedures of global governance for states at both the supra- and transnational levels."[13] Habermas explains, "one can construe the political constitution of a decentered world society as a multilevel system" in which a "world organization" such as a "suitably reformed" UN could secure peace and promote human rights "at the *supranational* level" while "at the intermediate, *transnational* level the major powers would address the difficult problems of a global domestic politics," such as "global economic and ecological problems."[14] In order to negotiate policy on a level playing field with the United States in such a scenario, "nation-states in the various world regions would have to unite to form continental regimes on the model of an EU equipped with sufficient power to conduct an effective foreign policy of its own." Thus, there would still be "foreign policy" between nations (or "continental regimes"), but the distinction between domestic and foreign policy would be blurred; a "modified form" of international relations would basically become a "global domestic politics" among the United States and various continental regimes such as the EU.

Nations would continue to exist. There would be no one-world government. But Habermas does not waver from the utopian goals he has for global governance: world peace and worldwide respect for universal human rights. And in order to achieve these goals, there would be a world organization – the UN – that, while purportedly not a world government, would be endowed with for-midable power on a global scale, the power to decide questions of war and peace and to enforce those decisions, and to impose glob-ally a particular vision of human rights. This is a level of power that would dwarf that of any nation-state, including the United States, the most powerful nation-state in the history of the world. As Habermas puts it, this would be "a global domestic politics without a world government... embedded within the framework of a world organization with the power to impose peace and implement human rights."[15]

What does this all mean? Could the democratic nation-state, directly accountable to its citizens, survive in such a system? Are global governance and liberal democracy compatible, or are they mutually exclusive? John Fonte gets to the heart of the matter in his masterful analysis of global governance, *Sovereignty or Submission: Will Americans Rule Themselves or Be Ruled by Others?* Here, Fonte strips the "postdemocratic and postliberal" agenda of the global governance movement down to the essence of what it would mean for those who cherish self-government: it would "shift power from democracies to supranational institutions and rules, and thus severely restrict democratic decision making in indepen-dent states."[16] Although the advocates of global governance may think of themselves as supporters of democracy, "the effect of their policies would be fundamentally at odds with the basic prin-ciples and practices of democratic self-government."[17] Ultimately, says Fonte, this is a "moral conflict" revolving around the ques-tion: "Do Americans, or other peoples, have the moral right to rule themselves or must they share sovereignty with others?"[18]

The global governancers, whether they openly admit it or not – whether they consciously realize it or not – believe that people do not have a right to self-government. They subscribe to what they consider a nobler ideal, in which "global norms and universal human rights" constitute the highest authority. As Fonte explains, "They regard the 'new' international law, embodying the latest (and most progressive) concepts of global human rights and universal norms, as superior to any national law or the constitution of any democratic nation-state."[19] Accordingly, global governancers aim to establish a "global rule of law" to which all national law would be subordinate.[20]

This is not about one-world-government conspiracy theories or the black helicopters of the UN. As Fonte explains, the advocates of global governance do not aim to create "a single global government, or any form of tyranny, but rather 'governance' through a hybrid of national, transnational, and supranational legal and regulatory regimes."[21] Nevertheless, if a "global rule of law" is to be established under some kind of global authority, "liberal democracy will be replaced by postdemocratic governance."[22] When all is said and done, the global governance ideology is engaging the Western democracies in a zero-sum conflict between two irreconcilable visions for political life, a conflict centering on the most basic question of politics: "Who determines the laws under which we shall live?" Again, this is "a moral struggle over the *first principles* of government and politics."[23]

Regardless of the opposing currents represented by sovereigntists such as Margaret Thatcher, nationalists such as Charles de Gaulle and pragmatists such as Tony Blair, the European project has always been motivated by a vision of supranational governance for Europe and global governance for the world, such as has been articulated by people like Robert Schuman, Jean Monnet, Alcide De Gasperi and Helmut Kohl. It is a grand and attractive and ambitious vision of a better world – a vision that many good people are espousing. John Fonte acknowledges that "the advocates of global governance hope for a better world – more humane, just, and democratic."[24] Indeed, after the bloody conflicts and totalitarian regimes of the twentieth century, writes Habermas, "The historical success of the European Union has confirmed Europeans in the conviction that the *domestication of the state's use of violence* also calls for a *reciprocal* restriction of the scope of sovereignty at the global level."[25]

Like the desire for peace that underlay the creation of the European Coal and Steel Community in the aftermath of World War II, the intentions of today's global governancers may be good, even noble. But, as Fonte so conclusively demonstrates, "their proposed policies would, in fact, shrink and usurp democratic self-government."[26] Even as committed an advocate of global governance as Pascal Lamy admits that there is a democratic deficit in the European experiment: "We are witnessing a growing distance between European public opinions and the European project.... In spite of constantly striking institutional flints over the past 50 years, there has been no resulting democratic spark."[27]

That is what global governance comes down to: the *usurpation of democratic self-government* by a democratically unaccountable group of globalist elites. In the next section we will step back and examine how this postdemocratic, postliberal project began. An overview of the history of postwar European integration will reinforce how the noble illusion of supranational governance runs like a red thread through the story of the EU.

PART TWO

INTENDED AND UNINTENDED CONSEQUENCES

CHAPTER 4:
OUT OF THE ASHES

Five years and a day after World War II had ended in Europe with Germany's unconditional surrender, the Schuman Declaration was presented, on May 9, 1950. The French foreign minister, Robert Schuman, was proposing the establishment of what would become the European Coal and Steel Community. The Schuman Declaration was a powerful symbol of a new Europe emerging from the ashes of the most destructive war the world had ever known.

The immediate purpose of the ECSC was to eliminate the perpetual rivalry between France and Germany, which had led to repeated conflicts and untold suffering for so many generations. By placing French and German coal and steel production under a common High Authority, which would administer both countries' coal and steel industries independently of their respective governments, the ECSC would bind together the economic interests of the two nations. Thereby, war between France and Germany was to be relegated to the past. According to the Schuman Declaration, "The solidarity in production thus established will make it plain that any war between France and Germany becomes not merely unthinkable, but materially impossible."[1]

The idea of making war between France and Germany impossible was a powerful and noble idea indeed. In World War II, approximately 5 million German soldiers, 1 million German civilians, 400,000 French soldiers and 400,000 French civilians had died, to say nothing of the millions of wounded and the war's estimated economic costs of 4 trillion dollars. And this is to say nothing of World War I, which had ended only twenty-one years before the beginning of World War II.

But of course, World War II and Nazism did not affect only France and Germany. On the continent of Europe, it claimed the lives of approximately 15 million people, including the 6 million Jews murdered in the Holocaust. Outside of Europe, the war dead numbered 6 million people. The United States mourned 290,000 American soldiers who died in Europe and Asia.

The war's end finally came in August 1945, when the United States dropped atomic bombs on the Japanese cities of Hiroshima and Nagasaki, killing approximately 120,000 people. But the specter of another war, one that could destroy civilization, soon loomed on the horizon. On August 29, 1949, the Soviet Union tested its first atomic bomb. Now there were two rival world powers armed with nuclear weapons that could cause devastation on a scale unimaginable even in the wake of the recent war.

In the midst of all this, the Schuman Declaration and the ECSC were not just about preventing war between France and Germany. That was only the starting point for building a new Europe – and via this new Europe, for achieving world peace. The very name of the "European Coal and Steel Community" made clear that this new supranational entity was not to be limited to Germany and France. Jean Monnet, who would serve as the ECSC's first chairman, invited the core Western European nations to the negotiations to establish the ECSC. Great Britain, protective of its national sovereignty, declined. Italy, the Netherlands, Belgium and Luxembourg accepted and, with the entry into force of the Treaty of Paris in July 1952, joined France and Germany as the six founding members. They formed the nucleus of what was eventually to become the European Union.

The Schuman Declaration attributes the recent war, at least

in part, to the failure to achieve "a united Europe," and takes as a presupposition that Franco-German reconciliation is only a first step to the greater goal of uniting Europe: "The coming together of the nations of Europe requires the elimination of the age-old opposition of France and Germany."[2] Likewise, the preamble to the Treaty of Paris establishing the ECSC speaks of building Europe, saying it can be done "only through practical achievements which will first of all create real solidarity, and through the establishment of common bases for economic development ...."[3]

From the beginning, the primary movers behind the ECSC were aiming toward a united, post-nation-state Europe. "The indispensable first principle," according to Jean Monnet, was "the abnegation of sovereignty in a limited but decisive field." Cooperation alone was not enough; there must be "a fusion of the interests of the European peoples and not merely another effort to maintain an equilibrium of those interests...."[4] The signatories to the Treaty of Paris, in founding the ECSC, declared themselves resolved "to create, by establishing an economic community, the basis for a broader and deeper community among peoples long divided by bloody conflicts; and to lay the foundation for institutions which will give direction to a destiny henceforward shared...."[5]

The ECSC High Authority was perhaps the first example of a supranational institution that was endowed with real authority over its member states. The six member states of the ECSC had truly ceded a significant aspect of their sovereign powers – control of the production of coal and steel. This was something not only central to their economies in general, but also necessary for building the weapons and machinery to wage war successfully. Clearly, the ECSC was meant to usher in a radically new, united Europe.

FROM EUROPEAN DREAMS TO INSTITUTIONAL REALITY

The idea of European unity did not appear out of nowhere with the ECSC. It has a long history. Perhaps the most significant intellectual antecedent of the European idea came from the German Enlightenment philosopher Immanuel Kant, with his proposal for achieving perpetual peace through "a league of a particular kind, which can be called a league of peace (*foedus pacificum*), and which... seeks to make an end of all wars forever." Kant suggested that this concept of federation "should gradually spread to all states and thus lead to perpetual peace...."[6]

Before and after Kant published his idea for a league of peace, many people had thought about or proposed a unification of some kind among European nations, or some sort of "United States of Europe." After World War I and until the ECSC's founding, the idea of European unification picked up steam. The Austrian count Richard Coudenhove-Kalergi founded the International Paneuropean Union in the 1920s, with the goal of uniting Europe. The French prime minister Aristide Briand advocated a federation of European nations at the League of Nations in 1929. Several books were written in several countries promoting a United States of Europe. Seeking a way to achieve lasting peace, Winston Churchill, in a famous speech in 1946, said, "We must build a kind of United States of Europe." In 1948, Churchill was honorary president of a Congress of Europe, which preceded the founding of the Council of Europe the next year. Today the Council of Europe has forty-seven member states, including all of the member states of the EU.

The idea of union among nations for the purpose of achieving world peace was not solely a European one. It was President Woodrow Wilson who proposed the first aspirationally global organization, the League of Nations, with the aim of securing a lasting international peace after World War I. In his "Fourteen Points" speech before Congress on January 8, 1918, Wilson called for a "general association of nations... formed under specific covenants for the purpose of affording mutual guarantees of political independence and territorial integrity to great and small states alike."[7] Because of opposition in the Congress, though, the United States itself never joined. For this and other reasons, the League was weak and ineffectual from the beginning. By the time World War II broke out, the League was all but defunct. It was formally dissolved in 1945 when the United Nations officially took over its functions.

The United States was also central to the establishment of the United Nations. In fact, it was President Franklin D. Roosevelt who first coined the term "United Nations," referring to the twenty-six countries allied against the Axis powers during World War II. Over the course of the war, the idea of the UN was developed under American leadership, and the UN Charter was agreed upon at a conference in San Francisco, in June 1945, entering into force on October 24.

The United States also played a large part in getting Europe on a practical path to unity. Tired of war and wary of Soviet designs on Western Europe, the U.S. promoted European economic integration with the Marshall Plan. U.S. officials also supported the idea of political and military integration. The ECSC enjoyed U.S. support and the U.S. even backed the idea of a supranational European army. As we will see, the war-weary Americans did not fully realize what kind of project they were helping to set in motion.

The key to translating the aspirations for European unity into institutional reality was Jean Monnet and his brilliant modus operandi, dubbed the "Monnet method."[8] Monnet embedded the utopian objective in a gradualist strategy that slowly moved forward toward the supranationalist goal but never clearly defined it. The strategy was to begin in the economic realm, avoiding openly political proposals, and with care never to take a step that would be unacceptable to people at any given stage of integration. A British Conservative author, Adrian Hilton, characterized the Monnet method so well that for years his words were wrongly attributed to Monnet himself: "Europe's nations should be guided towards the superstate without their people understanding what is happening. This can be accomplished by successive steps, each disguised as having an economic purpose, but which will eventually and irreversibly lead to federation."[9]

So a secret to the EU's success has been its eschewal of any Great Leap Forward. Instead, the EU is moving toward its utopian goal in small, achievable steps, occasionally taking an unavoidable step backward. Charitably, one might say that a kind of benign deception is at the heart of this strategy. The purpose of proceeding incrementally is to avoid alerting average citizens to the fact that the objective is slowly to hollow out the power of their country and its government, the power that they best understand and that is accountable to them. Only the insiders – who see themselves as long-range thinkers and believe they understand best the complexities of international relations – can be allowed to know what is really happening. The EU would not be the EU without this culture of government by insiders and elites.

But the elites are deceiving themselves too. Neither Monnet nor most of his followers have seemed to know exactly what they are striving for. And even if they think they do, can anything based on deception – including self-deception – be good?

THE UTOPIAN IDEA OF WORLD PEACE

While the goal of the European project eludes precise definition, one thing is certain: it has never been only about Europe. It began with no lesser aim than ending warfare globally; it was a child of Kant's ideal of perpetual peace. Thus the opening words of the Schuman Declaration: "World peace cannot be safeguarded without the making of creative efforts proportionate to the dangers which threaten it."[10] This statement, in almost exactly its original wording, became the first clause of the preamble to the Treaty of Paris, thereby establishing the safeguarding of world peace as the ECSC's fundamental reason for being.

A radically restructured, supranational Europe heralding the advent of world peace: this dream was a mirror image of the other political ideologies that had made the fate of twentieth-century Europe. In the aftermath of Nazi Germany's genocidal pan-European dystopia of evil, and in the midst of Soviet communism's ongoing global campaign to subjugate whole nations and peoples to its vision of a brave new world, the European idea was another political utopia brewing in the world. It is a utopianism of good, a soft utopianism, but it is utopian nonetheless.

And despite all the ways the do-gooder utopianism of the European Union is different from the "hard" utopianism of Nazism and communism, it has another thing in common with its totalitarian cousins: its ultimate goals are unachievable. But the pursuit of these impossible goals, like the pursuit of any utopian idea, cannot but cause real damage to real people. Seventy years after the end of World War II, the European idea is shaping up to be a tragedy of unintended consequences – the antidemocratic consequences of good people's determination to prevent the reoccurrence of the tremendous evil they have witnessed. If the supranationalist vision of the European project prevails, democracy and self-government will steadily be eroded in the vain pursuit of an unachievable world peace.

CHAPTER 5:
THE TRANSFORMATION OF EUROPE

The European Coal and Steel Community was unprecedented. But from the very beginning it was meant to be only the first step to an integrated, united Europe. Thus it was bound to be supplemented by organizations, institutions and agreements that would bring Europe closer to the integrated continent that the founders and their successors envisioned.

From 1952 to 1957, the ECSC was the only established institution advancing the supranational integration of Europe. During this period, though, there was an attempt to create another integrative organization, the European Defense Community (EDC). This was a truly audacious initiative by the six member states of the ECSC to launch a common European army. It proved to be a step too far, breaking Monnet's rule of taking incremental steps that would not arouse opposition. The project was dropped in August 1954 when the French National Assembly rejected the EDC treaty.

FROM COMMUNITY TO UNION

Soon, in June 1955, negotiations began toward the next phase of European integration, the European Common Market. The result was treaties in 1957 establishing the European Economic Community (EEC) and the European Atomic Energy Community (Euratom), the latter intended to develop a common market for the peaceful use of atomic energy. The Treaty Establishing the European Economic Community (TEEC), commonly known as the Treaty of Rome, is celebrated today as the most significant step toward the European Union until its formal establishment in 1992. Article 2 of the TEEC states:

> It shall be the aim of the Community, by establishing a Common Market and progressively approximating the economic policies of Member States, to promote throughout the Community a harmonious development of economic activities, a continuous and balanced expansion, an increased stability, an accelerated raising of the standard of living and closer relations between its Member States.[1]

At that time, the participants were still only the six founding members of the ECSC: Germany, France, Italy, the Netherlands, Belgium and Luxembourg.

Another milestone in European integration came in July 1967, when the European Economic Community merged with the European Atomic Energy Community and the European Coal and Steel Community to form the European Communities, also referred to unofficially in the singular, as the European Community (EC).[2] The change from "European Economic Community" to "European Community" is an example of how the integrationists use language in artful ways to advance their agenda under the radar. Steeped in their own technocratic universe, they have developed a body of jargon understandable only to insiders. Using this EU-speak, European elites have long been adept at disguising the ongoing process of integration in linguistic subtleties that escape the notice of the uninitiated. Like the Monnet method, EU jargon forestalls opposition by veiling the long-term objective while at the same time quietly asserting it.

In this vein, the disappearance of the word "economic" from "European Economic Community" was highly significant: the European Community was moving beyond the economic sphere and taking on a political dimension. Europe now formed a community, encompassing anything implied in that vague but evocative word, not just the pursuit of better economic performance. Thickening the fog even further, the 1993 Treaty of Maastricht (more on that soon) *officially* created a European Community within the European Communities. As a European Union website states tersely, "After the Treaty of Maastricht the EEC became the European Community, reflecting the determination of the Member States to expand the Community's powers to non-economic domains."[3]

But European integration moves forward in fits and starts, sometimes taking a step backward and sometimes stalling. The establishment of the EC in 1967 came after much resistance to further integration from the French president, Charles de Gaulle, in the first half of the decade. Concerned to prevent the erosion of French sovereignty, de Gaulle opposed the inclusion of new members in the EEC, especially his cultural rival the United Kingdom. In addition, he was determined to prevent the possibility of France's being overruled on important policy decisions. De Gaulle's resistance sparked what is known as the "empty chair crisis," when France boycotted all EEC meetings for seven months in 1965–1966. The boycott ended only after an agreement was reached to roll back some provisions of the Treaty of Rome, and thus to require unanimity on important issues rather than the qualified majority votes stipulated in the treaty for certain policy areas.

De Gaulle's successor, Georges Pompidou, agreed in 1969 to consider letting new members into the EC. After long negotiations, Denmark, Ireland and the UK joined in 1973, becoming the first additions to the original six member states. This was the beginning of an enlargement process that has continued to the present day, with Greece joining in 1981; Spain and Portugal in 1986; Austria, Finland and Sweden in 1995; ten new members – Cyprus, Malta, Poland, the Czech Republic, Slovakia, Hungary, Slovenia, Lithuania, Latvia and Estonia – in 2004; Romania and Bulgaria in 2007; and Croatia in 2013. The EU currently counts twenty-eight member states, with the prospect of gaining additional members in the future.

Meanwhile, along with a *widening* of the EU, there has been a *deepening* via institutional changes that promote closer integration. After the European Communities were merged in 1967, the next significant institutional step was the creation of the European Monetary System (EMS) in 1979, which established the

European Currency Unit (ECU), a reference unit valued at the weighted average of all participating European currencies. The EMS required currencies to maintain a value within a narrow band around the ECU in order to reduce exchange-rate fluctuations and lay the basis for an eventual monetary union. That year also saw the first direct elections to the European Parliament, which until then had been an appointed body made up of representatives from national parliaments. Henceforward, all members of the European Parliament would be elected to five-year terms. In 1987, the Single European Act (SEA) came into force; it set a deadline of December 31, 1992 to achieve the single market with free movement of capital, people, goods and services across borders throughout the European Community.[4]

The European Union was officially birthed with the ratification of the Treaty on European Union, commonly known as the Maastricht Treaty, in 1993. Here I note again the change from "community" to "union." Few people had the time to reflect on the deeper implications of now being a "union." The Maastricht Treaty included arrangements for a European Monetary Union (EMU), with a single currency to be in effect by 1999 and with monetary policy to be transferred from member states' national central banks to a European Central Bank (ECB). The treaty also included measures toward the development of a common EU foreign and security policy. These were huge steps toward supranational integration at the expense of the national sovereignty of the member states in core policy areas. The more sovereigntist UK and Denmark received an opt-out on the common currency, retaining their own currencies and keeping their national powers in the realm of monetary and fiscal policy. They were not subject to the treaty's measures related to the ECB and the European System of Central Banks.[5]

The Treaty of Maastricht was followed, in 1999, by the Treaty of Amsterdam, which is mainly known for increasing EU powers in the areas of "external border control and visas, asylum and immigration policy, and judicial cooperation."[6] Again, these policy areas traditionally represent core aspects of national sovereignty, as the refugee crisis overwhelming Europe in 2015 makes painfully clear.

In the early years of the new century, the EU continued its inexorable evolution toward a higher level of integration. On January 1, 2002, monetary union became a day-to-day reality for everyday people. Euro coins and notes replaced national currencies in twelve EU member states. The eurozone now comprises nineteen out of twenty-eight EU member states. We will discuss this huge leap toward supranationality in greater detail in Chapters 9 and 17.

Then, on February 1, 2003, the Treaty of Nice came into effect. Its main purpose was to reform the EU institutions to prepare for the upcoming enlargement, in 2004, from fifteen to twenty-five member states. This involved measures such as adjusting the weighting of votes in the Council of Ministers to give the more populous member states a greater voice, and redistributing the votes among the much larger number of member states; reapportioning seats in the European Parliament to accommodate the new member states; extending qualified-majority voting (as opposed to requiring unanimity of all member states) to about thirty new policy realms, affecting areas such as immigration, refugee and asylum policy, the introduction of the euro, and trade in services, so that the enlarged EU could function more easily even without unanimity in many areas; strengthening and streamlining the "enhanced cooperation" option, to allow member states the possibility of choosing more often to move forward together on common initiatives even if some member states opted out.[7]

These measures, especially those regarding enhanced cooperation and qualified-majority voting, all paved the way for a much larger and more deeply integrated EU, with more power centralized in Brussels. Several other steps the Nice Treaty made toward greater European integration were (1) the establishment of a way for the EU Council to step in if it believes that a member state's actions pose a danger of a serious violation of citizens' "fundamental rights" and to "recommend" measures the member state should take to avoid that violation; (2) the establishment of a legal basis for the EU to regulate EU-level political parties, especially regarding their recognition as parties and their funding; and (3) and (4) measures to increase cooperation at the EU level on defense and criminal justice. All of these measures represent an attempt to strike a balance between increasing the pooling of national sovereignty at the EU level and maintaining cherished prerogatives of the member states. Balance or not, by wading into areas such as fundamental rights, political parties, defense and criminal justice, the Treaty of Nice clearly anticipates a diminishment of national sovereignty in key policy arenas.

In 2002–2003, roughly at the same time as the ratification process for the Treaty of Nice, a Convention on the Future of Europe, or European Convention, was called into being. After about a year and a half of debate and negotiation, the convention produced a draft of what was formally called the "Treaty Establishing a Constitution for Europe," though it was generally known as the European Constitution. Meant to be reminiscent of the United States Constitution, but without establishing a United States of Europe, the draft was in reality a treaty and was officially so called, but the term "treaty" in the title was played down by EU elites. The concept of a "European Constitution" better reflected their aspiration: to establish in Europeans' hearts and minds a sense of European unity and patriotic attachment to the EU, expressed in a constitution crafted – like the U.S. Constitution – by a group of enlightened leaders, on behalf of their people, to found a new political "city on a hill" in Europe.

Again, language was manipulated in order to serve the cause of supranational European governance, with the treaty being sold to the public as a constitution. But the tactic backfired. Introducing a "constitution" for Europe was too big a step, violating Monnet's rule of incrementalism. Europeans already had their own national constitutions. They didn't want an EU constitution. In national referenda in 2005, the French and the Dutch rejected the European Constitution.

"A CONSTITUTION THROUGH THE BACK DOOR"

After getting hammered by French and Dutch voters, EU leaders beat a tactical retreat. They fell back on the legacy of Monnet and the strategy of deception. They made cosmetic amendments to the European Constitution and renamed it the Reform Treaty initially, before settling on Treaty of Lisbon. According to the European Commission website, the Lisbon Treaty, which entered into force on December 1, 2009, "reforms the EU institutions and improves the EU decision-making process; strengthens the democratic dimension of the EU; reforms the internal policies of the EU; [and] strengthens the external policies of the EU."[8] No mention is made of the fact that the Lisbon Treaty is, for all intents and purposes, the EU constitution with new clothing.

Jens-Peter Bonde, a leading Euroskeptic, effectively brought this reality to light. A longtime member of the European Parliament from Denmark and a member of the European Convention, Bonde undertook an exhaustive comparison of the Lisbon Treaty and the failed European Constitution.[9] He found that there was virtually no difference between the two, except that the Lisbon Treaty was packaged as a set of amendments to the existing EU treaties in order to obscure that fact. The Lisbon Treaty, he concluded, was "a constitution through the back door."[10] Bonde further characterized the European Constitution / Lisbon Treaty as a "Constitution without democracy," explaining, "A constitution usually protects citizens from politicians. It sets limits to what those elected may decide on between elections. The EU Constitution and the Lisbon treaty are different in this respect. They protect bureaucrats and politicians from the normal democratic influence of voters."[11] Furthermore, the Lisbon Treaty represents a massive transfer of power from member states to the EU. Bonde's analysis showed a "power shift from voters to Brussels in 113 points. There was and is not a single instance of power going the other way."[12]

The Lisbon Treaty brought a myriad of structural changes to the EU. For example, the EU now has two "presidents." In addition to the president of the European Commission, a post that has existed since 1958, there is now a president of the European Council, who presides over the summit meetings of the EU member states' heads of government and of state. Lisbon created the post of high representative for foreign affairs and security policy, basically a de facto EU foreign minister, and an EU-level diplomatic corps, the European External Action Service (EEAS), under the leadership of the high representative. Lisbon also increased EU power in justice and policing.

Another important innovation of the Lisbon Treaty is that it conferred upon the EU a legal personality. This made the EU into a real actor in international affairs, completely distinct from the member states, and thus enabled the EU, among other things, to negotiate and be a party to international treaties. Significantly,

Lisbon also incorporated the Charter of Fundamental Rights of the European Union, thereby making it legally binding. In that way, Lisbon has established a stronger legal basis – or at least a legal pretext – for the pursuit of a supranational human rights policy at EU level, a topic we will examine in Part Four of this book.

The symbolism of Lisbon is just as important as its transfer of considerable powers from the member states to the EU. Lisbon made the EU look more like a sovereign entity, endowing it with many of the characteristics of state sovereignty. An EU-level president of the European Council now "presides" over the EU national heads of government, at least symbolically. The EU now has a proto–foreign minister, its own diplomatic service, and a sovereign state–like legal personality. In enshrining the Charter of Fundamental Rights in the Lisbon Treaty, the EU has given itself its own "bill of rights." Perhaps most fraught with implications is Lisbon's elaboration – both explicit and implicit – on the rights and privileges conferred by the common EU citizenship of all member-state citizens, the "citizenship of the Union" that was first introduced in the Maastricht Treaty. EU citizenship exists over and above the national citizenships and, in case of conflict, trumps the privileges and duties of national citizenship.

These new attributes of sovereignty join two symbols adopted in 1985: the official anthem of the EU, Beethoven's setting of Friedrich Schiller's *Ode to Joy*, and the EU flag, a circle of twelve golden stars against a blue background, which is now the featured emblem on more automobile license plates throughout the EU than any national flag. The importance of this accumulation of symbols is difficult to exaggerate. In the EU universe, such symbols mean more than they do elsewhere. Taken all together, they vest the EU with the readily recognizable trappings of state sovereignty. In this context, it should not be forgotten either that the European Parliament has been a directly elected parliament since 1979.

How is all this best to be understood? The road from the ECSC to the EU of today has been long and winding, with many twists and turns and several switchbacks. But somewhere along the way, Europe truly was transformed. A continent of sovereign nation-states has become a continent of EU member states. And the governments of these member states have ceded, step by step over more than six decades, an incalculable magnitude of sovereignty to Brussels. This drawn-out, elite-driven process has largely escaped the notice of average Europeans. Certainly, in its bureaucratic obfuscation, its rarefied, legalistic complexity and its self-contained universe of insider jargon, the EU has developed in a way that most people have not had the time or energy to comprehend. The institutional growth of what is now the EU has come about through an unbending and dogged pursuit of "ever closer union," imposed from the top down, by a process shrouded in obscurity and crowned with a series of significant triumphs. In the next chapter we will examine the role that this key three-word phrase, "ever closer union," has played in the history of European integration.

CHAPTER 6:
THE CLOAK OF CONSTRUCTIVE AMBIGUITY

As we have seen, the EU and its institutional predecessors have been undergoing virtually continuous change. This includes tremendous growth in size and membership since the ECSC was launched with six founding members. Since the first new member states joined in the 1970s, the EU has reached the point where now, with twenty-eight members, it stands on the cusp of becoming almost pan-European. Just as importantly, though, the EU has steadily been changing institutionally over the course of six decades. Ever more power has been transferred, step by step, from national capitals to Brussels. According to best estimates, anywhere from 40 to 60 percent of the laws affecting the average Swede or Italian or Spaniard or Dane have their origin in Brussels.[1] And almost all of this has happened not in a straight line of logical progression, but along a curvy, sometimes broken path on which reality differs from language, practice diverges from law and regulation, and the European Union (like the *ten* different "configurations" of the supposedly *one* Council of Ministers) can appear to be all or none of the very different things that people of various nationalities and diverse ideologies want it to be.

But through all of the postmodern flux, one key foundational phrase has remained. It appeared at the very beginning of the 1957

Treaty of Rome establishing the European Economic Community, encapsulating the meaning of the entire treaty in three words: the determination of the signatories "to establish the foundations of an *ever closer union* among the European peoples ...."[2]

HOW "EVER CLOSER UNION" HOLDS THE PROJECT TOGETHER

In the hearts of believers in the European idea, "ever closer union among the peoples of Europe" is a noble aspiration. Arising as it did out of the postwar European longing for peace, "ever closer union" expressed not just the meaning of the Rome Treaty, but also the essence of what became the EU.

It also encapsulates the EU's "bothness." For the supranationalists, "ever closer union" captures better than any other formula their fervent adherence to the ideal of a unifying supranational governance. On the other hand, the phrase lacks clear objective content – and therein lies the key to its success. It is broad and open-ended. It means something, and yet it means nothing. And a key to understanding the EU project as a whole is understanding how the broadness and ambiguity of the phrase "ever closer union" function within the EU, and what these attributes tell us about the EU and the European idea.

Exemplifying the Monnet method at its finest, "ever closer union" leaves open what must for now be left open, namely, exactly what it will ultimately mean. Will it mean political union? Will it mean a common economic governance, but without political union? Will it mean developing as much political and economic cooperation as possible while retaining the distinct member states? Does it mean Luuk van Middelaar's "in-between-ness," in which EU elites act in a space "between" the member states and the EU itself, a space apart from both poles?[3] It could mean any of these. Anyone can interpret it in any way.

"Ever closer union," again, leaves room for the "bothness" of the EU – togetherness and separateness, dependence and independence. If one takes the larger phrase, "ever closer union among the European peoples," one sees the paradox at its heart. Joseph Weiler, one of the most brilliant academic experts on the EU, writes that "one of Europe's articles of faith" is that "the Community and Union were about 'lay[ing] the foundations of an ever closer union among the *peoples* of Europe.' Not the creation of one people, but the union of many."[4]

Another expression of this "union of many" is the slogan "unity in diversity," which has become a catchphrase for what EU elites believe is the heart of European identity.[5] Contrasting "unity in diversity," *In uno plures,* with the U.S. motto *E pluribus unum,* "out of many, one," a 1993 experts' report states: "We are Europeans, and are proud of it. What is happening is that we are realizing our identity.... We are many in one: *In uno plures,* and we want to keep and nurture our diverse cultures that together make us the envied focus of culture, civilization, intellectual life and savoir-vivre in the world."[6]

So where does the balance fall between unity and diversity? Is one more important than the other? Can both be equally important? In an insightful analysis of EU cultural policy, Cris Shore comments, "From the EU's perspective, 'unity in diversity' is intended to project the idea that the EU seeks to celebrate and promote cultural pluralism.... But it also suggests that the EU offers a new layer of identity under which the regions and nations can unite."[7] Shore goes on to assert that the underlying purpose is not safeguarding cultural diversity, but promoting "Europe's overarching unity."[8] That is probably correct, but no one really knows. And no one is supposed to know. The ambiguity wraps the agenda in the warm fuzziness of a noble-sounding phrase that means nothing and thus threatens nothing. A clearer definition of "ever closer union among the European peoples" would generate much more opposition because there are no unqualified "Europeans." The Dutch remain Dutch, the Czechs Czech and the Poles Polish. The primary allegiance of the overwhelming majority of Europeans is not to Europe, but to their home country and to their separate linguistic and cultural identities.

But the ambiguity is also for EU elites, among whom there is no consensus on the EU's ultimate form. "Ever closer union" is vague enough to be put aside by those who are busy keeping the day-to-day machinery of the EU in working order. Many of them are trapped in the EU agenda and need a way to avoid thinking that they might be eroding their own nation's sovereignty by their daily participation in the EU project. The average national minister from an EU member state spends overwhelming amounts of time attending EU meetings in Brussels, then transposing EU regulation into national law, and finally enforcing laws and regulations that originated in Brussels. In fact, EU and national jurisdiction in virtually every policy area are so hopelessly intertwined that the British government took more than two years and spent around 5 million pounds (7.7 million dollars) on a "Balance of Competences Review" meant to clarify how and where EU powers affect Britain and British sovereignty. When the review was finished in December 2014, the British government did not offer an overall assessment of the results. The conclusions to be drawn remained in dispute, and adding an official governmental evaluation would probably have been politically too explosive.

In such a predicament, it is very important to EU elites – both the sovereigntists and the integrationists – that there is no common definition of "ever closer union." The phrase has performed quite a service. It has proved open-ended enough to keep the supranationalists, such as Schuman, Kohl and Barroso, together with the nationalists such as de Gaulle and Thatcher.

THE WORLDVIEW AND DIRECTION OF EVER CLOSER UNION

"Ever closer union" is not only a way of keeping the EU project going despite a lack of agreement on ultimate goals. It also expresses a worldview. Whatever its meanings when the Treaty of Rome was signed in 1957, "ever closer union" has by now come to reflect a postmodern, relativistic worldview in which nothing is fixed or certain. Everything is constantly moving, constantly changing. The EU is like an amoeba continuously changing shape as the fluctuating currents push its outer membrane in all directions. "Ever closer union" has become the animating idea behind this state of constant change, because it can be reinterpreted at whim to fit every shape and every current, expressing an aspiration vague enough that everyone can implicitly share in it.

The haziness is deceptive, though. Underneath the soothing flux of postmodernity lurks a steely determination to achieve supranational governance. After all, while ever closer union is ambiguous, it is inspirational enough to serve as a rallying cry for the supranationalists, spurring them on to further European integration. Upon closer reflection, if one resists being lulled to intellectual sleep by the vaguely noble-sounding "ever closer union," the phrase aims at more than merely a free-trade area or a traditional international organization of sovereign member states.

The framework for relations between sovereign members of traditional international organizations is fixed, decided by a mutually understood balance between members' national sovereignty and their cooperation within the organization. In contrast, "ever closer union" entails fluid, undecided, evolving relations among the EU member states as they move toward some sort of political union. The British prime minister David Cameron seems to understand this. In an important speech in January 2013, he called for a stop to the push for ever closer union, advocating instead a flexible EU of cooperating, sovereign member states. (More on Cameron's speech in Chapter 17.) And Cameron is not alone in this view. Even the Netherlands, a core member state, shows signs of pulling back decidedly from the supranationalist model. In a press release in June 2013 after its own review of EU vs. national powers, the Dutch government said, "The Netherlands is convinced that the time of an 'ever closer union' in every possible policy area is behind us."[9]

As European integration has unfolded in the real world over the past sixty-five years, the EU's striving toward "ever closer union" has taken on a distinctly postdemocratic coloring, as we will see in the next section. And in the final analysis, despite the attempts of the British and the Dutch and others to push back, "ever closer union" symbolizes the victory of the visionaries over the pragmatists. Lost in their focus on hard facts, the pragmatists are too complacent. They seriously underestimate the power of ideas, dreams and worldviews, especially if they seem unrealistic or logically incoherent. Meanwhile, the supranationalists have it in black-and-white: "ever closer union" is the declared purpose of the Rome Treaty, and every member state has signed up for it.

PART THREE

CASE STUDIES IN SOFT UTOPIA

CHAPTER 7:
GETTING IT RIGHT THE SECOND TIME

"Europe's nations should be guided towards the superstate without their people understanding what is happening... which will eventually lead to federation."[1] Adrian Hilton's synopsis of the Monnet method could not be more apt. By stealth and subterfuge, ever closer union is to be made inevitable. This means overriding any voters, even majorities of voters, if they stand in the way.

Perhaps the most blatant indicator of the EU's disrespect for democracy is its refusal to accept the results of votes in the EU member states that do not turn out "correctly." It is a disturbing story. More unsettling is that so few people seem to care that their voices are slowly being silenced. It might be more accurate to say that few are fully aware of what has been happening, because of the sheer distance of Brussels and the disarming rhetoric of democracy that EU leaders employ.

GETTING THE DANES TO YES

The first time that EU elites refused to accept a democratic vote occurred more than twenty years ago. On June 2, 1992, Denmark held a referendum on the Treaty on European Union, or the

Maastricht Treaty, which had been signed that February. By a 50.7% vote, with 83.1% of voters participating, the Danes rejected the treaty. This was a major setback for European integration, delivered directly by voters themselves.

The reaction of EU elites was largely a combination of shock and incomprehension, followed by resolve to keep moving forward, with or without the Danes. Jacques Delors, president of the European Commission at the time and a mythic figure in supranationalist lore, said, "the Commission takes note of the views of the Danish people, who are fully entitled to make these views known and have done so in accordance with democratic procedure." Nevertheless, he went on, "the Commission is bound to say that it fears the result will have consequences not only for the Community itself but also for Denmark and the Danes." Delors expressed the Commission's hope that member states would "proceed to ratify on schedule."[2]

Even some of those associated with Euroskeptics did not want to listen to the Danes. After all, the negotiations had been so arduous. According to John Major, then the British prime minister and a member of the generally Euroskeptic Conservative Party, "The Maastricht treaty began to build the kind of European Community that we wish to see.... I do not believe that a substantial renegotiation of the Maastricht treaty is a practical proposition at this time. We must wait and see what action the Danish Government will take, but I still hope that the full provision of the Maastricht treaty will be carried forth into law."[3] The Danish prime minister, Poul Schluter, sounded somewhat nonplussed: "We all know that we must find a solution which does not necessitate re-ratification processes in the other countries," he said, adding that he thought such a solution was possible.[4]

Clearly, the verdict of the Danish voters could not be allowed to stand. Unless all EU member states ratify a treaty, it cannot come into effect. And Maastricht *had* to come into effect. The dream depended on it. It was the Treaty on European Union, heralding the birth of the EU and charting the path toward the common currency, which was to unify Europe not only economically, but also politically. Exactly there, of course, was the rub. The Maastricht Treaty impinged extensively on national sovereignty.

Therefore, at their December 1992 summit, European Community leaders concluded the Edinburgh Agreement, giving the

Danes opt-outs from the Maastricht Treaty to allow them to guard
their national prerogatives in areas they considered vital to
national sovereignty. Denmark thus opted out of closer cooperation on matters related to national defense. Neither would it participate in the common currency. It would not be subject to
monetary or fiscal measures related to the euro, and would remain
outside the jurisdiction of the European Central Bank. The Edinburgh Agreement also clarified that "citizenship of the Union" as
foreseen in the treaty did not "in any way take the place of national
citizenship," nor would it "create a citizenship of the Union in the
sense of citizenship of a nation-state."[5]

Denmark then held a second referendum, in May 1993. The
defeat of the first referendum was largely due to Danish voters'
desire to retain Danish national sovereignty and not be subject to a
supranational entity that was not directly accountable to them.
After concluding the Edinburgh Agreement, the Danish political
elite took it as a given that the Edinburgh opt-outs had satisfied
Danish voters' concerns. They downplayed the broader question
of the democratic legitimacy of transferring powers from a democratically accountable national government to a poorly understood,
much more loosely accountable European Union. Upon wrapping
up the agreement, Prime Minister Schluter had commented, "We
can now expect a clear 'yes' in the next referendum. I am very
happy that our future participation in European co-operation now
seems ensured...."[6] With seven of the eight political parties in the
Danish parliament pushing for it, those in favor of the Maastricht
Treaty won a strong victory: 56.7% of voters said yes, with an
86.5% turnout.

The other countries that held a referendum on the Maastricht
Treaty were France and Ireland. Voters in both countries approved
the treaty. In Ireland, 69.5% voted in favor, with a 57.3% turnout. It
was different in France: with an overall 69.7% turnout, the yes votes
just squeaked by, at 51%. Serious misgivings about the ushering in
of "European Union" were clearly not limited to Denmark.

TEACHING THE IRISH A LESSON OR TWO

Ireland has traditionally looked favorably on EU membership and
closer European integration, as demonstrated in the voters' approval

of the Maastricht Treaty by almost 70%. There are two main reasons for this. The most commonly cited reason is that EU membership gave Ireland access to EU markets and massive amounts of EU "structural funds," fueling its economic boom and its rise from one of the poorest Western European countries to one of the richest. It is quite true that Ireland had seen impressive growth by the time the eurozone crisis hit, and boasted a per capita GDP rivaling that of the very richest member states. The second reason, less often cited but just as important, is the troubled history of Great Britain's dominance of Ireland. The Irish believe that EU membership gives them independence and freedom to maneuver vis-à-vis their much larger neighbor to the east, between Ireland and the continent. Nevertheless, the Irish have twice failed to vote the "correct" way, and consequently have twice been called upon to "get it right the second time."

In June 2001, Irish voters rejected the Treaty of Nice by a solid majority. This treaty was ostensibly an effort to reform the EU in order to handle the upcoming enlargement from fifteen to twenty-five member states (with most of the new ones coming from the former Eastern Bloc). In reality, though, it was also an attempt to deepen European integration, taking more powers from the member states and handing them to the EU. In Ireland, 53.8% of voters said no to the treaty, with only 34.8% of registered voters participating in the referendum.

According to common wisdom, Irish voters were concerned that the Treaty of Nice might threaten Irish neutrality (as Ireland is a convinced neutral militarily and is not, for example, a member of NATO), and they worried that it gave too much power to the large member states, putting smaller ones at a disadvantage. But the Nice Treaty vote was also a wake-up call to both Irish and EU leaders. The Irish voters wanted their voices to be heard by their elected leaders. At the same time, the low turnout for the referendum was an example of a growing trend in EU-related votes: a great many voters are becoming complacent and apathetic toward a distant and complex EU that they do not understand. They become resigned to their lack of a voice, and give up.

As was the case after the Danish rejection of Maastricht in 1992, loud and insistent voices from Brussels and other member-state capitals asserted that the Irish result was not acceptable.

Another vote must be held so the Irish could get it right. The Irish government acquiesced, but first managed to obtain the Seville Declaration,[7] upholding Irish military neutrality, among other concessions. A second referendum on the Treaty of Nice was held in October 2002. Under massive pressure from throughout the EU, Irish voters approved the treaty by a resounding majority of 62.9%, with a turnout of close to half of registered voters.

The whole scenario repeated itself several years later when the Treaty of Lisbon – the repackaged EU constitution – came up for approval. On June 12, 2008, Irish voters rejected the treaty by 53.4%, with a 53.1% turnout. That this result was a great surprise to the Irish political establishment is testimony to the gulf between the decision makers and the average voters.

The predictable uproar ensued. Jean Asselborn, Luxembourg's foreign minister, said that Ireland would need to have a second vote, adding, "The question is how can we prepare it so that it can be won."[8] Elmar Brok, a senior MEP from Germany's Christian Democratic Union (Angela Merkel's party), declared controversially that Ireland would need to vote again and that a new referendum would decide whether Ireland stayed in the EU or not.[9]

Now the Irish political establishment was worried. They saw themselves between the rock of revealing their disrespect for Irish voters yet again, and the hard place of finding themselves shame-faced and excluded among their peers in the EU elite.

After sixteen months of renewed pressure from European leaders and intense campaigning in Ireland, the Irish voters got it right on their second try, approving the constitutional amendment allowing ratification of the Lisbon Treaty on October 2, 2009. Again, the vote was quite a turnabout: 67.1% in favor, with 59% of registered voters participating. Why the reversal? The most noticeable argument of the yes side was a blatant scare tactic: the suggestion that a no vote would isolate Ireland economically, closing EU markets and ending the Irish economic miracle. An Irish taxi driver summed it up well in a conversation with me just after the second referendum. When I asked why such a huge majority voted for Lisbon after so many of the same people had rejected it the first time, he said, "They scared the Bejesus out of us. Why, I didn't believe a word they said, and I was *still* so scared that I voted yes."

Between the Irish cases of Nice in 2001–2002 and Lisbon in 2008–2009, voters in France and the Netherlands (as mentioned earlier) handed EU integrationist elites what was perhaps their biggest defeat, at least symbolically, when they voted against the proposed European Constitution in 2005. Irish voters did not play a role this time only because the French and the Dutch beat them to it, rejecting the constitution before the Irish could schedule their referendum. Irish elites were undoubtedly relieved that for once they were not the ones on the hot seat in Brussels.

The European Constitution was born of the creative opportunity seeking of EU federalists. Curiously, their chance came with the attacks on the United States of September 11, 2001. The Belgians, who held the six-month rotating EU presidency at the time and who had a government of convinced federalists led by Prime Minister Guy Verhofstadt (author of *The United States of Europe*),[10] completely redirected their presidency in response to the terrorist attacks. They believed the attacks laid bare the need for a more unified EU that could take "concerted action" and show European leadership in the fight against terrorism, and they proceeded to take steps to create just such a unified "Europe." Thus, the crowning achievement of the Belgian EU presidency came into being: the Convention on the Future of Europe, or European Convention, named purposefully in reference to the Constitutional Convention in Philadelphia, where the U.S. Constitution was hammered out by the revered American Founding Fathers.

The aspiring founders of the New Europe were led by Valéry Giscard d'Estaing, former president of France, with Giuliano Amato and Jean-Luc Dehaene – former prime ministers of Italy and Belgium respectively – as vice chairmen. Convention participants, as the European Commission explained, "were drawn from the national parliaments of member states and candidate countries, the European Parliament, the European Commission, and representatives of heads of state and government." The European Convention first met in February 2002, and then once or twice a month in plenary session.[11] After more than two years of negotiations, the Treaty Establishing a Constitution for Europe was finally agreed on, and signed in October 2004.

This tangled web of jargon, vagaries and overreach still had to face some of the voters in the EU, though. In France and the Netherlands, the voters clearly said no, and EU leaders judged it politically impossible to call for a revote this time. Unlike Ireland and Denmark, the Netherlands and France are founding members of the EU. They are also much larger and more influential member states. Moreover, EU leaders had publicly committed to accepting the referendum results. And by this time, everyone realized that calling this treaty a constitution had been too big a step. No one could plausibly claim that voters did not know what the issue was when they voted: whether the EU had the right to establish a constitution, and thus symbolically assert EU governing authority over the member states and their citizens.

But surely, not being able to call for a revote could not possibly mean it was necessary to accept unwanted results. Here, necessity was the mother of creative invention, as EU leaders called an intergovernmental conference, repackaged the European Constitution as the Lisbon Treaty, and pushed it through without going back to the French or Dutch voters. The stubborn Irish put up a roadblock with their unmistakable no vote. But they were just the Irish, after all, so they were sent back to the polls, and they approved the Lisbon Treaty in the second vote under massive pressure and fear-mongering. And so the European Constitution, though voted down three times, is now, for all intents and purposes, in force in the European Union.

CHAPTER 8:
ÉCRASEZ L'INFÂME:
RELIGION AND THE EU CONSTITUTION

A constitution is not only a legal document, establishing a basic law for a people. Just as importantly, it is an expression of a people's identity. An effective constitution binds a people together in a compact that both lays out the fundamental rules of their life together and engenders the sense of unity that is necessary in order to have a flourishing, cohesive polity based on self-government under the rule of law.

The U.S. Constitution is a good example of this identity-affirming function. With the American people having already asserted their oneness and their Americanness, before God and the world, in the Declaration of Independence, and then having forged it in the hardship of revolutionary war, the U.S. Constitution begins with a reassertion of the existence of an American people and their intent to create a stronger union among themselves: "We the People of the United States, in Order to form a more perfect Union...."[1] Similarly, the postwar West German constitution, called the Basic Law, now the constitution of the unified Germany, refers to the German people as a single entity and, in a reference to the devastation of World War II, avows their responsibility and their determination to be a unifying force for good in Europe and the world: "Conscious of their responsibility before God and man, Inspired by the determination to promote world peace as an equal partner in a united Europe, the German people, in the exercise of their constituent power, have adopted this Basic Law."[2]

The Polish constitution refers to the Homeland, the Polish Nation, God, and the Polish people's ideals and identity forged in the struggle for independence and self-government:

> Having regard for the existence and future of our Homeland,
> Which recovered, in 1989, the possibility of a sovereign and democratic determination of its fate,
> We, the Polish Nation – all citizens of the Republic,
> Both those who believe in God as the source of truth, justice, good and beauty,
> As well as those not sharing such faith but respecting those universal values as arising from other sources,
> Equal in rights and obligations towards the common good – Poland,
> Beholden to our ancestors for their labours, their struggle for independence achieved at great sacrifice, for our culture rooted in the Christian heritage of the Nation and in universal human values,
> ....
> Hereby establish this Constitution of the Republic of Poland ....[3]

CREATING A EUROPEAN IDENTITY

A lofty, identity-forging document is what EU leaders hoped to create for the European Union when they called a constitutional convention in the wake of September 11, 2001. This was an attempted coup d'état of the utopians, dispensing with the frustratingly slow strategy of incremental progress and instead seizing the reins of history to make a Great Leap Forward toward real European union. The hope was that positing the existence of something that required a constitution would somehow make that something come into being. Draft a constitution, they thought, and the nation (or the postnational polity, or the supranational state, or

whatever it would be) that it constitutes would follow. The utopian unreality of it all was reflected almost poignantly in the
self-contradictory title, "Treaty Establishing a Constitution for
Europe."[4] This was a strained attempt to assert that the treaty was
creating something much more than a treaty can create – a higher,
European identity.

It was all about creating Europe. Blazing the trail to the
longed-for identity and cohesiveness of a unified European polity
and a unified European people. For many centuries, Europe was
Christendom and Christendom was Europe, so it was inevitable
that a debate would arise about whether European identity was
grounded in Christianity, and whether this should be acknowledged in the constitution. It was equally inevitable that this debate
would be passionate and contentious. It raged virtually from the
first session of the Convention on the Future of Europe in February 2002 until after the constitution was rejected by French and
Dutch voters in 2005.

Of course, lofty ideals were not the only motivation behind
the EU constitution. There was also a very hard-knuckled, practical
agenda: crafting rules to transfer more powers from the member
states to the EU. And there was what you might call a technocratic
reason to negotiate yet another EU treaty, namely, the sense that
"European governance" needed to be made more transparent, efficient and democratic. But the crucial issue in the negotiations was
how the constitution would define Europe and its people. What is
Europe, and what is the European people? This was the heart of
the matter. And so the fight over whether to mention religion in
the European Constitution became the pivotal symbolic battle in
the war for Europe's soul.

TRADITIONALISTS VS. PROGRESSIVES, AND A STUBBORN FRENCHMAN

No one can plausibly deny that the Christian faith was a primary
formative force in the development of European civilization. For
centuries, European civilization *was* Christendom. The debate at
the convention was not really about that history. It was principally
about three questions: (1) Is it appropriate to mention Christianity
as a defining element of European culture, while excluding other

traditions that have shaped Europe or that exist in Europe today, such as classical humanism, secularism or Islam? (2) Is Europe's Christian heritage something to be celebrated, or was it a negative influence to be overcome? (3) How do we want to define Europe and European identity, knowing that this definition will be a guide for Europe's future direction?

Given the foundational character of these questions, it was natural that certain groups and interests lined up decisively on each side of the debate. Who would line up where was relatively predictable. Those who argued for a recognition of Christianity were, in general, the traditionalists: the center-right, especially from Christian Democratic circles, and the established churches, especially the Catholic Church. This side included member states with center-right governments and a tradition of close affiliation with the Catholic Church, such as Poland, Italy, Ireland, Slovakia and Malta. Those opposed to recognizing Christianity were principally the progressives: the left and center-left, secularists and adherents of the French tradition of *laïcité*, the radical separation of religion from public life. This side included, in addition to France, member states that either had their own secularist tradition, or had center-left or secularist-oriented governments, such as Belgium, the UK, Denmark, Sweden and Finland. Some member states, such as Germany, Austria, Hungary and the Czech Republic, remained relatively neutral, generally because they had strong leaders and deeply rooted constituencies on both sides of the issue.[5]

As chairman of the Convention on the Future of Europe, Valéry Giscard d'Estaing was undoubtedly the most prominent voice for keeping Christianity out of the European Constitution, and a decided advocate of his country's tradition of *laïcité*. In an interview in the German weekly *Die Zeit*, Giscard was asked whether God would have a place in the constitution. His answer, disingenuously projecting France's *laïcité* onto the entire continent, described a double heritage of Europe since the nineteenth century – a "religious-spiritual" heritage and a "purely secular political system, in which religion plays no role."[6] He also claimed that Europe had become religiously diverse. Giscard's attitude seemed matter-of-fact to a point verging on indifference: "A reference to God seems to me personally inappropriate," he said. "Others think differently: I've just come back from Poland. For a Pole, 'God' simply means Christ. By far most people there are Catholic.

In France it's different – there are Protestants, Jews, Muslims. 'God' no longer has the same content."[7]

It is important to note that *laïcité* does not necessarily entail a consciously antireligious attitude, but Giscard sometimes made it seem that way. He infuriated traditionalists by simply presenting successive drafts of a constitution without reference to God or Christianity. When the convention's praesidium, which Giscard headed, first unveiled a skeleton draft in October 2002, it included nothing on religion at all. This omission sparked intense debate. The praesidium presented a draft of the opening articles of the constitution, covering objectives, goals and values, on February 6, 2003, and Christianity was again absent. What the text included was this distinctly secularist statement: "The Union is founded on the values of respect for human dignity, liberty, democracy, the rule of law and respect for human rights, values which are common to the Member States."[8] In response, there was fierce debate among convention delegates, and many calls for amendments came from both sides of the issue. Giscard then attempted to bridge the divide, telling reporters on February 27 that religion should be mentioned in the constitution's preamble, but not in the legally binding articles.[9] In an additional comment that could have made people wonder just how vague this reference might be, Giscard suggested that "the future constitutional treaty might borrow from the EU charter of fundamental rights, which refers to the bloc's 'spiritual and moral heritage.'"[10]

When the praesidium presented a first-draft preamble on May 28, 2003, there was no sign of the reference to God that Giscard had suggested. Instead, there was only a Giscard-like nod to the "cultural, religious and humanist inheritance of Europe," with the Enlightenment listed as a part of that heritage, but not Christianity. Two days later, the second draft of the constitution was released, without specific mention of Christianity or God. Another draft, a few weeks later, still lacked any such reference. Since this draft was the convention's final product, to be presented to member states for negotiation, Giscard and the secularists were handing a fait accompli to the traditionalists, who would now have to campaign for a change to the constitution as presented by the body charged with drafting it. By employing a good dose of Gallic stubbornness, and taking advantage of the lack of democratic accountability typical of negotiations in the realm of transnational governance, Giscard had succeeded in blocking the traditionalists.[11]

Emotions continued to rage over the issue until the constitution's final death. In early 2003, the former Irish prime minister John Bruton, a center-right praesidium member, joined a petition pushing for an article reminiscent of the Polish constitution's reference to God: "The Union values shall include the values of those who believe in God as the source of truth, justice, good and beauty as well as of those who do not share such a belief but respect these universal values arising from other sources."[12] Gianfranco Fini, deputy prime minister of Italy, proposed that the European Union be defined as a "community that shares a Judeo-Christian heritage," while a German deputy, Erwin Teufel, spoke of European civilization being built on three hills: the Acropolis of Athens, the Capitoline in Rome, and Golgotha in Jerusalem.[13]

The center-right traditionalists had a persistent ally in Pope John Paul II, who was a determined advocate of affirming Europe's religious heritage. In his apostolic exhortation *Ecclesia in Europa* (June 28, 2003), for example, the pope wrote, "There can be no doubt that the Christian faith belongs, in a radical and decisive way, to the foundations of European culture. Christianity in fact has shaped Europe, impressing upon it certain basic values. Modern Europe itself, which has given the democratic ideal and human rights to the world, draws its values from its Christian heritage."[14] A bit further on, he added: "I wish once more to appeal to those drawing up the future European constitutional treaty, so that it will include a reference to the religious and in particular the Christian heritage of Europe."[15] Other church officials, including Archbishop Christodoulos of the Greek Orthodox Church, also weighed in on behalf of the "Christian roots of the EU's spiritual and cultural traditions."[16]

The center-left and the secularists fully matched the traditionalists' passion. One British MEP, Linda McAvan, said that any explicit reference to Christianity would "offend those many millions of people of different faiths or no faith at all"; and the Belgian foreign minister, Louis Michel, forcefully declared that "Europe is not mono-religious."[17] Jacques Chirac, the president of France, was more nuanced, saying, "The Christian origins of European civilization are undeniable, but France is a secular state and so is not accustomed to having a statement of a religious nature in a constitutional text."[18]

The issue remained very much alive after the convention had

finished its work. In May 2004, on the eve of the summit of EU leaders set to make the final decision on the constitutional text, seven member states wrote a letter urging them to acknowledge a "historical truth" by making specific reference to the "Christian roots of Europe" in the EU constitution. "This issue remains a priority for our governments as well as for millions of European citizens," the letter explained.[19] The other member states were not enthusiastic about this idea. Spain's center-left foreign minister, for example, commented that "Spain is a Catholic country, but in the European constitution our government is rather secular, and in this sense we want to respect the text as it currently stands."[20]

Even after the constitution itself was dead, though being readied for a covert resurrection as the Lisbon Treaty, the issue of God in the constitution – and Christianity as a constituting factor in European identity – refused to die. After a meeting with the new pope, Benedict XVI, nearly a year after the defeat of the EU constitution, the German chancellor Angela Merkel, a Christian Democrat, said, "I underlined my opinion that we need a European identity in the form of a constitutional treaty and I think it should be connected to Christianity and God, as Christianity has forged Europe in a decisive way."[21]

A POST-CHRISTIAN EUROPEAN IDENTITY?

The result of the debate was not surprising. Instead of unequivocally recognizing the role of Christianity in Europe's history, the opening clause referred generally to "the cultural, religious and humanist inheritance of Europe, from which have developed the universal values of the inviolable and inalienable right of the human person, freedom, democracy, equality and the rule of law...."[22] This formulation carried Giscard's fingerprints, but it was also a typical EU compromise. Bloodless and rootless, vague and vapid, it represented an attempt to satisfy everyone, inevitably satisfying no one.

Looking at a deeper level, it is hard to deny that the utopian nature of the European idea influenced the outcome of this debate. After all, insofar as the European idea is a utopian commitment, religion cannot but be perceived as a *competitor*. A utopian political ideology bends reality to its political objective, rather than vice versa. It can brook no opposition from the real world, especially from a powerfully identity-shaping legacy that it is attempting to overcome. And the reality-bending nature of the European idea was fully apparent in the project of establishing an EU constitution. As was remarked earlier, referring to a treaty as a constitution seriously blurred the line between reality and fantasy. Attempting to create a European Constitution when no nation of Europe existed was an exercise in utopian fantasy, with no place for Christianity – the real progenitor of European civilization.

But the reference to Christianity was rejected not only because of an anti-Christian animus or in deference to the French tradition of *laïcité*, or even because of the utopian idea, but also because it would have been unambiguous. It would have clearly defined the roots of European identity. Worse, it would have pointed to a single, indisputably primary root of European identity. Such clarity is unacceptable. It could bring everything to a grinding halt.

The fuzzy ambiguity of "ever closer union" cloaks the lack of consensus in Europe regarding the EU and Europe's future. It obscures the persistent absence of "ever closer union" among peoples whose values, histories, languages and so much more remain identifiably distinct. The EU *has to be* a postmodern narrative – inventing and reinventing itself in order to keep together what stubbornly refuses to be the together-ness so deeply aspired to. The EU must create its own reality. It must tell the story it has chosen for itself in order to make the foundational myth of "ever closer union" real. Such an entity cannot logically acknowledge its roots in Christianity, a religion holding that there is an objective truth that cannot be reinvented.

Ironically, it is perfectly fitting that the European Constitution contained no substantive reference to Christianity, given that the EU elites aspired to create a European identity and polity from nothing but their own words. After all, calling what eventually became the Lisbon Treaty the European Constitution was nothing less than an attempt to declare their Europe into existence *ex nihilo*. How then could there be room in it for God? In the biblical creation story, the Spirit of God hovered over the waters and said, "Let there be light." And there was light. The delegates to the European Convention said, "Let there be *our* Europe." But *their* Europe stubbornly refuses to be.

CHAPTER 9:
THE EUROZONE CRISIS AND
THE POLITICS BEHIND THE MONEY

Speaking about the eurozone crisis, Herman van Rompuy, then the president of the European Council, said in October 2011 that the answer to the crisis was "more Europe." He also tried to shame the Euroskeptics:

> The euro began as a political project, and so it remains. Admittedly, even the fairest and most inclusive ideal cannot survive without a sound and stable economic foundation. But nor should we forget the basic reasons for this enterprise, which – far beyond the question of money – stem from values, from that idea of peace, democracy and a social market economy which we call the European model.... The great enemy of any project is the scheming mind that asks "What do I get out of it?" ... Those who say they want less Europe should be answered with more Europe.[1]

This was an astounding statement, accusing those who had suffered economically under the euro of being self-serving "enemies" of the grand European project, with "scheming minds." It illustrates another characteristic of political utopia: major policy decisions are based not on the concrete policy merits but on what is perceived to serve the realization of the utopia. The most glaring example of this pattern in the history of the EU is the introduction of the euro.

As van Rompuy affirmed, the euro was a political project. He said nothing at all about the economic pros and cons of having a common currency, only about how more European solidarity was needed to make the euro work. To have introduced the euro without serious regard for economic considerations was bad enough, but it was worse than that. The decision was made *against* all economic fundamentals. Introducing a common currency into countries of radically different cultures and levels of economic development and production has shown itself to be disastrous.

BEST-LAID PLANS

John Peet and Anton La Guardia, in their book *Unhappy Union: How the Euro Crisis – and Europe – Can Be Fixed*, summarize particularly well how the eurozone crisis grew in large measure out of the common currency and EU monetary policy, which is set for the entire eurozone by the European Central Bank (ECB) independently of eurozone governments and treats very different economies in a one-size-fits-all manner:

> In the early 2000s, years that became known as the "great moderation," when money was cheap, euro-zone countries were able to build up large external imbalances (15% of GDP in Greece). Had they still had national currencies, this would surely have provoked a response from markets. Instead, everybody benefited from low interest rates. Thus was born the great paradox of economic and monetary union. In order for countries to survive within it, they needed to make deeper structural reforms to improve their competitiveness; and yet the pressure to push through those reforms was reduced by the benign mood of financial markets. Many had hoped the creation of the euro would force ossified countries like Italy to change their ways. Losing the ability to devalue meant that competitiveness could be recovered only by "internal devaluation" (that is, bringing

down wages and prices relative to others), boosting pro-ductivity, or both. This meant liberalising labour and product markets, and promoting competition. But for coun-tries used to high inflation and high interest rates before the launch of the euro, any loss of competitiveness could be masked for a long time by cheaper money.

By about 2005 ... [the weaker economies] were enjoy-ing a boom fuelled by lower interest rates. At the other end of the spectrum, mighty Germany was growing anaemi-cally, but with very low inflation. To some extent the ECB's one-size-fits-all interest rate exacerbated this polarisation: interest rates were too low for overheating countries, but too high for Germany (the situation is reversed today).[2]

Of course, this wasn't supposed to happen. The euro was sup-posed to bring a windfall of economic benefits. From the publica-tion in 1970 of the Werner Report on how to achieve economic and monetary union, to the creation of the European Monetary System and the European Currency Unit in 1979, to the decision to form an Economic and Monetary Union as enshrined in the Maastricht Treaty in 1992, to the introduction of euro notes and coins in Jan-uary 2002 into the twelve member states that originally joined the euro, the advocates of currency union did all they could to tout its purported economic advantages.

Tellingly, most of their arguments focus more on European integration than on improved economic performance, as if inte-grating Europe economically would automatically mean a more prosperous Europe. The "Report on Economic and Monetary Union in the European Community" prepared in 1989 by a committee chaired by Jacques Delors, president of the European Commission, is emblematic. It predicted that "a single currency would clearly demonstrate the irreversibility of the monetary union, considerably facilitate the monetary management of the [European] Community and avoid the transaction costs of converting currencies. A single currency ... would also have a much greater weight relative to other major currencies than any individual Community currency."[3] Throughout, the report reflects three common assumptions about the benefits of the euro: (1) that a single currency would force closer macroeconomic cooperation and promote convergence of economic performance among the member states; (2) that a single currency would help realize fully the goal of a single market with free cross-border movement of people, goods, services, and capital; and (3) that a single currency would enhance the European Community's economic weight and influence in the world.[4]

The arguments of the Delors report were echoed in a 1994 speech by Henning Christophersen, the European commissioner for economic and financial affairs from 1985 to 1995, a time encompassing the decisions to establish a single market and a common currency: "To reap the full benefits of the single market... [it] must be supplemented by a better coordinated economic policy, a single monetary policy conducted by a European central bank and a single currency.... A single currency will eliminate transaction costs and uncertainty caused by exchange rate movements. It will truly integrate the European markets for goods and services."[5]

Today, despite the ravages of the eurozone crisis, the arguments haven't changed. And the purely economic ones – those that don't mention European integration – are disappointingly weak. As of this writing in early 2015, the EU Council website says: "The euro makes it easier for consumers to compare prices, and no exchange fees or transaction costs have to be paid when buying goods and services in other member states in the euro area."[6] The ECB website feebly echoes the argument that the euro results in a "high degree of price stability," the "removal of transaction costs," and "no exchange rate fluctuations."[7] Without a presupposed commitment to European integration, there's not much "there" there when it comes to the purported economic benefits of the euro – unless worrying about transaction costs keeps you up at night.

The conclusion is obvious: in essence, the economic arguments have always been perfunctory. What EU advocates were hoping, and quite openly saying, was that monetary union would force political union. And all of the arguments, economic or otherwise, were and are interwoven in the larger fabric of the European integration agenda. In fact, the euro and its supposed benefits are not even meant to be understood apart from European political integration. European union, and not a better-performing European economy, was the real reason for the euro. Helmut Kohl, the chancellor of Germany when the euro was agreed upon in Maastricht and perhaps the most influential figure in the push for the single currency, once said, "I wanted to bring the euro because to me it meant the irreversibility of European development," and that the euro was "a synonym for Europe going further."[8] The economic and financial affairs section of the European Commission's website highlights the euro as "a symbol of European identity... one of the strongest tangible symbols of European integration and the shared values of Europe, the European nations and Europeans themselves."[9] Similar statements by European leaders affirming the political motivation for the euro could go on forever.

But Great Leaps Forward always meet with opposition, too. The desires of the European dream almost always clash with waking, concrete interests – even the interests of those who dream sweet dreams of European integration. And so it was with the euro. As the German weekly *Der Spiegel* reported, "The efforts toward monetary union were continually foiled by the conflicting interests of the inflationary countries in the South and the so-called hard-currency belt around Germany and the Netherlands."[10] When the Cold War ended and the Berlin Wall fell, the French president François Mitterrand used Germany's wish for reunification as a lever to strengthen Kohl's resolve to commit to the euro. Mitterrand thought the euro would bind a unified Germany to Europe – helping maintain French influence over Germany and rendering more likely a German acquiescence to the easier monetary policy that France favored.[11] And so, ironically, the Germans' desire for German unification cleared the way for a big step in the dream of supranational European unification. Helmut Kohl, a committed European integrationist if there ever was one, took that and ran with it.

And what did the people in the street think? Not surprisingly, the countries that were most in favor of the euro were those with weak currencies and a habit of overspending.[12] People in countries such as Germany that had strong national currencies tended to be much more reticent about giving up what they had for the euro.[13] In typical EU manner, the benighted skeptics were scolded by their enlightened leaders for their lack of European vision.

THE TSUNAMI HITS

Political union did not come with the euro, however. This foolish utopian policy decision was an economic disaster-in-waiting, and in the eurozone crisis it hit Europe like a tidal wave. When the American subprime bubble burst, European banks proved to be even more exposed than American banks. Soon, several eurozone countries found themselves having to prop up failing banks. Then, in October 2009, a newly elected Greek government announced that Greece's deficit was twice as high as the previous government had claimed. That was enough, in the generally escalating panic, to cause interest rates on Greek bonds to go so high that "insolvency threatened" by the following spring.[14] Portugal also corrected its deficit estimate upward in 2009.

Investors seemed to realize, for the first time, that the euro had not transformed the eurozone countries into equally safe investment opportunities. It dawned on the markets that the creditworthiness of the individual eurozone countries differed radically. Meanwhile, the bursting of Ireland's and later Spain's real estate bubbles – which developed because of the "explosion of credit and economic activity" fueled by too low, one-size-fits-all interest rates after the euro's introduction – brought those countries into the crisis.[15] More and more, the crisis was showing the potential to spread to the entire southern flank of the eurozone.

Bailouts came to be seen as unavoidable. First, in 2010, came the initial bailout of Greece to the tune of 110 billion euros. This was followed in 2012 by a second rescue package of 164 billion euros. The year 2015 saw two snap elections called because of the bailout crisis. The first, in January, brought the left-wing anti-austerity party Syriza to power. The second, in September, gave the Syriza prime minister, Alexis Tsipras, the mandate he was seeking – against the radicals in his party – to accept the terms of a third bailout. This third rescue package, agreed to in the summer, could provide up to 89 billion euros to Greece over a three-year period. Meanwhile, Greece remains highly indebted, with a staggering unemployment rate and the obligation to its creditors to impose austerity measures that will prolong the suffering for the foreseeable future. Realistically, there is no end in sight to Greece's need for outside financing as long as it remains a part of the eurozone.

But the need for bailouts was not confined to Greece. Ireland too received a bailout in 2010, a sum of 85 billion euros, and Portugal got 78 billion. In 2012, Spain needed approximately 40 billion euros to bail out its banks. In 2013 came the rescue of Cyprus to the tune of 10 billion euros.[16]

From 2010 to 2013, the economically weaker countries seemed to be falling like dominoes. Contagion was the monster lurking behind the curtains – the possibility of massive insolvency, the failure of the euro and economic collapse in the eurozone. There were fears that other countries might need bailouts, and the specter of having to rescue the highly indebted Italy and the economically rigid and profligate France haunted EU leaders. Italy and France would have toppled the euro for good – and still could. They are too big to allow to fail and too big to be able to save.

As of this writing, the markets have calmed down. But despite upturns in Ireland, Spain, Portugal and Cyprus, the economic fundamentals of the eurozone, a monetary union of widely divergent economies, are askew. As the British economist Roger Bootle dryly observes, "In economics textbooks, countries decide whether or not to form monetary unions with other countries on the basis of their economic suitability to each other."[17] The cost of the euro has been enormous and its political and economic pitfalls huge.

THE FUTURE OF THE EURO

The "economic governance" of the eurozone, with its economics-for-the-sake-of-politics, is bound to undermine growth, argues Hans-Werner Sinn, the president of the highly respected Ifo Institute for Economic Research in Munich and a passionate advocate of an integrated Europe. As Sinn explains, the eurozone looks not so much like a free market as a planned economy, radically distorting and attempting to steer the market in order to salvage the political goal of integrating Europe:

> We have created a quasi centrally planned system in which capital is steered toward southern Europe by two organizations, the ECB and the European Stability Mechanism [the EU bailout facility] under conditions that are politically determined... not market-determined.... What is happening in the euro zone right now undermines the foundational rule of the market economy... that behind every commitment of capital stand assets and the owner of those assets who endeavors to direct his money into investments that are as safe and as profitable as possible. This careful attention, that arises out of personal responsibility, is the lifeblood of the capitalist market economy.... By what we are

doing in Europe right now, we are sacrificing this lifeblood and replacing it with central planning authorities.... With the decisions of the euro-countries, more and more government-backed and state-directed capital flows will go into politically desired but inefficient investment projects that will further undermine the forces of growth in Europe.[18]

Moreover, he says, continuing on the path the EU has taken until now to save the euro will not only fail to solve the problems of the EU south, but also result in the impoverishment of the currently prosperous north, particularly Germany: "At the latest in 15–20 years we will feel the pinch everywhere."[19] Sinn explains, "Many people seem to think that because we have weathered the financial crisis, everything will be okay. Politicians and the media are doing their part to rock people in the cradle of a false sense of security. But most people fail to see that the only reason the markets have calmed is that they, as taxpayers and pensioners, have triggered the debts of the southern countries with new loans, and that sooner or later they will have to foot the bill."[20]

The growing tensions between the north and the south of the EU, especially the Greek resentment of Germany, attest that the effects of the euro have not been confined to the economic sphere. They have been social and political as well, and the consequences of a misbegotten euro threaten to get worse. Commenting on how the eurozone crisis created festering animosities between the prosperous north of the EU, mainly Germany, and the profligate south, Sinn predicts that if the policy response continues unchanged, "it will bring the peoples of Europe into conflict with each other."[21] He elaborates, "The effort to create a European equivalent of the dollar and impose a fiscal union on top of it, despite the absence of a common European state, is bound to fail. It will turn member countries into debtors and creditors to each other, stoking even more animosity."[22]

Sinn goes further to predict a crisis of democracy: "At some point people will notice that a part of their wealth is already lost. They'll notice that they can no longer afford the standard of living that they wanted to guarantee for their old age with their savings because of the loss of wealth caused by politicians. Even if people still don't understand how it all happened, and even if it's also too late to undo any of that loss of wealth, people will still react by rejecting the government." Politicians are thus "risking the flight of the people out of traditional parties and institutions."[23] As we will see in Chapter 19, this process is already well underway.

If the EU continues along its current policy path of "saving the euro" at all costs, the debt crisis and the demographic crisis – the phenomenon of fewer and fewer young people working to finance the retirement of more and more old people – will combine to land a double blow against the prosperity of Germany, the EU's economic engine. This has the potential to cause severe social unrest, warns Sinn: "If things keep developing according to the same logic as they have so far, I believe that significant social fault lines will arise in a few years in German society that will shake the very economic and political foundations of our state." Given the low birthrate of 8.1 children per 1,000 inhabitants, along with the burden of funding bailouts of weaker economies, "a good part of the supposed savings of the Germans will go up in smoke."[24] In a nutshell, Sinn concludes, "We are ensnared in the euro. Now we have to escape from this prison."[25]

PART FOUR

TRANSFORMING HUMAN RIGHTS

CHAPTER 10:
ABSOLUTE AUTONOMY:
THE GLOBAL ETHIC OF WOMEN'S RIGHTS

In a world where people are routinely disadvantaged, persecuted, imprisoned, even killed because of their religious faith, their political beliefs, their race, their sex, or their sexual orientation, robust engagement in behalf of human rights is not only a moral imperative, it is also wise. Respect for human rights, after all, is what has made Western Europe and North America beacons of stability, peace and prosperity where life can be good and human beings can flourish. In many ways, the EU's advocacy for human rights around the world has been exemplary.

On the other hand, what human rights *are* and which rights matter most are not axiomatic. What you believe *human rights* are depends on what you believe *human beings* are. And here, a transformation of worldview has occurred throughout the West, but especially in Europe – a switch from a basically Judeo-Christian culture rooted in tradition and truth, to a secular culture characterized by relativism, novelty and choice. This change has had a profound effect on the idea of human rights. In Europe, this transformation has taken place roughly simultaneously with the growth of the global governance ideology and is intimately connected with it.

Cursory observance of the human rights–related activities of the EU reveals a pervasive concern for women's, children's and LGBT rights. They are being "mainstreamed" into all areas of EU policy making, with the intention that each new EU initiative promote these rights.

Why this emphasis on rights asserted in behalf of particular categories of people, rather than on the classical freedoms that all people share in common? One might say it is because the classical freedoms have already been achieved in the EU. But there is a much deeper reason for the EU's focus on women's, children's and LGBT rights. As conceived by the postmodern secularists, including the EU, these rights have one characteristic in common: they are based on the notion of the absolute autonomy of the individual – the notion of choice taken to its ultimate extent. They are *transformative* and *liberationist*, like the global governance ideology itself.

What is meant by "transformative and liberationist"? Despite innocuous official statements and guidelines that keep largely to unobjectionable generalities, the EU's view of human rights promotes a transformation of the idea of what people *are*, redefining them as radically autonomous individuals who can choose to change their very nature and thus liberate themselves from the constraints of traditional familial and social bonds. In the case of women's and children's rights (to be analyzed in Chapter 10 and Chapter 12 respectively), liberation from the constraints of the family is a core concern. In the case of LGBT rights (to be discussed in Chapter 11), the transformative aspect is central, as the push for gay marriage and the concept of flexible gender identity are aimed at liberating human beings from both moral and physical constraints, to the extent of ignoring the empirical reality of the sexual nature of the human being as either man or woman.

Certainly, women and children and LGBT persons have as great a claim to human rights as anyone else. But the transformative and liberationist model of human rights – which, it must be said, has taken root among most of the elites in the United States and Canada as well as in Europe – is a complete departure from the traditional Western view of human beings out of which the concept of human rights first emerged. The classical human rights, originally called political rights or civil rights, were based on the

Christian/Enlightenment view of human nature. This view is expressed in the American Declaration of Independence: "We hold these truths to be self-evident, that all men are created equal, that they are endowed by their Creator with certain unalienable Rights, that among these are Life, Liberty and the pursuit of Happiness. – That to secure these rights, Governments are instituted among Men, deriving their just powers from the consent of the governed . . . ."[1]

It is directly from this view of human nature that the classical rights spelled out in the Bill of Rights – such as the freedoms of religion, speech and assembly – were derived. But I would argue that these classical rights can also be grounded in plain old common sense and observable reality. For people in the Western democracies, at least, it is a manifest fact of everyday life that human beings are individuals who, on the one hand, possess dignity and therefore rights independently of others, as individuals. On the other hand, individuals are connected to others, and they *want* to be connected to others. Human beings are individuals, but they are social. They are embedded in communities, and it is eminently appropriate that they live within the roles they bear in those communities and according to the values and the rights that are commonly accepted there – commonly accepted because they promote, or at the very least are believed to promote, the flourishing of those communities.

Nearly the world over and certainly in the West, the common-sense value that is the keystone of the flourishing society is the family. But the family requires a significant and permanent commitment of the individual to the other family members, and a considerable subordination of the individual's supposed interests and rights to the needs of others. This subordination of individual choice and autonomy flies in the face of the transformative and liberationist view of human rights as propagated in the EU and the global governance ideology, a view of human beings as radically free to define themselves as they wish, unfettered by traditional values or family obligations.

Thus, the family must unavoidably be undermined as a consequence of the global governance view of human rights propagated in the EU. That is why women's rights and children's rights have been skewed and redefined, along with marriage and human sexuality, and human beings themselves. And these skewed, redefined rights are the rights that matter in the EU, precisely because they oppose the traditional value of family – the most powerful institution of Western society that militates against personal autonomy and choice. Human rights reinterpreted as the right of atomized, self-defining individuals to determine "what's true for them" have become weapons against the traditional family and other social institutions that respect traditions and entail obligations. The new "human rights" are a means to separate individuals from each other, alienating them from the roles they would fill in communities and breaking the ties that would bind them to other people.

LIBERATING WOMEN FROM THEIR CHILDREN

A woman's right to equal pay for equal work, to equality of opportunity in the workplace, not to be subject to domestic violence – in short, the right to be treated as well as men – is indisputable. But in EU policy, the women's right *sine qua non* is "the right to choose." The right to an abortion, in other words. The absolute autonomy of every woman to do whatever she wants "with her own body" trumps everything else, including the right to life of the weaker, innocent party, the unborn child.

The fact that the EU promotes abortion at all is a mark of real dedication to the cause of "choice." Abortion policy actually falls within the remit of the member states, meaning that the EU may not officially make abortion policy at EU level. In fact, abortion is either illegal or highly restricted in three member states: Malta, Ireland and Poland. Nevertheless, EU institutions and officials have managed to make support for abortion a centerpiece of EU activity in the area of women's rights.

This is apparent first of all in the EU's vocal support for what have become the cornerstones of the abortion lobby's claim to international legitimacy: the Program of Action of the International Conference on Population and Development, held in Cairo in 1994, and the Platform for Action of the Fourth World Conference on Women, held in Beijing in 1995, both sponsored by the UN. In fact, the Cairo agenda is one of the EU's stated legal bases for funding projects related to women's sexual and reproductive health.[2] EU implementation of the Beijing Platform for Action, which contains repeated references to sexual and reproductive health, reproductive rights and family planning, has been mandated by the EU Council of

The Cairo and Beijing documents themselves, it is true, do not declare support for abortion. And EU officials – when compelled by parliamentary questions from pro-life members of the European Parliament – have explicitly said that EU support for Cairo and for "reproductive health" does not include abortion.[3] At both conferences, the EU and most EU member states wanted the right to abortion to be declared an international human right, but in order to get an agreement, abortion had to be dropped.

Since then, however, abortion activists have ensured that the conferences in Cairo and Beijing, and terms such as "reproductive health," have come to mean support for the right to abortion – regardless of the fact that it is nowhere specified in any UN agreement. Here again, as described in Chapter 5, language is manipulated to advance an agenda. In order to preserve deniability, clear definitions are avoided. "Reproductive health" in the mouths of pro-lifers might not mean abortion; in the mouths of abortion advocates, it almost always does. Subtle changes in phrasing send signals that insiders understand, but rarely specify openly. The primary example of that in this context is "sexual and reproductive health and rights," or SRHR, which everyone involved in UN discourse, both pro-choice and pro-life, understands as referring to the right to abortion. SRHR has become EU abortion advocates' rallying cry, and they take pains to link SRHR to Cairo and Beijing. To name just one of many examples, in an EU statement at the UN on the twenty-year anniversary of the Cairo conference, the ambassador who made the statement took care to include support for "sexual and reproductive health and rights," saying: "The EU and its Member States remain committed to the promotion, protection and fulfillment of all human rights and to the full and effective implementation of the Beijing Platform for Action and the Programme of Action of the International Conference on Population and Development and the outcomes of their review conferences and, in this context, sexual and reproductive health and rights."[4] Thus, Cairo and Beijing have come to mean abortion rights in EU-speak.

Beyond the declared support for the Cairo and Beijing platforms, if you want to see what EU policy on women's rights really is, follow the money. The EU is one of the world's largest providers of development assistance, and many of the projects it funds in developing countries are aimed at "improving women's health" in ways that include abortion. Two of the EU's biggest recipients of funds to carry out such projects are the two largest abortion providers in the world: the International Planned Parenthood Federation (IPPF) and Marie Stopes International (MSI).

In a meticulously researched report, the organization European Dignity Watch – despite the egregious delaying tactics and apparently intentional obfuscation of the European Commission – convincingly documents how the EU has funded tens of thousands of abortions or abortion-related services through MSI and/or IPPF projects in Cambodia, South Africa, Bangladesh, Papua New Guinea, Bolivia, Peru and Guatemala. These services include "menstrual regulation," a procedure employed before a pregnancy has been verified, which "empties a uterus" by means of "high-powered suction," typically of sufficient violence to "completely dismember and deconstruct the fetus... leaving only a mass of unidentifiable, bloody tissue...." Menstrual regulation is often done in order to circumvent the law in countries where abortion is illegal.[5]

The EDW report goes on to show how SRHR is a top priority in the EU's development assistance budget, consuming millions of euros. As EDW reports, a European Commission–financed study in 2011 ranked the EU as the world's fourth largest contributor of official development aid to reproductive health, behind the United States (shamefully), the Netherlands and Great Britain.[6]

Making a connection that is truly mystifying to all those not steeped in the SRHR-related code language of the international aid and abortion industries, EU officials have even linked fighting HIV/AIDS to promoting the right to abortion. Poul Nielson, then the European commissioner for development, put all of the standard pieces together – HIV/AIDS, fighting poverty, the Cairo commitments, reproductive rights and abortion – in a speech on June 3, 2004. While Nielson avoided mentioning abortion explicitly, he tacitly admitted that EU money was used for abortion when he referred to a "comprehensive approach" to SRHR and lamented the obstacles presented by the "global political climate," particularly the "Mexico City Policy" of the United States:

> Reproductive health services including family planning are in the front line of HIV/AIDS prevention and maternal health.... European civil society organisations are well

placed to work on sexual and reproductive rights issues.
They are not restricted by policy limitation on sexual and
reproductive health and rights like the US organisations are.

The European organisations can take full advantage of the
principles laid down in the International Conference on
Population and Development (ICPD) from 1994. The ICPD
was a watershed event that gave us a new, comprehensive
approach to sexual and reproductive health and rights. In
Cairo, for the first time ever, the global community declared
that women must be the centre of our efforts to address
reproductive health, population and development issues.
The EU fully endorses the Cairo commitments and supports their full implementation.

However, now in the year of the 10th anniversary of Cairo,
several factors are threatening the achievement of the
ICPD goals. In particular, I note that development aid funds
are not increasing sufficiently to improve reproductive
health services, the HIV/AIDS pandemic is devastating
social and economic structures, and the global political climate is hampering progress in reproductive health. In this
context, I am referring in particular to the GLOBAL GAG
RULE or MEXICO CITY POLICY as reinstated by President Bush. Without access to reproductive health information and services and the freedom to make reproductive
decisions, significant poverty reductions will not be
possible.[7]

The Mexico City Policy (or "global gag rule" as its more fervent
opponents like to call it) was the policy that required all organizations receiving U.S. funding not to perform abortions nor to promote abortion overseas. President Obama rescinded the policy as
one of his first acts in office. It was about abortion, and only about
abortion. Thus, when Nielson talked of "reproductive health services," "family planning," "sexual and reproductive rights," and the
"Cairo commitments," he was not just including abortion, but thinking of abortion as a top priority. For proponents of abortion the
world over, the ICPD's "comprehensive approach" means support

for abortion, whether they are honest enough to admit it or not. Clearly, the EU's constant refrain about its support for the ICPD is an affirmation of EU support for abortion.

The European Parliament (EP) also plays a huge role in supporting SRHR. A coalition of pro-abortion organizations including IPPF and Marie Stopes concluded that EP voting on SRHR during its 2009–2014 term had shown "the continuous commitment of the EP to maintaining the EU's role as the world's biggest supporter of development assistance... and Global health (as measured by two specific policy areas: sexual and reproductive health and rights (SRHR) and poverty-related and neglected tropical diseases (PRNDs))."[8] The report documents that the EP in its latest term had passed nine out of ten resolutions that endorsed SRHR, in the context of EU development policy, human rights, the Cairo agenda and the Millennium Development Goals of the UN. Most of these resolutions passed by convincing majorities that usually spanned the political spectrum. Resolutions specifically promoting the right to abortion or clearly specifying "sexual and reproductive *rights*," as opposed to "sexual and reproductive *health*," encountered more opposition from the right side of the spectrum.[9]

With its heavy support for SRHR, the EU – along with many in the United States, Canada and elsewhere – has reinvented women's rights. What the EU calls "women's rights" are not asserted, for example, to protect the role of women as mothers to the next generation who nurture and cherish their offspring, subordinating their own interests to their children's needs. Rather, the term "women's rights" has come to mean liberation from the constraints of motherhood, and a right to abort one's children if one so chooses. For International Human Rights Day in December 2014, EP members Heidi Hautala and Sophie in 't Veld, the co-chairs of the EP Working Group on Reproductive Health, wrote an op-ed piece titled, "Abortion: Choice Is a Human Right." Citing the EU's "longstanding track record" of providing "development aid funding for family planning and sexual and reproductive health," they declared, "It is of utmost importance this funding is maintained and the access to safe and legal abortion is not restricted...."[10]

Not all EU member states and not all MEPs support abortion. There is a small but significant minority who are staunchly and courageously pro-life. But they face an overwhelming wave of those promoting the global redefinition of women's rights according to a relativistic paradigm that values choice and individual autonomy above all. This large majority has effectively appropriated the language of global governance and universal human rights as promoted by the UN and its global agreements. In response, many pro-lifers in the EU seem to see no alternative to using the language of supranational governance to make their own arguments.

One example is the intrepid pro-life MEP Anna Zaborska's minority opinion on a draft EP resolution endorsing SRHR including abortion. Zaborska writes:

> This non-binding resolution violates the EU Treaty and cannot be used to introduce [the] right to abortion.... No international legally binding treaty nor the ECHR [European Convention on Human Rights] nor customary international law can accurately be cited as establishing or recognizing such right. The ECJ [European Court of Justice] confirms... that any human ovum after fertilization constitutes a human embryo which must be protected. The UN Declaration of the Rights of the Child states that every child has the right to equal protection before as well as after birth....[11]

Zaborska's argument relies mostly on the authority of international courts, agreements and treaties, not on the far more fundamental fact that abortion is a grave injustice and a moral abomination. Thus, the argument implicitly concedes the rightness of the transformative and liberationist worldview, which does not recognize objective truth, but only the treaties and institutions of global governance. Thereby, the argument undermines itself. If the political situation in the UN or in the EU were to change enough to allow a UN or EU agreement that would declare abortion to be an international human right, would that make it so?

SRHR AND THE GLOBAL GOVERNANCE OF HUMAN RIGHTS

With the major UN conferences in Cairo and Beijing as the declared bases for promoting SRHR, the EU is pursuing its women's rights policy within the framework of its larger global governance agenda. In fact, it is shaping the development of a global human rights ethic with a significant focus on SRHR. The UN is often nominally in the lead in this process, but the EU is pulling the strings behind the scenes.

The examples of this strategy are legion. One is an EU-funded publication called "An Advocate's Guide: Strategic Indicators for Universal Access to Sexual and Reproductive Health and Rights," produced by the Asian-Pacific Resource and Research Centre for Women to mark the twentieth anniversary of the Cairo conference. It proposes indicators to improve the monitoring of progress toward "universal access" to SRHR throughout the world, and explicitly defines sexual and reproductive health to encompass abortion, including for "adolescents." This definition is derived from "the ICPD Programme of Action and subsequent interpretations."[12] Showing the connection between different aspects of the transformative view of human rights, the document also proposes indicators for monitoring progress on LGBT rights, advocating same-sex marriage, adoption by same-sex couples, and legal protection of "a person's subjectively felt gender identity [that] may be at variance with their sex or physiological characteristics."[13]

The document makes several references not only to financial assistance from the EU but also to its leading role in the project. At the same time, the cover page includes a disclaimer allowing the EU to deny it is participating in a policy area reserved to the member states: "This publication has been produced with the assistance of the European Union. The contents of this publication are the sole responsibility of the Asian-Pacific Resource & Research Centre for Women and can in no way be taken to reflect the views of the European Union."[14]

The EU is also involved in promoting the ideology of transformative rights through the UN's Sustainable Development Goals (SDGs), adopted in September 2015. Perhaps the most important building block in the global governance project at the moment, the SDGs are the successor to the Millennium Development Goals that were agreed upon at the UN in 2000 and intended to show the way toward eradicating poverty and achieving sustainable development worldwide by 2015. Now that we have reached the year 2015 and poverty has not been eradicated, the global governancers are trying it again, and giving themselves another fifteen years to solve the world's problems.

In the midst of this effort is the EU, helping to set the ideological framework of global correctness. With its endless repetition of globalist mantras, sterilized and purged of all color and any hint of ideological impurity, the EU is involved in establishing the jargon whose obscurity keeps the insiders in and the outsiders out – the quasi-theological language of global governance that mesmerizes those who immerse themselves in it. All three principal EU institutions have spoken officially on the SDGs, all of them emphasizing that the "post-2015 agenda" must be global, sustainable, transformative and rights-based. They have all declared women's rights (as well as children's rights and, explicitly or implicitly, LGBT rights) to be central to a rights-based agenda, and where possible they endorse SRHR as the most important aspect of women's rights.

In its endorsement of the SDGs, the European Commission says, "Eradicating poverty and achieving sustainable development are fundamental global challenges... and need a global response. Addressing them requires strong political commitment and determined action at all levels and by all stakeholders.... The EU and its Member States have emphasized their commitment to work inclusively with all partners and stakeholders to build consensus for a new transformative post-2015 agenda." The Commission stresses that the post-2015 agenda "should be rights-based and people-centered." Among the main concerns in the area of health are to "reduce child mortality, maternal mortality, and ensure universal sexual and reproductive health and rights...."[15]

The European Parliament speaks of the need for a "transformative" and "global" development agenda, with SRHR front and center. It also spotlights LGBT rights. According to the EP, "the global sustainable development framework after 2015 should be transformative," and it should be based on "the universality, indivisibility and interdependence of all human rights of all people, without discrimination on any grounds, starting with the fundamental right to dignity of all human beings, with particular attention to the human rights of women and girls, including the promotion of universal access to sexual and reproductive health and rights, as well as the protection and respect of the rights of migrants and minorities, including LGBTI people...."[16]

The Council of Ministers echoes the key words and mantras that the Commission and the EP use, and underscores its concern that the SDGs should build on all of the established instruments of global governance in order to "address some of the key global

issues facing the world today in a truly transformative manner."
The post-2015 agenda "should be truly global and universal, with
all countries and stakeholders playing their full part." Moreover, it
is "crucial to ensure that the agenda has a rights-based approach
encompassing all human rights and that it respects, supports, and
builds on existing multilateral agreements, conventions, commitments, and processes."[17] Because the Council of Ministers includes
representatives of EU member states that restrict abortion, it does
not highlight SRHR as strongly as the Commission and the EP do.
Nevertheless, it pays homage to the Cairo and Beijing protocols,
and in this context it declares SRHR to be central to the global
agenda: "We reiterate that the empowerment and human rights of
women and girls, and ending both discrimination in all its forms
and violence against women and girls, must be at the core of the
post-2015 agenda.... We remain committed to the promotion, protection and fulfillment of... sexual and reproductive health and
rights."[18]

THE LANGUAGE AND FAITH OF GLOBAL CULTURAL CHANGE

When it comes to the transformative and liberationist model of
human rights, why focus on the EU? Why not shine a light on the
United States? After all, it has one of the most liberal abortion
regimes in the world, and under Obama as under Bill Clinton before
him, the U.S. government has expended considerable energy pushing for SRHR, LGBT rights, and the skewed type of children's
rights that we'll discuss in more detail in Chapter 13.

The reason for this focus is global governance. Unlike the
U.S., the EU is making the potentially revolutionary connection
between global governance and the transformative and liberationist model of human rights, thereby posing, in principle if not yet in
noticeable effect, a dire and literally global threat to liberal democracy and self-government, and to human rights rightly understood.
As the EU statements above illustrate, the EU is pursuing nothing
less than "global cultural change," to borrow a term from Marguerite Peeters, one of the most perceptive analysts of the globalist
postmodern revolution as exemplified by the UN and the EU. In
her monograph on the "new global ethic" she pulls all the major
strands together. The global ethic, she writes, is an all-encompass-

ing agenda. It aims to include all "global citizens," or, as the Council of Ministers puts it, to be "truly global and universal, with all countries and stakeholders playing their full part."[19]

Like the EU itself, the global ethic described by Peeters "posits itself *above* national sovereignty," and like the EU's transformative and liberationist human rights policy, it places itself "*above* the authority of parents and educators, even *above* the teachings of world religions."[20] This global ethic, like the EU and the global governance movement, is a child of postmodernity, the basic tenet of which is "that every reality is a social construct, that truth and reality have no stable and objective content – that in fact they do not exist." Thus, the EU's globalist human rights policy "exalts the arbitrary sovereignty of the individual and his or her *right to choose*." Human rights as understood in the global ethic promote "the 'liberation' of man and woman from the conditions of existence in which God has placed them." Personal autonomy trumps all outside constraints and truth claims, since "the individual, in order to exercise his *right to choose*, must be able to free himself from all normative frameworks." In fact, "the *right to choose*," as Peeters observes, "has become the fundamental *norm* governing the interpretation of all human rights."

In a reference to deconstructionist literary criticism, Peeters writes at one point that for postmodernity, "reality would be a *text to be interpreted*," since truth and reality are merely social constructs without any objective content. This notion is reflected in the sterile, ritual terminology of EU statements and of the global governance movement. The examples of the new language of global cultural change that Peeters lists are all reminiscent of EU jargon: "global citizenship, sustainable development, good governance, right to choose, gender mainstreaming, transparency, inclusion, women's rights, children's rights, reproductive rights, sexual orientation, the rights approach, indicators of progress, multistakeholder consensus," etc. It is a striking sign of the relativistic spirit of global governance that "the new global language," as Peeters points out, "tends to exclude words specifically belonging to the Judeo-Christian tradition, such as truth, morality, conscience, reason, heart, chastity, husband, wife, father, mother, son, daughter, service, faith, charity, hope, suffering, sin, friend...."

The examples of the new globalist language above display another representative characteristic of the jargon of the EU and the global governance movement: the language of globalism is vague and ambiguous. Peeters asserts that "the absence of clear definitions is the dominant feature of all the words and expressions of the new global language," because providing such clarity would "contradict the norm of the right to choose." Instead, the globalist concepts "are processes of constant change, enlarging themselves... as often as possibilities for new choices emerge." Seen from this vantage point, the vagueness of the EU's support for abortion – its failure to name the thing by its name – reveals more than just the EU's deceptiveness. It also reveals the world-view of global governance as described throughout this book. It is not only the EU that is an unanswered question shrouded in ambiguity. For the postmodern global governancers, *life itself* is an unanswered question. And vagueness, the lack of clear truth-telling, reflects the loss of belief in objective, definable truth.

Encapsulating all the EU stands for in its policy on women's rights, children's rights and LGBT rights, Peeters concludes her monograph with a trenchant observation on what happens when the absolute autonomy of the individual is taken to its logical conclusion, where "the individual becomes the 'free' creator of his own destiny." The transformative ethic dictates that a person "can choose to be homosexual today and bisexual tomorrow," while children "can choose their own opinion, irrespective of the values they receive from parents." In this postmodern world, "We are all equal citizens with equal rights, bound together by contractual relations without love.... What the global ethic deconstructs is the very anthropological structure of the human person." The speed with which this deconstruction of human nature has occurred is truly breathtaking. In the next chapter we will see how far it has already gone.

CHAPTER 11:
THE DECONSTRUCTION OF
HUMAN NATURE: LGBT RIGHTS

In the European Union, "human rights" no longer means the right to practice that which promotes the flourishing of human beings based on human nature and the embeddedness of individuals in social groups that depend on a commitment to truth about humankind and human society. Rather, "human rights" now stands for the right of the atomized individual to transform himself or herself in whatever way he/she chooses and to be liberated from the constraints imposed by the outside world.

This development is manifested most radically in the current EU push for LGBT rights, underpinned more and more by gender theory. Again, LGBT persons have as much claim to human rights as anyone else. But more than any other phenomenon, the new view of LGBT rights reflects how adherence to objective truth has been upended in nothing less than a Nietzschean transvaluation of all values.

THE GRANDCHILDREN OF NIETZSCHE

In her book *The Global Sexual Revolution: The Destruction of Freedom in the Name of Freedom*, Gabriele Kuby observes that "The strategic agenda of the EU seems to aim at a new image of the human person that threatens to topple the very foundations of what has been the social order until now."[1] Kuby demonstrates this with extensive documentation of EU efforts in "gender mainstreaming, sexual orientation, gender identity, sexual diversity, anti-discrimination, homophobia [and] same-sex 'marriage.'"[2] To cite just one example that Kuby discusses, approximately 70 percent of the financing of the European Region of the International Lesbian, Gay, Bisexual, Trans and Intersex Association (ILGA-Europe) comes from the EU.[3] ILGA-Europe then turns around and uses that money to lobby the EU institutions and influence EU policy. Among other things, it concentrates on "strategic litigation in the European courts" so as to compel individual member states "to end discrimination on the grounds of sexual orientation and gender identity," and on "working closely with the European institutions in order to promote the right to equality and freedom from discrimination and enhance the appreciation of diversity by lobbying and advocacy."[4]

The language, as always, is obscure and innocuous. It sounds laudable, too, in the sense that real human rights belong to everyone, including LGBT people. But what is it really intended to mean?

An EU Foreign Affairs Council statement of June 24, 2013 makes clear upon close reading, despite its generally circumspect style, that the EU has taken a firm stance on the side of organizations such as ILGA-Europe, with their transformative view of human rights for LGBT people. Titled "Guidelines to Promote and Protect the Enjoyment of All Human Rights by Lesbian, Gay, Bisexual, Transgender and Intersex (LGBTI) Persons," the document states that "The EU is committed to the principle of the universality of human rights and reaffirms that cultural, traditional or religious values cannot be invoked to justify any form of discrimination, including discrimination against LGBTI persons."[5] At first glance, this statement might seem unobjectionable. But what does it mean, in this context, to be "committed to the principle of the universality of human rights"? What is meant by "any form of discrimination"? And why are "cultural, traditional or religious values" set up as the villain?

The central point to note in the EU statement is that LGBT rights trump cultural, traditional or religious values. The latter are demoted to a subordinate role, where they possess a possible claim to validity only if they reinforce LGBT rights. Moreover, LGBT rights are declared to be absolute and universally valid in all times and situations, while cultural, traditional or religious values are implicitly relativized. They are not "universal." Rather, they reflect only the limited perspective of the culture, tradition or religion in question. Finally, the word "values" speaks volumes. "Values" are subjective. The EU statement ignores the possibility that certain cultural, traditional or religious beliefs might be *true*. It acknowledges only that people *value* them. In effect, the word reduces culture, tradition and religion to personal or, at most, societal preference, with no claim at all on anyone who does not share those particular preferences. It is especially ironic that religion, which in the West has kept the idea of objective truth alive, is declared by the relativists to be of only subjective validity – and that this is done in the service of their own absolutist, universal notions.

Perhaps without realizing it in most cases, relativists are inventing a new objective truth by declaring LGBT rights to be "universal human rights," thus investing them with absolute, worldwide validity. But the core doctrine of the campaign for universal LGBT rights is that each individual's feelings and opinions are valid for that individual regardless of any claims from outside the person. The only thing that is *objectively* true is my *subjective assessment* of what is true for me. Similarly, the relativists reject the idea that there is any truth claim that is valid regardless of the feelings or opinions of any individual or group. How then can the claim to universal LGBT rights be truly universal?

The rest of the EU's "Guidelines to Promote and Protect the Enjoyment of All Human Rights" continues in the same vein, starting from a largely unelaborated premise that LGBT rights mean the absolute right to live and affirm every aspect of the LGBT lifestyle, both publicly and privately, and that any attempt by any society to limit the expression of the LGBT lifestyle where it conflicts with culture, tradition or religion amounts to persecution or discrimination.

Tellingly, the "Guidelines" also include a reference to the Yogyakarta Principles (YP).[6] Drafted by a self-proclaimed "distinguished group of international human rights experts," the YP purports to be a "set of international principles relating to sexual orientation and gender identity," providing "a universal guide to human rights which affirm binding international legal standards with which all States must comply."[7] At the center of the YP is the idea of each individual's right to define his/her own gender identity, to the point of an implicitly complete denial of empirical facts such as the physical characteristics that make men men and women women. The YP defines gender identity as "each person's deeply felt internal and individual experience of gender, which may or may not correspond with the sex assigned at birth…."[8] The document asserts throughout that the right to define one's sexual identity is central to an individual's very being as a human person.

One example is "Principle 3: The Right to Recognition Before the Law," which states, "Everyone has the right to recognition everywhere as a person before the law…. Each person's *self-defined* sexual orientation and gender identity is integral to their personality and is one of the most basic aspects of self-determination, dignity and freedom."[9] In line with this principle, the YP demands that "all State-issued identity documents… reflect the person's *profound and self-defined* gender identity."[10] This is a truly radical denial of any objective truth about human nature that is valid independently of an individual's subjective preferences, and an audacious claim of an individual's right to social recognition of his or her particular twist on reality, regardless of whether it corresponds to empirical, physical fact.

Have EU foreign ministers really committed themselves, in the name of LGBT rights, to this radical redefinition of human nature and empirical reality? The "Guidelines" do not clearly say whether the EU considers the Yogyakarta Principles to be valid and foundational for the LGBT rights it promises to promote and protect, but the implication is that it does. If EU foreign ministers are prepared to endorse the denial of empirical reality in the name of LGBT rights, is there any higher commitment that could be left standing? Did the EU foreign ministers who signed off on this document even understand what they were doing?

While the "Guidelines" just examined provide the official basis of EU policy on LGBT issues, the European Union Agency for Fundamental Rights (FRA) is at the foreground of the battle to base LGBT rights on a redefinition of human sexuality and thus of human nature. Founded in 2007, the FRA has as its tagline: "Helping to make fundamental rights a reality for everyone in the European Union."[11] According to its website, the FRA accomplishes this by assisting the "EU institutions and EU Member States in understanding and tackling challenges to safeguard the fundamental rights of everyone in the EU."[12]

In pursuing this mission, the FRA works fully out of the liberationist and transformative view of fundamental rights. One recent example is a conference held on October 28, 2014, called "Tackling Sexual Orientation and Gender Identity Discrimination." The event was cohosted by the FRA and the government of Italy, in its capacity as the holder of the six-month presidency of the Council of the EU. A member of the European Commission was a featured speaker. Among the conference conclusions was the recommendation that legislation in member states "should ensure the full legal recognition of a person's preferred gender," according to the person's self-determination.[13] The EU itself stands fully behind this recommendation.

A principal objective of the conference, by the way, was to push for adoption of a sweeping new antidiscrimination directive. As we will see in Chapter 12, this legislation represents a proto-totalitarian imposition of the LGBT agenda on virtually every area of public life, and it promises to restrict the religious freedom of orthodox Christians severely.

BLAZING THE TRAIL FOR GAY MARRIAGE

In the public mind, the principal focus of LGBT rights activism is probably the fight for the right to gay marriage. In keeping with the EU's supranational governance, the trail for gay marriage has been blazed in the EU Charter of Fundamental Rights, which became binding for all EU member states (except the UK, Poland and the Czech Republic, who opted out) when it was made a part of the 2009 Lisbon Treaty. The Charter opens the way to gay marriage with a subtle, unremarked change from an earlier document upon which it is largely based. Article 9 of the Charter states, "The right to marry and the right to found a family shall be guaranteed in accordance with the national laws governing the exercise of these rights."[14] This is a small but significant shift from the language of the European Convention on Human Rights (ECHR), which entered into force in 1953. Article 12 of the ECHR, on the right to marry, states, "Men and women of marriageable age have the right to marry and to found a family, according to the national laws governing the exercise of this right."[15] The Charter of Fundamental Rights pointedly omits the ECHR's mention of "men and women."

The European Court of Human Rights, representing the forty-seven member states of the Council of Europe, officially noted this change in its 2002 *Goodwin* decision, in which it found, among other things, that the plaintiff Christine Goodwin, a male-to-female transgender, had the right to marry under Article 12 of the ECHR: "The Court would also note that Article 9 of the recently adopted Charter of Fundamental Rights of the European Union departs, no doubt deliberately, from the wording of Article 12 of the Convention in removing the reference to men and women...."[16] Because of this change in language, argues Jackie Jones, a British law professor and human rights specialist, "[as] substantive equality is one of the foundational values and principles of the EU, the CJEU [Court of Justice of the European Union] has to rule in favour of letting same-sex couples marry. Any other course of action would mean the supremacy of EU law is in doubt."[17]

This reasoning is convincing. The supremacy of EU law, not incidentally one of the most blatant violations of national sovereignty in the EU system, has made eventual EU-wide imposition of same-sex marriage virtually inevitable – and this in spite of the fact that marriage and family law fall under the competence of the member states according to the EU treaties, and not under the jurisdiction of the EU. In fact, it is actually *because* the member states decide marriage and family law that it must be imposed at the EU level if the EU court wishes to uphold the principle of substantive equality. The EU court is the only power that can impose a policy that some member-state governments are bound to resist; and resistance is likely in the six EU member states – Bulgaria, Croatia, Latvia, Lithuania, Poland and Slovakia – whose constitutions effectively ban same-sex marriage by defining marriage as a union between a man and a woman.

You might or might not agree, as I do, with the traditional idea of marriage as a comprehensive union of a man and a woman, "inherently ordered to procreation and thus the broad sharing of family life, and calling for permanent and exclusive commitment." You might agree or disagree that the well-being of children, and thus the "health and order of society" depend on traditional marriage's being promoted and protected in law.[18] The principal point here, though, is that same-sex marriage should not be imposed

tional European court interpreting a supranational charter of fundamental rights.

LGBT RIGHTS AND THE DWINDLING OF FREEDOM

The redefinition of human rights is of course not only a European Union phenomenon. All of this is happening in the United States, Canada and elsewhere as well. But there is a crucial difference between the promotion of this transformative and liberationist paradigm in the European Union and its advocacy in the United States. A Judeo-Christian-tinged worldview underpins the foundational American doctrine expressed in the Declaration of Independence that human beings have rights that are inalienable because they derive from our nature as creatures of a Creator, and this worldview still holds sway in the United States. In the European Union, by contrast, a transformative and liberationist concept of human rights is entwined with the global governance ideology at the bottom of the entire EU project. As long as the EU remains committed to its utopian ambition of transforming the world into a sort of global community of peace, prosperity and international law, it must logically continue to push the transformative and liberationist view of human rights.

And this transformative and liberationist model must logically continue to deconstruct freedom, because it denies the obvious, commonsense reality of an essentially constant, objective human nature, and it cannot permit the obvious to be stated. To point out the obvious is to kill the attempt to declare the absurd commonsensical. When the emperor has no clothes, no one can be allowed to say so. Thus arise the draconian hate-speech laws and antidiscrimination regulations that are gaining ground in the EU. We will go into the implications for free speech and religious freedom of this transvaluation of all values in more detail in the following chapter.

CHAPTER 12:
ANTIDISCRIMINATION AND RELIGIOUS FREEDOM
IN A POST-CHRISTIAN EUROPE

A human rights policy based on a transformative and liberationist ethic will not only target the family, unborn children, and human sexuality itself. It will necessarily target any of the traditional human institutions derived from a belief in objective truth. Above all, it will target the church and, ultimately, the very worldview that gave rise to the values and traditions of Western society that the postmodernists are striving to overcome – the Christian faith.

The postmodern globalist human rights lobby and the sexual left have opened up three major fronts in their war against objective truth and the Christian faith: the campaign to criminalize "hate speech"; the effort to achieve all-inclusiveness in antidiscrimination legislation; and the indoctrination of children in a gender-flexible view of human nature under the guise of children's rights.

HATE SPEECH

Whether it should or should not be legally prohibited, real hate speech is reprehensible. But what is hate speech? For that matter, what is hate? That depends on the ideological framework from which one sees things. The Merriam-Webster online dictionary, presumably speaking with no ideological agenda, defines hatred as "a very strong feeling of dislike," or a "prejudiced hostility or animosity."[1] Hatred may be something that people recognize when they feel the emotion themselves, but hate speech is something considerably more nebulous. As the Legal Project, an organization established to protect freedom of speech, explains, "there is not even a universally agreed upon definition for what constitutes hate speech.... Delineating the line between speech that is considered rude and that which is considered insulting for the purposes of criminal prosecution is an utterly subjective undertaking, and a distinction that governments are ill-suited to determine."[2]

The website of the European Region of the International Lesbian, Gay, Bisexual, Trans and Intersex Association (ILGA-Europe), in its discussion of what hate speech is, refers to a statement by the Committee of Ministers of the Council of Europe. (Remember, the CoE is not a part of the European Union, even though all EU member states are also CoE members, and the EU itself intends to accede to the CoE's European Convention on Human Rights.) According to the Committee of Ministers, the term "hate speech" includes "all forms of expression which spread, incite, promote or justify racial hatred, xenophobia, anti-Semitism or other forms of hatred based on intolerance, including intolerance expressed by aggressive nationalism and ethnocentrism, discrimination and hostility towards minorities, migrants and people of immigrant origin."[3] This statement, one of those most commonly cited in discussions of what hate speech means for Europeans, doesn't succeed in drawing clear lines.

Elsewhere on its website, ILGA-Europe defines what it considers to be hate speech, and specifically "LGBTI-phobic" hate speech, as follows:

> Hate speech is public expressions which spread, incite, promote or justify hatred, discrimination or hostility towards a specific group. LGBTI-phobic... hate speech is... speech and/or aggression towards LGBTI people due to their actual or perceived sexual orientation, gender identity and/or gender expression. ILGA-Europe usually refers to LGBTI-phobic... hate speech as *bias motivated speech* as it is a more precise definition as it underlines the bias as the main reason for the violence or speech.[4]

So "bias" is a key concept. But isn't "bias" often just another way of saying "an opinion with which we disagree"? In this case, it appears so. Elsewhere on the ILGA-Europe website, a click on the word "bias" leads to a Wikipedia page that opens with the following definition: "Homophobia encompasses a range of negative attitudes and feelings toward homosexuality or people who are identified or perceived as being lesbian, gay, bisexual or transgender (LGBT). It can be expressed as antipathy, contempt, prejudice, aversion, or hatred, may be based on irrational fear, and is sometimes related to religious beliefs."[5]

There is good reason to suspect that, in ILGA-Europe's ideological world, "negative attitudes... sometimes related to religious beliefs" include orthodox Christianity and the teaching that homosexual behavior goes against the will of God and is sinful. This example shows that the concept of hate speech has been shaped to a considerable extent by the secularist, globalist agenda that is its principal sponsor.

In this light, what happened to Ake Green in Sweden is not overly surprising. Green, a Christian pastor, was convicted in 2004 of inciting hatred against homosexuals after preaching a sermon on the biblical view of homosexuality. In the fire-and-brimstone sermon,[6] he minced no words as he endorsed the view shared by all traditional Christian confessions that homosexual behavior is sin. But he also stressed another view shared by all orthodox Christians: that with repentance, God's grace is for all sinners, including homosexuals, and he talked of Jesus' showing to everyone he met a "deep respect for the person they were."[7] For this "crime," Pastor Green was sentenced to thirty days in prison, but the sentence was suspended. Later, he was acquitted by an appeals court, but Sweden's chief prosecutor ordered a review. Finally, after a judicial nightmare of approximately two years, and arguably only because of persistent international pressure, Green was acquitted once and for all by Sweden's supreme court.

Ake Green's case is perhaps the most famous "hate speech" case against free expression of religious faith, but there have been many others. Paul Coleman documents over thirty hate speech cases from fifteen EU member states in his book *Censored: How European "Hate Speech" Laws Are Threatening Freedom of Speech*.[8] (A case from Romania and one from Croatia occurred before those countries joined the EU.) Coleman examines civil actions and cases brought under criminal law, including cases in which charges were dropped after an investigation, as well as cases that were prosecuted, some of which ended in conviction. While observing that "relatively few of these cases resulted in actual convictions,"[9] Coleman quotes another analyst's point that "the real danger posed by Europe's speech laws is not so much guilty verdicts as an insidious chilling of political debate, as people *censor themselves* in order to avoid legal charges and the stigma and expense they bring."[10]

Of the 34 cases that Coleman documents, 16 were sanctions of speech perceived to be hateful toward homosexuals, and 11 were cases of perceived defamation of Islam. As for the targets of the charges, 16 cases were actions against Christians for expressing aspects of the Christian faith that other people might find offensive, usually pertaining to homosexuality. Here is an astounding fact: only 6 of the 34 cases did not involve one or more of the following: objection to some aspect of the Christian faith, perceived homophobia or perceived Islamophobia. *None* of the cases had to do with a perceived defamation of Christianity or hatred of Christians. Clearly, some categories of protected persons are more equal than others.

ANTIDISCRIMINATION LAW

While the repression of free speech – especially speech expressing views derived from the Christian faith – relentlessly gains momentum, an ever more comprehensive body of antidiscrimination law is like a roaring lion prowling about, seeking to devour religious freedom. Just as "hate speech" has been defined expansively, "discrimination" has been redefined to include anything that any alleged victim feels uncomfortable about – in effect, any attitude short of active acceptance and vocal support of the behavior in question. And those pushing a political agenda of LGBT rights don't even necessarily wait for discrimination, even discrimination that barely clears their very low bar, before acting to lay the groundwork for ever more restrictive antidiscrimination laws.

The "European LGBT Survey" is a particularly egregious

example of this tactic. A report of the EU Fundamental Rights Agency (FRA) on "discrimination against LGBT people in Europe," released in May 2013, it goes to great lengths to find discrimination anywhere it might reasonably, or unreasonably, be found.[11] European Dignity Watch exposes the survey's lack of credibility and its manifest purpose of "provid[ing] for the FRA's pre-fabricated report and political agenda a false appearance of 'being founded on serious social research.'"[12] While claiming to reveal pervasive discrimination against LGBT people in Europe, the survey is in fact hopelessly biased and spurious.

As European Dignity Watch points out, the European LGBT Survey allows only self-identified LGBT people to participate, rather than a representative sampling of the overall population. Its length of fifty questions virtually guarantees that only those highly motivated to demonstrate widespread discrimination against themselves as LGBT people are likely to take the time to complete the survey. The discrimination reported in the survey includes incidents not reported to police, of which there is thus no verifiable outside record. Above all, the survey itself – the questions and multiple-choice options for the responses – reveals that (1) the emphasis is on subjective perceptions, feelings and opinions about whether discrimination has occurred rather than on verifiable incidents of discrimination; and (2) the desired responses suggest the need for more pervasive regulation and monitoring of behavior, to a point that comes unsettlingly close to coercion. Everyone's active affirmation of the LGBT lifestyle in all areas of everyday life is obviously, in the view of the FRA, the only state of affairs that is acceptable. And the FRA is prepared to push for law and regulation that is intrusive and totalitarian-tinged enough to bring about that state of affairs.

These examples of the survey's questions and multiple-choice responses, focused on personal feelings and unverifiable perceptions of the attitudes of others, speak for themselves:

Have you ever received negative reactions because you behave or have behaved in a too feminine or masculine way?[13]

What would allow you to be more comfortable living as a transgender person in the country where you live?

[Possible choices include:]
* Workplace anti-discrimination policies referring to gender identity
* Measures implemented at school to respect transgender people
* Better acceptance of differences in gender identities by religious leaders[14]

In your opinion, how widespread are the following in the country where you live?
[Possible choices include:]
* Casual jokes in everyday life about [LGBT] people
* Same-sex partners holding hands in public
* Heterosexual partners holding hands in public
* Positive measures to promote respect for the human rights of transgender people (for instance equality plans, public campaigns, specialised services, etc.)[15]

What would allow you to be more comfortable living as a lesbian, gay or bisexual person in the country where you live?
[All of the multiple-choice responses aim either at legally recognizing same-sex marriages or partnerships and same-sex adoption, or at more regulation and monitoring of behavior in the workplace, schools, government offices and churches.][16]

In the last 12 months, in the country where you live, have you personally felt discriminated against or harassed because of being perceived as [LGBT]?[17]

During the last 12 months, have you personally felt discriminated against because of being [LGBT] in any of the following situations:
[Possible choices include:]
* when looking for a job
* at work
* when looking for a house
* at a cafe, restaurant, bar or nightclub
* at a shop[18]

In the last six months, in your day-to-day life, how often have any of the following things happened to you because you are or are assumed to be lesbian, gay, bisexual and/or transgender?

[Possible choices include:]

* You have been treated with less courtesy than other people
* You have been treated with less respect than other people
* You have received poorer services than others (e.g. in restaurants, shops)
* People have acted as if they thought you were not clever[19]

According to European Dignity Watch, ILGA-Europe, which conducted the survey with the help of Gallup, received FRA funding – in other words, EU funding – of 370,000 euros for the project.[20]

In the last few years, similar illustrations of seeing LGBT discrimination everywhere have multiplied exponentially. But this phenomenon is not new. Perhaps the first incident that came prominently to public attention revealing the chilling effects on religious liberty of the EU's LGBT rights obsession was the European Parliament's rejection of Rocco Buttiglione, a Catholic thinker and statesman, as a European commissioner. It was a flagrant example of how religious people lose hands down when they express beliefs that have been deemed discriminatory against LGBT people within the European transformative and liberationist human rights paradigm.

In 2004, the center-right Italian government nominated Buttiglione, then Italy's European affairs minister, to serve as Italy's commissioner for the 2004–2009 term of the European Commission. He was to be the commissioner for justice, freedom and security, a portfolio that included civil rights and antidiscrimination policy. At his confirmation hearing before the European Parliament, an MEP from the Dutch Green-Left Party asked him his views on homosexuality. Buttiglione responded honestly, saying that "there is a clear distinction between morality and law." He added that he "may think homosexuality is a sin," but said he endorsed the European Charter of Fundamental Rights, which forbids discrimination on the grounds of sexual orientation, and affirmed that he was "willing to defend it."[21]

This honesty was too much for the enlightened secularists in the EP and their supporters in the media. It was unacceptable to believe that homosexuality is a sin, and an affront to refined sensibilities to say it. "How can I trust this man when he says he'll protect homosexuals from discrimination if he thinks homosexuality is immoral?" asked the Dutch Green MEP.[22] The Italian government ultimately saw no alternative but to withdraw Buttiglione's candidacy. The incident suggested that orthodox Christians who confess their faith anywhere other than in private are no longer qualified to hold office in the European Union. And from the viewpoint of the advocates of the new human rights, keeping Christians from holding office makes perfect sense.

Nominees for high office in the EU are not the only ones endangered by the Orwellian antidiscrimination fervor. The long arm of EU antidiscrimination regulation threatens to touch everyone, everywhere, and in almost any activity they might undertake. This sweeping reach makes the EU's proposed general antidiscrimination directive quite probably the most serious threat to religious freedom and political liberty on the antidiscrimination front. Officially titled "Council Directive on Implementing the Principle of Equal Treatment between Persons Irrespective of Religion or Belief, Disability, Age or Sexual Orientation," and first proposed in 2008, it has not yet become EU law, mainly because of opposition from Germany motivated by German industry's fears regarding the burdens that would be imposed on businesses. Nevertheless, it is very much alive and is being pushed by the European Commission and the European Parliament. The first two paragraphs of the explanatory memorandum accompanying the directive state:

> The aim of this proposal is to implement the principle of equal treatment between persons irrespective of religion or belief, disability, age or sexual orientation outside the labour market. It sets out a framework for the prohibition of discrimination on these grounds and establishes a uniform minimum level of protection within the European Union for people who have suffered such discrimination.
>
> This proposal supplements the existing EC legal

framework under which the prohibition of discrimination on grounds of religion or belief, disability, age or sexual orientation applies only to employment, occupation and vocational training.[23]

Soothing as it might appear at first reading, this statement – with phrases such as "implement the principle of equal treatment… outside the labour market," and "uniform minimum level of protection" – makes clear that this regulation would open the door to an "unprecedented" degree of "governmental control over the social and economic behavior of citizens in the widest possible sense," as Sophia Kuby of European Dignity Watch puts it.[24] The directive employs an exceedingly vague definition of discrimination, in principle allowing anyone who feels he has been discriminated against to bring a complaint against the alleged discriminator. Moreover, it shifts the burden of proof from the accuser to the accused, who is guilty until proved innocent. The result would be a perilous situation of legal uncertainty in which "nobody can ever be sure not to be found guilty of infringing the law."[25]

The directive also requires EU member states to establish independent entities that would oversee the "promotion of equal treatment" in each member state. Judging from human nature and the behavior of regulatory agencies everywhere, it is reasonable to assume that such agencies, in order to justify their existence, would be zealous in finding and pursuing alleged discrimination wherever they can.

But again, some rights to nondiscrimination are more equal than others. Given the secularist climate in the EU, the promotion of unlimited LGBT "rights" against anyone perceived to be anti-LGBT, such as orthodox Christians, would be a primary, probably *the* primary, upshot of this directive. This prediction is supported by trends in the United Kingdom, where antidiscrimination legislation has already expanded beyond the labor market to the provision of goods and services – the sort of expansion foreseen by the EU directive. As Paul Coleman and Roger Kiska of the Alliance Defending Freedom point out, the UK Equality and Human Rights Commission has been exceedingly activist, siding unequivocally with the LGBT side against traditional Christians and Christian organizations, even to the point of "making *unsolicited* legal submissions."

Among many other abuses of its remit, the commission has

advocated forbidding Catholic charities to place children for adoption because of their opposition to adoption by same-sex couples, and has tried to forbid Christians from foster-parenting children if they hold traditional Christian views of homosexuality. Also, UK courts, with or without the prodding of the Equality and Human Rights Commission, have consistently confirmed both a dramatically expanded scope of antidiscrimination legislation and the positive obligation of all those covered by the legislation to "promote equality" actively. This trend is playing out to the detriment of religious liberty for Christians and to the injury of common sense, sometimes with almost comical absurdity. Coleman and Kiska note that "a government funded guidance document stated that it is 'potentially unlawful' for schools to require pupils to wear gender-specific clothes (such as skirts for girls)," and that "a local council was prompted to carry out an expensive two-month investigation to decide whether the historic city of Canterbury was 'sufficiently gay.'" In April 2012, a church in the city of Norwich was banned from handing out literature, as it had been doing for several years, because the material essentially argued that "Christianity is correct and Islam is incorrect." This was judged to be "hate motivated."[26]

Coleman and Kiska point out how courts in the UK have consistently treated sexual orientation more favorably than religious belief, although both are covered in UK antidiscrimination law. Whereas the British courts have consistently ruled that the protection of sexual *orientation* entails also the protection of sexual *practice*, they have drawn a distinction between religious *belief* and religious *practice*, the latter presumably including the public expression of unpopular religious beliefs. The courts have consistently denied religious people the right to "manifest their deeply held convictions on marriage." Again, when LGBT rights and religious freedom collide, LGBT rights win hands down. With the proposed EU directive mirroring the UK legislation in all of those key aspects, there is little reason to believe the results of the directive would be any different elsewhere in the EU. As Coleman and Kiska write, these results include "the large implementation costs, the increases in litigation, the constant legal clashes, the removal of religious freedom and the overriding of individual conscience in the marketplace...."[27]

Gudrun Kugler, of the Observatory on Intolerance and

Discrimination against Christians in Europe, and Sophia Kuby observe that implementation of the directive "would end up turning entrepreneurial freedom, private autonomy and religious freedom from the rule to the exception." They ask, "Is it really the government's job to enforce the alleged advancement of society through laws prescribing how citizens should (or should not) believe?"[28]

To be sure, this general antidiscrimination directive has not been passed. But it has been proposed as such by the European Commission, approved by the European Parliament and agreed to in principle by at least twenty-two of the twenty-eight member states.[29] After conducting a review of older, not-yet-approved directives with an eye toward dropping as many of them as possible, the 2014–2019 European Commission under the presidency of Jean-Claude Juncker has kept the latest directive on its agenda. Even if it never becomes EU law, it is a chilling illustration of the totalitarian impulse beneath the soft utopia of the EU and its global governance ideology.

CHILDREN'S "RIGHT" TO RE-EDUCATION

"Hate speech" and "discrimination" against LGBT people are only the most visible fronts in the ideological war against religious freedom. A less well known front is children's rights, defined as the right to choose a sexuality unencumbered by traditional, supposedly "restrictive" views on gender, sex and the innocence of childhood. Here too, the aggressively secular state works in alliance with the postmodern sexual left, often unwittingly, to force a secularist agenda onto schools and families.

In the EU, the state is more and more asserting *its* right over parents to decide how children are brought up. Not surprisingly, this is happening especially to Christian parents. The examples are abundant. In Germany, for instance, four Christian parents were sent to prison after they chose not to allow their nine- and ten-year-old children to participate in four days of mandatory "sexual education" classes.[30] There have been several cases of parents' losing custody because they kept their children out of sex education classes on account of disagreement with what was being taught about the morality of all forms of sexual activity.[31] German homeschooling parents, usually Christians who object to

the secularist education in German schools, face forcible seizure
of their children by police, loss of custody, fines and imprison-
ment. One German family is now living in the United States after
paying almost $9,000 in fines and being threatened with further
legal action. The U.S. government has granted them the right to
stay indefinitely in the United States,[32] and there is now a bill before
Congress that would allow asylum for families who are "persecuted by their governments for homeschooling their children."[33]

In 2009, a seven-year-old Swedish boy was taken from his
parents, without a warrant or criminal charges, because they were
educating him at home. As of this writing almost six years later,
the parents have not yet regained custody despite unanimous testimony to their fitness as parents.[34] In Spain, mandatory "Education for Democratic Citizenship and Human Rights" classes that
many parents believed promoted homosexual behavior, among
other things, were added to the curriculum in 2006. After numerous complaints and years of lawsuits, Spain's supreme court in
2009 decided that parents had no right to keep their children out
of the classes.[35]

Concentrating on Germany and Austria principally, Gabriele
Kuby extensively documents how the transformative and liberationist redefinition of children's rights is being promoted in the
schools, at the expense of parental rights. With the support of
federal, state and local governments in Germany and Austria,
organizations such as the Federal Center for Health Education
(Bundeszentrale für gesundheitliche Aufklärung), the Institute
for Sexual Pedagogy (Institut für Sexualpädagogik) and Pro
Familia – which is the German arm of the International Planned
Parenthood Federation (IPPF) and performs the majority of abortions in Germany – are making great strides toward revolutioniz-
ing education in support of an early sexualization of children
according to gender theory and the LGBT view of the human person. The IPPF website for teenagers illustrates this view: "Every
sexual orientation, whether it be lesbian, gay, bisexual, queer or
'straight,' is completely normal. If you get pregnant, you have three
options – abortion, adoption or parenting. Abortion is legal and
safe."[36] Sexual encounters between children as young as preschool
age are encouraged, as are, in Kuby's words, the "pluralization of
types of relationship, forms of love and lifestyles," and the "flexibi-
lization of gender identity and sexuality."[37] Sex education textbooks

for children and adolescents – and guidebooks for parents of children from infants to six years old – include graphic descriptions of all kinds of sexual encounters, sometimes with instructions, and encourage children to affirm almost all forms of sexual activity.

For the pioneers of the new rights of the child, this is a matter of complete liberation from the traditional view of the human person. According to a leading Austrian sexual education expert, "The occasional attempts of churches and other religious and social groups to spread their own moral-sexual convictions and standards for sexual behavior, to restrict the diversity of life possibilities and establish a sexual monoculture, is not a solution. Pluralism in the area of sexuality... represents the foundation for the unfolding of our human life possibilities. Sexual pedagogy must not be allowed to make itself the accomplice of social control and standardization."[38] The implication is, of course, that parents should not have the right to stand in the way of this liberation of children's sexuality. Kuby aptly sums up the transvaluation of values that the new children's rights advocates are advancing: "The moral standardization of sexuality upon which the family, European culture and *every* culture rest is being portrayed as robbing people of their freedom. The deregulation of sexuality, in contrast, is sold as pluralism and the victory of individual liberty."[39]

And the propagation, witting or unwitting, of gender theory is widespread in Europe, as previous examples from Germany, Austria, Spain and the UK show. For the 2013–2014 school year, the French government introduced a "compulsory sex education course based on the 'gender theory' for all children aged 6 and over." According to Julie Sommaruga, member of the French National Assembly's Cultural Affairs Committee, the purpose of this course was to "replace categories such as sex (...) with the concept of gender, which (...) shows that the differences between men and women are not based on nature but are historically constructed and socially reproduced."[40] Introduced as a pilot program in 275 schools, the plan was dropped in the summer of 2014 after helping ignite the massive Manif Pour Tous (Protest for Everyone) demonstrations in Paris and other cities.[41] Hopefully, grassroots groups in Germany, such as Besorgte Eltern (Concerned Parents), a group established to stop the early sexualization of children in schools and preschools, will have similar success.[42]

The EU is relatively careful to keep its distance from highly charged issues having to do with children, families and education. Under the EU treaties, the member states have jurisdiction over education. However, the EU does have the "competence to support, coordinate or supplement actions of the member states in education, vocational training, youth and sport,"[43] and it takes advantage of this "competence" wherever it can. As we have seen, the EU also promotes all of the new transformative and liberationist human rights, including children's rights, in its international development policy and in international forums such as the UN.

True to its commitment to global governance, the EU acknowledges the United Nations Convention on the Rights of the Child (CRC) as the basis of its children's rights policy. The fact that the CRC has been ratified by every UN member state except Somalia, South Sudan and the United States reflects nothing more than the skill of globalist elites in enshrining the new human rights in international agreements, especially when the subject seems as unobjectionable as "children's rights." As Professor Bruce C. Hafen of Brigham Young University points out, the CRC promotes "a broad but untested new legal concept – the autonomous child." He quotes an official UN document saying that the CRC would advance a concept of children's rights in which government takes on the "responsibility of protecting the child from the power of parents." The CRC's proponents speak of taking a "quantum leap" in formulating children's rights "more based on choice than needs" of children, and proposing that children should have the same rights as adults.[44]

How could such an agreement gain almost worldwide adherence? Well, let me ask another question: Who reads UN agreements? Mary Ann Glendon, a Harvard law professor and former U.S. ambassador to the UN, said in reference to the CRC, "There is an increasing tendency for advocates of causes that have failed to win acceptance through ordinary democratic processes to resort to the international arena, far removed (they hope) from scrutiny and accountability." Once they succeed in getting their ideas into UN documents, these advocates can then present them as "international norms."[45]

In an article on behind-the-scenes negotiations at the 1995

UN World Conference on Women in Beijing, Glendon provides an illustration of how determinedly the EU pushes the new transformative human rights away from the scrutiny of voters. She explains how the EU not only understands and shares the CRC's concept of the autonomous child but would go beyond the CRC if it could:

> A minority coalition, led by the powerful fifteen-member European Union negotiating as a bloc, was pushing a version of the sexual and abortion rights agenda that had been rejected by the Cairo conference. The EU-led coalition was so intent on its unfinished Cairo agenda that it was stalling negotiations on other issues. Equally disturbing, the coalition was taking positions with ominous implications for universal human rights.
>
> . . . the EU was opposing the inclusion of key, pertinent principles from UN instruments where the nations of the world had recognized certain core rights and obligations as universal. . . .
>
> Though the Beijing documents had identified the situation of the "girl child" as a "critical area," the coalition attempted to eliminate all recognition of parental rights and duties from the draft, even rejecting direct quotations from the Convention on the Rights of the Child. . . .
>
> In the stark vision promoted by the EU caucus at Beijing, there is no room for the idea that society has a special interest in providing the best possible conditions for raising children. Family life, marriage, and motherhood would be worthy of no more protection than any other ways in which adults choose to order their lives. The girl child, her parents nowhere visible, would be alone with her rights.[46]

One wonders whether the Beijing shenanigans were present in the minds of the proud drafters of the European Commission's document "Towards an EU Strategy on the Rights of the Child," when they wrote that the Commission would "address children's rights in political dialogue with third countries, including civil

society and social partners, and use its other policy instruments
and cooperation programmes to promote and address children's
rights worldwide."[47]

Another international arena in which the EU pushes this
deconstructionist model of children's rights is in its alliance with
the World Health Organization (WHO). In an initiative started in
2008, the WHO Regional Office for Europe and the aforementioned Federal Center for Health Education of Germany published
"standards for sexuality education in Europe," replete with praise
for IPPF and UNESCO definitions of "sexual and reproductive
rights." Decrying the fact that approaches to sex education differ
among European countries, the WHO recommends pan-European
standards for outcomes such as "to respect sexual diversity and
gender differences and to be aware of sexual identity and gender
roles;" and "to reflect on sexuality and diverse norms and values
with regard to human rights in order to develop one's own critical
attitudes."[48] According to the WHO, sex education in Europe
should begin before the age of four and should not be the exclusive
province of parents, as they "often lack the necessary knowledge,
particularly when complex and technical information is needed."[49]
For the youngest children, up to four years old, it should foster "an
awareness of their rights which leads to self-confidence" and "the
feeling that they can make their own decisions."[50] For those
between the ages of twelve and fifteen, it should help develop "a
personal view of sexuality (being flexible) in a changing society or
group."[51] For those fifteen years and above, the outcome should be
"a critical view of cultural norms related to the human body" and
of "different cultural/religious norms related to pregnancy, parenthood, etc.," as well as "acceptance that sexuality in different
forms is present in all age groups" and "celebration of sexual differences" such as homosexuality.[52]

The WHO document is filled with rights language, and it falls
decidedly within the autonomous-child paradigm by grounding
children's right to sex education in the CRC, saying, "The right of
the child to information has also been acknowledged by the United
Nations Convention on the Rights of the Child," which "clearly
states the right to freedom of expression and the freedom to seek,
receive and impart information and ideas of all kinds."[53]

Children's rights as understood in the age of relativism,

novelty and choice are, like women's rights, anything *but* rights that would allow real people – with real social roles and obligations – to flourish as members of families and communities. The new children's rights are not asserted to give children a safe and beneficial environment in which to be children, nurtured and disciplined by parents who teach them how to be adults with a proper understanding of their rights and obligations. Rather, children's rights in the global ethic are asserted *against* the parents and *against* parents' rights – and, moreover, against what children *are*. Proponents of this ethic fail to recognize that childhood is not an age of consent, and that children need to be protected from themselves and their incapacity to understand their rights properly, so that they can grow into the maturity they do not yet possess. And finally, the transformative children's rights are implacably opposed to Christian faith, tradition and the idea of objective truth.

TRICKLE-DOWN POSTMODERNISM

Clearly, the EU represents fertile ground for the postmodern sexual left's agenda of redefining human rights and the human person. Let me conclude with two reasons why. First, although the "silent majority" in Europe may still instinctively be opposed to the sexual left's agenda, the post-Christian man-in-the-street lives and breathes and has his being in the cognitive universe of postmodern secularism. He has come to share postmodernism's disapproval of all traditional truth claims and to sympathize with its pretense that reality can be reshaped in the service of individual choice. Thus, he has few intellectual or emotional resources with which to resist the pervasive glorification of sexual license. Instead, he joins in the celebration of it. A banal but telling example of this is the Austrian singer Conchita Wurst (given name: Thomas Neuwirth), the winner of the 2014 Eurovision song contest. A transgender female with a full beard, hair flowing past her shoulders and fluttering false eyelashes, she performed in a gold-embellished fishtail gown. Wurst was celebrated throughout the continent as a courageous hero of human rights. Her Eurovision victory generated 5,384,678 tweets.[54]

But it is not only Europe's more secular social context that explains why the transformative/liberationist paradigm and its concomitant threat to religious freedom have gone further in the European Union than in the United States. Another reason is the less democratically accountable supranational governance of the EU, which allows the utopian left much freer rein to impose its views on everyone else via international agreements made in international forums beyond the scrutiny of ordinary citizens. In the next section, we will see how the EU's commitment to supranational governance at the expense of democratically accountable national sovereignty has also seriously weakened the partnership of the United States and Europe as an effective force for good in the world.

PART FIVE

OUR BEST FRIENDS AND OUR WORST ANTAGONISTS

CHAPTER 13:
GLOBAL GOVERNANCE AND NATIONAL SOVEREIGNTY

"The United States will not accept any treaty requirement incompatible with the Constitution of the United States of America." This is a frequently seen reservation with which the United States has often qualified its adherence to international agreements. As John Fonte points out,

> For most of the past half century, the U.S. State Department has routinely qualified American ratification of international treaties with stipulations... that the United States will not accept anything in the treaty as valid if the treaty provisions violate the U.S. Constitution. If there is a point of dispute between an international treaty and the Constitution of the United States, the Constitution trumps the international convention.[1]

This is the core of national sovereignty in the American understanding. National sovereignty does not mean any sort of "splendid isolation" from international affairs or the renunciation of an active role in promoting international cooperation or participating in binding international agreements. It does not mean opposition to international organizations such as the United Nations, as long as those organizations do not attempt to usurp the sovereignty of their member nations. Rather, it simply means that the United States will insist on its right to participate in international affairs as a sovereign nation-state that retains the power to govern itself. It means that the U.S. government is responsible primarily to the citizens who hold it democratically accountable, and that its powers are circumscribed not by the desires of other nations but only by its own constitution, which is accepted by the American people as the basic law against which the legitimacy of all other laws, treaties and agreements must be judged.

And here, the "American people," the concept of "We the People," is key. It is what makes the U.S. idea of national sovereignty morally compelling, because it affirms the inherent dignity of the human person. Sovereignty resides in the citizens of a nation, "endowed by their Creator with certain unalienable rights," not in the government of the nation. The power and authority of the U.S. government are derived from the American people, and the American people alone. This is what John Fonte calls "Philadelphian sovereignty," or "democratic sovereignty," which means "the sovereignty of a self-governing, free people."[2] It is the heart of the model of government pioneered and elaborated by the framers of the U.S. Constitution at their convention in Philadelphia in 1787, and the most precious gift of America to the world. "The Founders viewed sovereignty as something that resided in the people themselves, rather than the government or the nation-state," Fonte explains. "It is the citizens who hold ultimate political authority."[3]

The Declaration of Independence affirms that governments derive "their just powers from the consent of the governed," and that whenever any government becomes destructive of the ends for which it was instituted, "it is the Right of the People to alter or to abolish it, and to institute new Government, laying its foundation on such principles and organizing its powers in such form, as to them shall seem most likely to effect their Safety and Happiness."[4] On this basis – the consent of the American people – rests the entire legitimacy of the United States government. Therefore, if any international actor claims any power over the American people or seeks to restrict the freedom of the American government to formulate constitutionally legitimate policy and act upon it on behalf of the American people, that claim is utterly illegitimate. It bears repeating: the Constitution is the supreme law to which the American people are subject. Anything that conflicts with the Constitution cannot be binding on the American people nor on the American government that serves them.

THE TRANSATLANTIC CLASH OF VISIONS

In the American system, it is because sovereignty rests in the people that the U.S. government does not have a right to transfer sovereignty to any other organization, government or group of governments. But in the EU, the member states have been ceding ever more sovereignty to "Europe" since the establishment of the European Coal and Steel Community in 1952. Sovereign power is exactly what the European Union exercises over the national governments of the EU member states. And again, for EU elites it is not just about Europe. Their vision of supranational governance is a global one, and that is why a political and moral clash between the American idea of democratic sovereignty and the EU's agenda is unavoidable. Regardless of the eerie ambiguity of the global governance ideology, which lets it appear to be almost anything to anyone, there is at least this one foundational certainty: the idea of global governance, at its core, cannot but be a sworn enemy to democratic sovereignty as practiced in the American system.

Because of this supranational vision for a wholly new world order, the European Union and its member states – along with Canada, Australia, Israel and Japan the best friends and allies of the United States – have become, at the same time, our worst antagonists. The EU's goal of creating a post-nation-state, supranationally governed world – in which nations give up key aspects of their national sovereignty to a web of international institutions that administer and enforce a body of international law – is diametrically opposed to Americans' instinctive refusal to recognize as legitimate any international organization, law or treaty that claims any authority over Americans above the U.S. Constitution, particularly if that organization, law or treaty contradicts the Constitution or violates Americans' constitutional rights. And it only makes sense that this American attitude is highly offensive to the global governancers in Brussels, Berlin and Paris. After all, how could such antiquated notions as national sovereignty and "We the People," or the arrogance of American exceptionalism, be allowed to stand in the way of a transformative global order of human liberation, human rights and international justice – or, as the UN puts it, "a world of prosperity, equity, freedom, dignity and peace"?[5] Ditto for Israel, a sovereign nation-state providing a safe haven of separation to an ancient religious group that has the audacity to defend itself militarily – rather than to seek peace at all costs – against those in its neighborhood whose hatred for Israel gives the lie to the vision of a free and peaceful world.

The UN statement above, echoed by countless EU declarations both official and unofficial, illustrates the aim of the global governance project to bring the world under control in order to transform it. The intellectual pioneers of the EU project foresaw this agenda and embraced it. In the early years of the European project, the EU founding father Jean Monnet said that the European Community was "only a stage on the way to the more organized world of tomorrow."[6]

It is impossible to exaggerate the overweening ambition of wanting to "organize the world," or the inherently totalitarian ramifications of the desire to impose global organization on a world of endless diversity and unpredictability. Leaving aside the question of what it means to organize the world and what aspects of life and society are to be organized, a big question is *how* does one achieve an organized world? Success would be possible only if one were prepared to impose one's vision – whether by the stealth of the Monnet method, by the intellectual intimidation of political correctness, or by the force of law – on those who resist, especially those who have the power to resist effectively and the influence to rally others in resistance. And this is the root of the global governancers' ineradicable anti-Americanism and strangely uniform opposition to United States policy.

America is big enough to stand in the way of the grand global governance plan. This is the huge exacerbating factor in the ideological clash between the United States and the European Union. The United States is not just any nation-state, clinging cluelessly to its outmoded national sovereignty. It is the dominant world power. It cannot be ignored, and there is no end-run maneuver that is likely to leave it behind. Jürgen Habermas, always anything but an impassioned advocate of transatlanticism, underscores this fact, saying that "the project of a cosmopolitan order is doomed to failure without American support, indeed American leadership.

The U.S. must decide whether it should abide by international game rules or whether it should marginalize and instrumentalize international law and take things into its own hands."[7] Thus, the United States not only harbors an opposing vision of the world and of international affairs – a world of sovereign nation-states voluntarily cooperating and entering into agreements when desirable and necessary – but as the sole remaining truly global power it also stands as an imposing obstacle to the realization of the EU's vision for the world. By its dominance in world affairs, the United States obstructs the fulfillment of the vision regardless of whether that is its intention or not. As a bare fact, the existence of the sovereign United States makes the EU vision seem like a soft-power fantasy without any meaningful effect on the real world.

Another role that the phenomenon of U.S. global power plays in the European idea is represented by a very common argument for European integration: the idea that Europe, if it is truly to have a say in international affairs in a world dominated by the military, economic, ideational and cultural power of the United States, must speak with one voice. A France of 62 million people, slightly smaller than Texas, has no chance to be an equal player with the United States. Great Britain, despite its history of empire, is now an island of 64 million people, barely more than one-fifth of the U.S. population. Even Germany, with its population of 80 million and its GDP of 2.66 trillion euros, the fourth-largest GDP in the world, is a dwarf compared to the United States. Only a truly cohesive European Union, of 500 million people and a total economic output of 13.5 trillion euros, can equal the United States. So goes the argument.

This almost nineteenth-century balance-of-power thesis, masking as it does the utopian European dream with foreign-policy pragmatism, is ubiquitous among European pundits and elites. In many people's minds, standing up to the dominance of the United States is one of the primary raisons d'être of the European Union. And to a great extent, it is completely understandable and legitimate. This does not necessarily mean anti-Americanism. Many steadfast friends of the United States and supporters of the transatlantic alliance have made this argument. The question is, does contesting the dominant role of the United States mean the legitimate and reasonable desire of Europeans to assert their own interests on the world stage and protect their right to decide for themselves how Europe will be ordered? Or does it mean actively seeking to undermine Americans' exercise of that same legitimate and reasonable desire? Does it mean actively seeking to undermine Americans' right to decide for themselves, as citizens of a sovereign nation, how the United States will be ordered?

CLASHING ALLIES, BUT ALLIES NONETHELESS?

In the following chapters we will examine the collision course that the global governance agenda puts the EU on against the United States. But if this opposition is as fundamental and inherent as I claim, why is it not more apparent? Why is the European-American partnership still, in many ways, as strong and vital as diplomats, presidents and prime ministers repeatedly affirm? After all, the U.S. and the EU remain committed allies. There are many reasons for this paradox. I will mention three of the most compelling.

First of all, the global governance ideology has not yet won the day in the EU. There are still many sovereigntists and pragmatists in Europe, and most of them are strongly committed to the transatlantic alliance. Second, and related to the first point, the vision of global governance competes with the everyday reality of a Europe of democracies, still rooted in centuries of Western, Judeo-Christian tradition, and still sharing, by instincts shaped through generations, the United States' commitment to the classical idea of human freedom and the bedrock, classical rights to life, liberty and the pursuit of happiness. Finally, the United States and the democracies of Europe need each other. By default, they remain each other's closest allies in a world full of urgent threats to liberty, prosperity and security. Despite all our differences, we are bound together both by the common values of our shared Western heritage and by existential threats to that heritage, including violent Islamism, the revanchism of Putin's Russia, and Iran's pursuit of a nuclear bomb.

But this does not change the fact that the ideology of supranational global governance is a dire threat to the transatlantic partnership. For decades, and with growing intensity, the global governance agenda has been actively undermining the shared transatlantic commitment to self-government properly understood. The EU's pursuit of its vision, in its arcane public statements filled with obscure jargon and its quiet leadership in building institutions of supranational authority in the rarefied councils of the global elite, is largely escaping public notice. But while unnoticed, it is not without effect. Already, despite the largely calm appearance on the surface, the U.S.-EU alliance is not only fraying at the edges but threatening to hollow out at its core. There are myriad examples of how the opposing visions of democratic sovereignty vs. global governance can lead to a very real rift between the United States and Europe. In the next chapter, the U.S.-EU dispute over the International Criminal Court will graphically illustrate the seriousness of the break this difference in worldview portends.

CHAPTER 14:
GLOBAL JUDICIAL DESPOTISM AND
THE INTERNATIONAL CRIMINAL COURT

The International Criminal Court (ICC) is not about bringing criminals to justice. It is about giving teeth to global governance. It is about giving enforcement powers to an international body that is not accountable to any electorate or to any elected government – powers that in many ways go beyond those of any duly constituted national court in a democratic country. For example, a U.S. citizen could conceivably be brought before the ICC on a charge that the U.S. government considers politically motivated and illegitimate, and be subject to prosecution and punishment without benefiting from several key rights that the U.S. Constitution guarantees to those who are prosecuted in U.S. courts.

With its sensitivity to national sovereignty and the constitutional rights of its citizens, the United States cannot accept this. The EU on the other hand, with its belief in global governance, is the world's most enthusiastic champion of the ICC. The EU's ardor for the ICC is undampened by the fact that its own citizens could be subject to arbitrary prosecution without enjoying rights that various EU member states guarantee their citizens – and this is testimony to how deeply committed the EU elites are to supra-national global governance.

The ICC is a logical outgrowth of the notion of universal

jurisdiction, which the American sovereigntists Lee Casey and David Rivkin define as the claim that "any state can define and punish certain 'international' criminal offenses, regardless of where the relevant conduct took place or what the nationality of the perpetrators or victims may be."[1] Universal jurisdiction suggests that any country can prosecute anyone for anything it has defined as a prosecutable crime, even if the alleged crime was committed thousands of miles outside of that country, and even if neither the perpetrator nor the victim of the alleged crime has ever set foot in that country and or had any connection whatsoever with that country. Presumably, the right of universal jurisdiction would be limited to certain types of crime and certain well-defined circumstances that have been internationally agreed upon.

Whether or not universal jurisdiction is limited in that way, however, it remains breathtakingly broad in scope, arrogant, intrusive and predatory upon national sovereignty. Any nation that presumes to apply universal jurisdiction to prosecute crimes that have not affected it or its citizens in any direct way is arrogating to itself the power not only to decide what is right and wrong for other countries, but to enforce that decision by supplanting the judicial processes of other countries and possibly imprisoning their citizens. Universal jurisdiction goes so far as to claim the right to prosecute officials of other governments for actions taken "in the execution of their official duties" even if those actions were "otherwise consistent with the laws and constitution of their own country."[2]

THE SPANISH JUDGE AND THE CHILEAN DICTATOR

Not surprisingly, universal jurisdiction has made the most headway in Europe. In fact, a single Spanish judge, Baltasar Garzón, played a huge role not only in making universal jurisdiction a compelling idea for many – the idea of making the powerful answer for their crimes against the oppressed and powerless – but also in coming close to actually exercising jurisdiction against the former dictator of Chile, Augusto Pinochet, who had committed his alleged crimes in Chile, not in Spain (where Garzón was an investigating magistrate), and mostly against Chileans, not against Spaniards. Garzón was primarily concerned with Pinochet's role in Operation

Condor, in which various South American security services worked together in an effort to eliminate leftist political opposition.[3] As the former president and commander in chief and as "senator for life," Pinochet enjoyed immunity under Chilean law, but when he traveled to Britain in 1998 for medical treatment, Garzón issued an international arrest warrant and requested his extradition to Spain.

For seventeen months, UK authorities held Pinochet under house arrest until the House of Lords finally ruled that he could be extradited to Spain (though the ruling was not made on the basis of universal jurisdiction). Jack Straw, then Britain's secretary of state for home affairs, chose a diplomatic solution, concluding that Pinochet was medically unfit for trial and allowing him to return to Chile. Significantly, though, Straw made a point of bowing deferentially to the supranational soft utopia, expressing his belief that "universal jurisdiction against persons charged with international crimes should be effective." It is also telling that in releasing Pinochet, Britain declined to accept extradition requests similar to Spain's from three other European countries – France, Belgium and Switzerland.[4]

After the Pinochet affair, Garzón did not waver in his quest to revive the legacy of Don Quixote in modern-day Spain. He also investigated, and in some cases indicted, many others who he believed might otherwise have escaped with impunity for human rights abuses they allegedly committed. His targets have included U.S. officials for alleged abuses in Guantanamo, Argentine officials for crimes committed during Argentina's Dirty War, and Osama bin Laden. Turning the tables, four charges have been filed against Garzón in recent years, for abuse or improper use of his authority. Garzón, who claims the complaints were bogus and politically motivated, was convicted on one of the charges and suspended from practicing as a judge for eleven years.

BELGIUM'S UNIVERSAL JURISDICTION LAW

While the Spaniard Baltasar Garzón is the individual official who has done the most for the cause of universal jurisdiction, Belgium is the country that has probably expended more effort than any other to realize universal jurisdiction. This is not surprising. Belgium, host to the principal EU institutions, is steeped in the ideology of global governance and the belief in the European idea perhaps more than any other country.

Belgium's adventures in universal jurisdiction began in earnest with the passing in 1993 of a law asserting jurisdiction for Belgian courts over serious violations of international humanitarian law, such as war crimes, regardless of where the crimes were committed, who was accused of committing them and who the victims were. The law also applied to foreign government officials, overriding diplomatic immunity. As could have been predicted, the law was eventually brought to bear against the United States as well as Israel. By 2003, complaints mostly related to the Iraq wars of 1991 or 2003 had been brought against Ariel Sharon, George H. W. Bush, Dick Cheney, Colin Powell, and General Tommy Franks, commander of U.S. forces in Iraq.[5] Not coincidentally, this occurred when Belgium, along with Germany, France and Luxembourg, was firmly in the camp of the EU's hard-core opponents of the 2003 Iraq war and insistently critical of U.S. "unilateralism."

Belgium eventually repealed the law after the U.S. secretary of defense, Donald Rumsfeld, implied that the United States would no longer participate in NATO meetings at its headquarters in Brussels, nor financially support a new 400-million-euro headquarters building for NATO, if U.S. officials had to fear prosecution in Belgium. Condemning "divisive politicized lawsuits," Rumsfeld said, "It would obviously not be easy for US officials" to travel to Belgium, and "It would not make much sense to build a new headquarters if they can't come here for meetings."[6] After all this, one would think that other EU member states would shy away from universal jurisdiction. That is quite decidedly not the case. All of the EU member states have some sort of universal jurisdiction law on the books, of varying levels of reach and intrusiveness. In the EU, the mission to build the soft utopia of a globally governanced world goes on.

THE INTERNATIONAL CRIMINAL COURT

The ICC is the next step in the universal jurisdictionists' quest for cosmic justice, as Thomas Sowell might put it.[7] As the first permanent international court dealing in criminal matters, the ICC "has competence to investigate, try and punish dozens of offenses," currently within three broad categories: genocide, crimes against humanity, and war crimes, with a fourth category, "aggression," to be included as of 2017 if approved by state parties.[8] What is truly unprecedented about the ICC is its supranational authority, which could reach even to citizens of countries that are not signatories of the Rome Statute, the treaty establishing the ICC. In violation of previously construed international law, the Rome Statute invests the court with the authority to prosecute citizens of non–state parties, even, under certain circumstances, for crimes committed on the territory of non–state parties. Also, like the Belgian law, the reach of the ICC extends to government officials who would traditionally enjoy official governmental immunity in the performance of their official functions.

Thus, an American citizen could conceivably be prosecuted by the ICC for an alleged crime committed on U.S. soil. For example, the ICC could prosecute a Pentagon official if the ICC believes an attack ordered by that official against a country with which the U.S. was at war to be a war crime. And it is by no means clear how it is to be determined that a "war crime" has occurred. It is quite conceivable that this Pentagon official could be accused of a war crime if civilians were unintentionally injured or killed or civilian property damaged.[9]

It is this pretense of supranational authority, crowned by an assertion of jurisdiction over non–state parties, that is the heart of the ICC's unacceptability to the United States. For the EU it is just the opposite. It is exactly *because* of this supranationality that the EU values the ICC as a major step forward for global governance. And the story of the decades-long dispute between the United States and the EU over the ICC is a chilling illustration of how the global governance movement aims to impose its vision on all who resist it. We cannot go into all of the details here, but rather will summarize the broad outlines.

As negotiations to establish an ICC began, the United States was supportive. It approved of the superficially noble goal of preventing the most egregious tyrants from getting off scot-free for heinous crimes that they could not be prosecuted for in their home countries. President Bill Clinton thought he could overcome the threats to national sovereignty inherent in the ICC idea and limit its jurisdiction to obvious cases of impunity for crimes against humanity, as in the Nuremberg trials of Nazi crimes.

However, in five years of tough negotiations before and after the adoption of the Rome Statute establishing the ICC, the Clinton administration met unappeasable resistance from European negotiators. This resistance was not tactical. It was based on a fundamental clash of worldviews that was emerging in the aftermath of the Cold War: a clash between the continuing American attachment to self-government and the growing European devotion to the idea of global governance. As one scholar reports, "In a formulation used almost identically by several officials and NGO observers, those European governments that refused to accommodate U.S. demands did so as a 'matter of principle.' Almost all interviewees, including U.S. government officials, cited normative concern – that is, concerns about state equality, justice, the rule of law or standards of diplomatic conduct – as a key motivation for European resistance to U.S. requests, and many even named them as the most important factor underlying European responses."[10]

On the deadline to sign the Rome Statute (December 31, 2001), and just a few weeks before leaving office, President Clinton reluctantly approved the signing, despite what he called "significant flaws in the treaty." He did so because, as he explained in his signing statement, the United States would otherwise not "be in a position to influence the evolution of the court," nor be able to enhance its "ability to further protect US officials from unfounded charges and to achieve the human rights and accountability objectives of the ICC."[11] In authorizing signature, though, Clinton declined to submit the treaty to the Senate for ratification, and he expressly urged his successor, George W. Bush, not to submit it to the Senate, either. In May 2002, the Bush administration wisely decided to "unsign" the Rome Statute.

THE DESPOTIC FACE OF GLOBAL GOVERNANCE

After the Rome Statute entered into force on July 1, 2002, the United States, not a party to the pact, sought to protect U.S. citizens from the possibility of arbitrary prosecution in the ICC by negotiating bilateral "Article 98" agreements with other countries. Also called "non-surrender" agreements, these were designed to shield U.S. citizens in those countries from being handed over to the ICC.

EU member states not only refused to enter into Article 98 agreements, but openly pressured other countries, even countries that were not party to the Rome Statute, to reject such agreements with the United States. This European policy of actively undermining U.S. attempts to protect U.S. citizens and their constitutional rights came from the top, animated by the EU commitment to building a world in which no country has the right to opt out of the pursuit of universal justice. Senior government officials from European countries including Germany and Belgium publicly criticized the Article 98 agreements and other U.S. efforts as "undermining justice," as "incompatible with the rule of law," and as "a blow to the credibility of international law."[12]

For the European global governancers, this was not just a disagreement over an isolated issue. Rather, opposing this core U.S. national sovereignty concern – the concern to protect U.S. citizens from an essentially unaccountable international court – had arguably become central to an emerging European identity. Many Europeans saw the dispute over non-surrender agreements as "a question of values regarding the role of international law," and an issue that went "to the core of the European perception of the world, of an emerging European identity."[13]

Of course, European advocates of the ICC insist that it poses no threat to the United States. They maintain that politically motivated prosecutions in the ICC are not possible. But as illustrated by the Belgian courts' inquiries into the actions of George H. W. Bush and Colin Powell, among others, there is no reason to believe that other U.S. and allied officials could not be subject to frivolous investigations by an unaccountable ICC. In fact, there have been many calls to bring George W. Bush, Tony Blair and other policy makers involved in the Iraq war before the ICC.

To give one recent example, on April 16–17, 2014, international lawyers and activists convened in Brussels (of all places) to explore ways to hold George W. Bush and Tony Blair, along with other British and American officials, legally accountable for "war crimes, crimes against humanity and crimes against peace for their roles in the Iraq invasion and occupation."[14] While acknowledging that the United States was not a member of the ICC, conference attendees reportedly said that Bush and various members of his cabinet, including Donald Rumsfeld, Colin Powell and Condoleezza Rice, were "guilty of war crimes for their roles in creating the conditions for the invasion and occupation of Iraq."[15]

One may think it absurd to imagine the ICC prosecuting officials of established democracies such as the United States or Britain for activities conducted in the lawful fulfillment of their governmental functions. But on May 13, 2014, a few weeks after the Brussels conference, the ICC prosecutor opened a "preliminary examination" into alleged crimes committed by British nationals during the Iraq War. According to an ICC statement, this was done partly on the basis of information received from the European Center for Constitutional and Human Rights along with the Public Interest Lawyers "alleging the responsibility of officials of the United Kingdom for war crimes involving systematic detainee abuse in Iraq from 2003 until 2008."[16]

The first announcement from the ICC in 2015 also confirmed the prudence of a healthy suspicion toward it. On January 16, 2015, the ICC prosecutor "opened a preliminary examination into the situation in Palestine," according to an ICC press release, which continued, "The Prosecutor's decision follows the Government of Palestine's... accepting the jurisdiction of the ICC over alleged crimes committed 'in the occupied Palestinian territory, including East Jerusalem, since June 13, 2014.'"[17] As Reuters reported, "This allows the court to delve into the war between Israel and Hamas militants in Gaza in July–August 2014 during which more than 2,100 Palestinians and 73 Israelis were killed."[18] This ICC action came little more than a month after the Palestinian Authority was accorded the status of "non-member observer State" at the UN, its first official recognition as a state, and days after the PA filed for ICC membership. Thus, in the twinkling of an eye, the ICC confirmed the longstanding fears of Israel, the United States and others of possible collusion between Palestine and the ICC to pursue politically motivated war crimes charges against Israel, which is not a party to the ICC. Palestinian officials greeted the announcement of the inquiry with joy. Israel's foreign minister, Avigdor Lieberman, correctly described it as "outrageous." To put it mildly, the ICC's action does not inspire confidence. Its emerging anti-Israel bias mirrors Israel's mistreatment in other UN councils and the visceral hostility of many EU elites toward the Jewish state.

In addition to its lack of accountability, its assertion of

authority over citizens of non–state parties, and procedures that are far below the standards of due process guaranteed by the U.S. Constitution, there is yet another reason why ICC abuses represent a clear and present danger: the very fact that ICC officials are taken from all corners of the earth. The ICC prosecutor Fatou Bensouda is from Gambia. Her predecessor was from Argentina. Under the Rome Statute, the ICC prosecutor has tremendous power and is, for all practical purposes, unaccountable even to the state parties of the ICC treaty. She has the authority to determine, on her own motion, whether to open an investigation in any given instance. The investigation can go forward if authorized by one of the two "pre-trial chambers," consisting of three judges each.

As Casey and Rivkin argue, the implications of endowing someone of a completely different cultural, political and social context with the powers of a prosecutor are explosive. The powers and discretion of federal prosecutors in the United States, they explain, are "tempered by democratic accountability" and by the prosecutor's understanding of the "needs of the community he serves."[19] By contrast, the ICC prosecutor is, in effect, completely unaccountable to anything or anyone, and is "entirely detached from the countries and localities where he exercises his authority."[20] Regardless of whether the ICC prosecutor is acting in good faith or not, the potential for serious miscarriages of justice is obvious.

The ICC has eighteen sitting judges. The current judges are from Argentina, Belgium, Botswana, the Czech Republic, the Democratic Republic of the Congo, the Dominican Republic, France, Germany, Hungary, Italy, Japan, Kenya, Korea, Nigeria, the Philippines, Poland, Trinidad and Tobago, and the United Kingdom. Only three of these eighteen judges – those sitting in a pre-trial chamber – need to approve for a case to go forward in the ICC. All of this raises the question: Why should the United States expose U.S. citizens to the possibility of being tried, convicted and sent to jail by people who are not in any way subject to the Constitution of the United States? Indeed, why should any country that cares about its citizens subject itself to the whims of the ICC? How could the EU support such an institution, unless the ideological blinders of global governance have completely distorted its perspective on reality?

If the European dream could remain a matter for Europeans

to decide, that would be one thing. But the dream is a global dream, and no matter how you try to twist it, global governance pursued to its logical end requires everyone to knuckle under. Joining the European cause of global governance would mean essentially the same thing for Americans as joining the ICC. In the words of Casey and Rivkin, it would "require the American people to accept that they no longer hold the ultimate authority over their own destiny but that they and their elected representatives must answer to a foreign power over which they have no control and precious little influence."[21]

The story of the ICC makes clear that the European commitment to global governance, while now still "manageable," could one day become as passionate and inflexible as it would have to be in order to realize the European dream on a global scale. If that ever happens, the price of maintaining a strong transatlantic alliance will have become a price too high to pay. In the next chapter, we will see how high a price in lost cooperation and support – and in open opposition – the European global governance ideology has exacted from the United States in its post-9/11 war against international terrorism.

CHAPTER 15:
BINDING THE LEVIATHAN IN ITS WAR ON TERROR

The ICC starkly illustrates how the American commitment to democratic sovereignty and the EU's global governance ideology put the transatlantic allies on a collision course. But the ICC debate, as serious as it is, could conceivably be firewalled off from the overall relationship. That is not true of this century's primary example of the ill effect of the belief in global governance on the U.S.-EU alliance: the U.S. war on terror since the attacks of September 11, 2001.

To be sure, here also we are talking of a difference that is often more in principle than in action. The United States and the EU are allies in the war on terror in many ways, and the UK – not coincidentally the most sovereigntist of the EU member states – has been America's most important ally in this struggle. In the immediate aftermath of September 11, everyone stood by the United States. On September 13, 2001, the French left-wing newspaper *Le Monde*, not generally known for its pro-Americanism, proclaimed, *"Nous sommes tous Américains"* – "We Are All Americans."[1] In the days and weeks following the attacks, as the U.S. State Department noted, "many European countries acted quickly to share law enforcement and intelligence information, conduct investigations into the attacks, and strengthen laws to aid the fight against terrorism."[2] The EU promptly took measures enhancing its ability to fight terrorism, such as freezing terrorist assets and combating money laundering.[3] Several EU member states contributed troops to the fight against the Taliban and al-Qaida in Afghanistan. A good number of EU member states even supported the U.S. invasion of Iraq.

That said, however, the EU's adherence to the ideology of global governance has severely damaged the efficacy of the transatlantic alliance in the most important foreign policy priority of the United States in the twenty-first century – the global war on terror. Even amidst the wave of sympathy for the United States in Europe after September 11, the transatlantic difference in worldview started to show quickly.

SEPTEMBER 11 AND EUROPEAN INTEGRATION

The Belgian presidency of the EU, as mentioned in Chapter 7, used the terrorist attacks as a pretext to promote further supranational European integration, including the idea of a European Constitution. EU leaders held an emergency summit on September 21, and in explaining their plans to support the United States and intensify the fight against terrorism, they called for "the broadest possible global coalition against terrorism, under United Nations aegis."[4]

One of the earliest policy measures announced to combat terrorism was the introduction of a European arrest warrant, something that integrationists had long been touting. The argument was that this would allow more effective EU-wide cooperation in apprehending terrorist suspects. What it also did, though, was make it possible for anyone to be arrested in any EU member state at the request of any other EU member state, and then to be transferred to the requesting state without going through traditional extradition procedures. Essentially, the European arrest warrant represents an EU-authorized demand on a country to arrest and hand over even its own citizens living in their own country, at the request of another member state, and even for an act that might not be prosecuted in the person's home country.

In his report to the European Parliament on the September 21 summit, the Belgian foreign minister, Louis Michel, said, "The terrorist threat is a test for European integration," and, "The crisis situation created by the attacks in New York and Washington has given impetus to European unification." Clearly looking to leverage the fight against terrorism to advance supranationalist integration, he stressed "concerted action" by the EU and the display of "genuine European leadership."[5]

The capstone of the six-month Belgian EU presidency was the Laeken summit of EU leaders on December 14–15, 2001 and the resulting "Laeken Declaration on the Future of the European Union." In her address at the summit's opening session, the European Parliament president, Nicole Fontaine, set the tone: "Turning to the fight against international terrorism, the tragic events of September 11 have given the Union the opportunity to demonstrate its political cohesion... and to make spectacular progress towards the establishment of a joint [EU-wide] area of freedom, security and justice."[6] The Laeken Declaration, proclaiming that "the eleventh of September has brought a rude awakening," concluded that "Europe needs to shoulder its responsibilities in the governance of globalisation." According to the EU leaders, citizens of member states were calling for a "democratically controlled Community approach, developing a Europe which points the way ahead for the world." Therefore, "the European Council has decided to convene a Convention on the Future of Europe," to consider whether to adopt "a constitutional text in the Union."[7]

The Belgian EU presidency managed to draw a straight line from September 11 to the Convention on the Future of Europe. In keeping with the unvarying priority of EU true believers, the EU in late 2001 sharpened the focus on the deeper supranationalization of the EU and the strengthening of global governance as ends in themselves, seemingly more important in the long term than actually fighting terror and providing security for Europeans and Americans. From that time on, an overriding concern of the EU, popping up everywhere in U.S.-EU deliberations on terrorism, has been the further development of an international/supranational institutional and legal architecture, and the limiting of the prosecution of the war on terror to policies and actions that strengthen this architecture of global governance. In every major action and policy in the war on terror, the ideology of global governance has arguably been the primary factor in European opposition to the United States.

Many Europeans, and the EU itself, supported the war in Afghanistan that quickly followed the 9/11 attacks. But the EU made it clear that its support was contingent on the United States' playing by the rules of global governance: "The EU confirmed its staunchest support for the military operations, which began on the 7 October 2001 in Afghanistan in line with UN Security Council Resolution 1368 and the right to self-defence as enshrined in the UN Charter."[8] Just so there would be no misunderstanding, the EU pointedly added: "The European Union has consistently underlined the central role of the *United Nations* in building an effective global framework against terrorism."[9] The EU also played a huge part in the reconstruction of Afghanistan, donating humanitarian aid, conducting other development projects, contributing to counternarcotics efforts, and engaging in many other initiatives. The EU insisted, though, that the UN – and no other organization or country – must have "the central coordination role" in the rebuilding effort.[10]

Of course, no war since World War II has enjoyed worldwide support, especially if the war was conducted by the powerful United States. And there is good evidence that majorities throughout the world did not support the war in Afghanistan, even in 2001. A Gallup poll of thirty-seven countries in late September 2001 revealed that majorities in almost all of the polled countries "preferred extradition and trial of suspects to a U.S. attack." According to that poll, the United States, Israel and India were the only countries in which majorities supported a U.S. attack, while 75% of respondents in Britain, 67% in France, 87% in Switzerland, 64% in the Czech Republic and 83% in Lithuania preferred legal to military action.[11]

IRAQ AND PREEMPTIVE WAR

The war in Iraq was, needless to say, quite a bit more controversial than Afghanistan. Here is where the global governance ideology of the EU began really to work its spell, nearly tearing apart the international coalition of democracies against al-Qaida and exposing the profound rifts within the EU, ever present just below the surface, between the sovereigntists/pragmatists and the supranationalists.

Despite the leading roles that France, Germany, Belgium and Luxembourg played in opposing the U.S. invasion of Iraq, there were many EU member states on the U.S. side, with significant support coming from the UK, Spain (until a socialist government took office in 2004), Italy, Portugal, the Netherlands and Denmark. But the divisions within the EU deepened so gravely that EU foreign policy cooperation seemed headed for paralysis. In early 2003, after France and Germany made a statement against war in Iraq, eight European countries, led by Spain and the UK, released a letter supporting the United States. This was followed by a letter from ten Eastern European countries, including seven soon-to-be EU member states, underlining their backing of the U.S.[12] President Jacques Chirac of France, furious over the insolence of the Eastern European EU membership candidates, fumed that they had "missed a good opportunity to shut up."[13]

People now remember the controversy over the war as revolving around whether there were actually weapons of mass destruction hidden in Iraq. But before the invasion, almost everyone – including the French, the Germans and, for good measure, the Russians – believed that Saddam Hussein *did* possess WMDs. The real dispute was whether a preventive attack was justified under international law and whether war could be legitimate without the approval of the UN Security Council. It was truly a battle of worldviews centered on the question of the legitimacy and authority of supranational governance. The French foreign minister Dominique de Villepin perhaps expressed it most succinctly when he said in a speech that the disagreement over Iraq was a matter of "competing visions of the world."[14] An address by de Villepin at the UN in 2003, in the midst of France's implacable opposition to UN authorization of the use of force in Iraq, overflows with the language of global governance:

> France has always said that we do not exclude the possibility of having one day to resort to force.... In any case, if that eventuality occurs it is the unity of the international community that would guarantee its efficacy. By the same token, it is the United Nations that will remain, whatever happens, at the heart of the peace to be constructed.... Faithful to its values, [France] desires to act resolutely with all of the

members of the international community. [France] believes in our ability to build a better world together.[15]

Jürgen Habermas goes so far as to describe the mass demonstrations in 2003 against the impending invasion of Iraq as quite possibly marking the emergence of a unified, EU-wide European public, saying that "February 15, 2003, the day on which the masses of demonstrators in London, Rome, Madrid, Barcelona, Berlin, and Paris responded to this coup... may go down in future history books as a signal for the birth of a European public."[16] He grounds this statement not merely in European opposition to U.S. Iraq policy, but in the broader, foundational conflict between the European vision of a supranational world order – a "progressive constitutionalization of international law" as he describes it elsewhere – and the "hegemonic unilateralism" of the United States.[17] Habermas deplores "the image of a superpower that uses its military, technological, and economic superiority to create a global order in accordance with its own religiously colored notions of good and evil and its geostrategic goals...."[18]

In the midst of being vilified by all comers as a unilateralist, President Bush tried to meet the globalists on their own territory and show why it was in their own interest to support the toppling of Saddam Hussein. In a speech to the UN General Assembly on September 12, 2002, Bush recounted the long list of previous UN resolutions that Iraq had flouted, and announced the U.S. intention to seek a new UN Security Council resolution authorizing the use of force in Iraq:

> The conduct of the Iraqi regime is a threat to the authority of the United Nations, and a threat to peace. Iraq has answered a decade of U.N. demands with a decade of defiance. All the world now faces a test and the United Nations a difficult and defining moment. Are Security Council resolutions to be honored and enforced or cast aside without consequence? Will the United Nations serve the purpose of its founding or will it be irrelevant?[19]

In retrospect, it is clear that Bush's appeal to the authority and credibility of the UN was doomed to failure, for while he attempted to argue in globalist terms, he was really speaking a different language. His very suggestion that the UN could possibly ever be rendered irrelevant, whether by its own inaction or for any other reason, was undoubtedly an unpardonable offense to many global governancers.

Even worse, Bush assumed that his first responsibility was to the American people and not to the "international community" as represented by the United Nations. This was an unconscionable breach of morality for the global governancers. Nothing else mattered – not the threat posed by Saddam Hussein to the security of the United States and its allies, not Saddam's brutal persecution of his own people, nothing. Perhaps President Bush would not have met such vehement opposition if he hadn't been so honest about where he stood and how he saw his responsibility. For global governancers, who are used to operating in a world of perceptions rather than reality – who in fact routinely endeavor to create reality by manipulating perception – an open rejection of their priorities by the president of the United States in facing the twenty-first century's most deadly threat to global security was unforgivable.

In the end, one can agree or disagree with the decision to invade Iraq, but it is indisputable that this was a decision that Bush had to make, that there were many uncertainties and complexities, and that there were good reasons in favor of invading. The global governancers could not see it that way, though. They saw only the United States taking "international law" into its own hands in the absence of unanimous international recognition of the threat posed by Iraq. As Habermas puts it, "The most powerful member of the United Nations disregarded its basic norm, the prohibition on violence."[20] And that was that.

CAN TERRORISTS BE POWS?

Another controversy in the war on terror that had everything to do with global governance was the debate surrounding Guantanamo. It is a good example of how the global governance ideology, while completely unrealistic, can gain many adherents among those who are not directly affected, and thereby do much damage. The decision to build a prison on the American base in Guantanamo, Cuba was a careful, considered solution to an unprecedented and complex problem: what to do with captured enemy

combatants who did not exhibit the salient characteristics of
enemy soldiers in the traditional sense and thus were not covered
under the Geneva Conventions establishing a basic law of war. It
was also a bipartisan solution, proposed by a commission that
included prominent Democrats as well as Republicans.

The objectives that had to be met were principally threefold:
(1) to treat the detainees humanely and in keeping with American
decency and the international law of war; (2) to gain intelligence
from the detainees that could help prosecute the war on terror
and save innocent lives; and (3) to keep the detainees from return-
ing to the battlefield and thus possibly killing more innocents.
Guantanamo accomplished all of these objectives to an acceptable
extent. It was an imperfect but workable solution to a pressing
problem that needed to be dealt with. President Bush explained
the matter clearly:

> To win the war on terror, we must be able to detain, question
> and, when appropriate, prosecute terrorists captured here
> in America and on the battlefields around the world.... It's
> important for Americans and others across the world to
> understand the kind of people held at Guantanamo. These
> aren't common criminals or bystanders accidentally swept
> up on the battlefield. We have in place a rigorous process to
> ensure those held at Guantanamo Bay belong at Guanta-
> namo. Those held at Guantanamo include suspected bomb-
> makers, terrorist trainers, recruiters and facilitators, and
> potential suicide bombers. They are in our custody so that
> they cannot murder our people.[21]

Why did so many, led by the Europeans, object to this solution?
Because they viewed Guantanamo through the spectacles of global
governance. The desire to build a global legal order was so overwhelming that it resulted in a denial that the war on terror *was* a
war – an insistence that it would be merely a legal problem to be
solved in the courts if it were treated as such. Dick Marty, who
investigated alleged CIA secret prisons in Europe for the Council of
Europe, reflected European right thinking on Guantanamo to a tee:

> At Guantanamo Bay, on the island of Cuba, several hundred
> people are being detained without enjoying any of the

guarantees provided for in the criminal procedure of a state governed by the rule of law or in the Geneva Conventions on the law of war. These people have been arrested in unknown circumstances, handed over by foreign authorities without any extradition procedure being followed, or illegally abducted in various countries by United States special services. They are considered enemy combatants, according to a new definition introduced by the American administration.[22]

Thus, the Guantanamo dispute was about global governance. And the global governancers pulled out all the stops in an effort to achieve the worldwide recognition of a global legal order that did not exist, one that would trump the national sovereignty of the United States and force it to treat foreign enemy combatants as if they were civilian criminals with a claim to all the rights that the U.S. Constitution guarantees to citizens – more rights than the ICC would deign to give Americans – to say nothing of any additional due process rights that the globalist elite could conjure up for them. And this in a time of war, in which the security of the United States and the safety of innocent Americans were at stake – along with that of non-Americans who could become victims of terrorism.

The Guantanamo dispute, like the Iraq dispute, struck at the heart of international relations – the issue of war and peace. In the face of both Iraq and Guantanamo, the EU global governancers attempted to transform the international law of war into a *supranational* law of war.

GLOBAL GOVERNANCE VS. INTERNATIONAL COOPERATION

Interestingly, the postmodern global governancers have consistently distinguished themselves in their black-and-white thinking about the war on terror. Honest people of good will disagree on much of what the United States has done to combat terrorism since 9/11. There has been little precedent to fall back on, and the information on which to base policy decisions is severely limited and often unverifiable. The issues are very complex. We are dealing with all shades of gray in the war on terror, and consequential mistakes have been made. In fact, we may never know in many cases whether we took the best approach. But the global governancers don't want to deal with the real world of uncertainty and complexity. They want to realize their globalist vision, based on a caricature of reality, and that agenda has immeasurably hindered the prosecution of the war on terror.

It must also be said that the supranationalist approach to the war on terror finds plenty of support outside Europe, including in the United States. One major example is President Obama's perennial desire to close Guantanamo, a desire which has been butting up against the common sense of the American people for seven years now. Still, his administration's globalist inclinations have been insufficient to keep the global governancers of the EU happy. Many in Europe vigorously oppose Obama's use of drone strikes to kill terrorists in the Middle East. The National Security Agency's interception of private communications, as dramatized by the leaks from Edward Snowden, the former CIA systems administrator and NSA contractor, have met with outrage throughout the world.

All of these issues – the Iraq War, Guantanamo detentions, drone strikes, the NSA interceptions – are complex issues with intelligent and informed people on both sides. And global governance considerations are not by far the only factors behind the disagreements. But it is clear that the foundational dispute between the U.S. and the EU regarding the prosecution of the war on international terrorism – between a global governance model and one of international cooperation among sovereign and democratic nation-states – shows no signs of abating. And the persistence of this dispute concerning the central foreign policy interest of the United States over the past fourteen years threatens to erode the U.S.-Europe alliance. Reality is stubborn. It will not go away just because one prefers to view it through the distorting lens of global governance ideology.

CHAPTER 16:
POST-CHRISTIAN EUROPE AND RELIGION IN AMERICA

Since before the turn of the century, the EU's commitment to global governance has given rise to notions and initiatives that are inimical to U.S. interests, such as universal jurisdiction, the International Criminal Court, and the attempt to subject the war on terror to a crippling regime of international law. There is a yet more fundamental difference between Europe and the United States: the fact that Europe is largely post-Christian while the United States remains, culturally if not in actual religious faith, Judeo-Christian. This is an important reason why the idea of global governance has taken root in Europe but not (yet) in the United States, despite the support it has among American academics and the left-liberal elite. Global governance stands little chance of winning a significant number of adherents in a religious society because it is essentially secularist and relativistic.

The prevalent stereotype of a secular Europe over against a religious America is basically accurate. This is so even after all the qualifications regarding the impossibility of assessing and aggregating the individual beliefs of 300 million Americans and 500 million Europeans. It is true that great majorities of Europeans as well as Americans say they are Christians, but I would maintain that this is an inaccurate way to measure real religious faith. It primarily reflects an identification with a culture in which Christianity has essentially been "everyone's religion" for many centuries.

Social scientists cannot look into another's heart, so they tend to agree that churchgoing, the most basic and empirically verifiable religious practice of Christians, is a more accurate measure of faith than self-identification. According to a Gallup survey, although 74.5% of Europeans belong to a church, less than 20% of adults in the majority of EU member states attend church or any organized religious activity weekly.[1] In contrast, 40% of Americans attend church regularly.[2] According to Pew Research Center surveys taken from 2011 to 2013, religion is important to a far higher proportion of Americans than to inhabitants of the eight EU member states surveyed. While 54% of Americans said religion was "very important" in their lives, only 13% of the French, 17% of the British and 21% of the Germans said religion was very important. In the most religious EU countries surveyed, only 35% in Greece, 30% in Italy and 24% in Poland said religion was very important. Only 9% of Americans said religion was "not at all important" in their lives, while the figures were much higher in most of the EU countries: 43% in the Czech Republic, 40% in Britain, 38% in France, 31% in Spain and 24% in Germany.[3]

If the transatlantic alliance rests upon our common values, as is declared by everyone from President Bush to President Obama, Chancellor Angela Merkel to Prime Minister David Cameron, then this religious-secular disconnect is bound to have consequences. And so it does.

The disconnect is consequential because religion is not just about self-fulfillment and the afterlife. A religious faith affects every area of life, and certainly one's political outlook, given that politics is about ordering society and world affairs for the good of human beings, an undertaking necessarily rooted in basic presuppositions about human nature, the purpose of life, and the nature of good and evil. And everyone who engages in politics or thinks about politics – whether an atheist, an agnostic, a Christian, a Jew, or an adherent of any other religion – starts from a worldview that is religious in the sense that it rests on fundamental presuppositions of that kind.

I could elaborate on all sorts of issues in which the difference in religiosity between Europe and America leads to different political perspectives, but a crucial point is what Americans and Europeans believe to be the role of government and politics in human society. America, founded upon principles derived from the Judeo-Christian worldview, has traditionally not put its primary hope in politics. As Americans generally see it, the purpose of government and politics is to ensure security and freedom, so that people can pursue more important things, such as faith, work, family and friends. The ultimate source of goodness is God, and perfect justice cannot be realized by humans on this earth. On the other hand, for most people in post-Christian Europe, this world is all there is. Thus, the highest justice must be determined by human beings and pursued via politics and government.

These fundamental beliefs most often operate at a preconscious level, but the consequences are real nonetheless. I will illustrate this by comparing emblematic expressions of American and European views of government and politics: *The Federalist Papers* and the EU pronouncements on the UN's Post-2015 Development Agenda.

THE AMERICAN VIEW OF GOVERNMENT

The Federalist Papers, written by Alexander Hamilton, James Madison and John Jay, and published as a series in 1787–88 to urge ratification of the new constitution for the United States of America, are both a brilliant defense of effective self-government and a definitive exposition of the American view of government. The authors, three of the greatest thinkers among the American Founding Fathers, ground their case for the constitution in a humble reverence for wisdom and experience, prudent realism and a sober view of human nature.

"Why has government been instituted at all?" asks Hamilton in *Federalist* 15. He answers, "Because the passions of men will not conform to the dictates of reason and justice without constraint."[4] There is no hint in Madison, Hamilton or Jay of any notion that human nature is malleable in a transformative way. They would have seen it as folly to attempt to fashion a new kind of human being through a political project. On the contrary, the entire point of the constitution was to structure the government in such a way that it would have enough power to be effective while also limiting and diffusing its power so as to constrain the irremediable flaws of human nature, such as the lust for power and the tendency to abuse the power one has. Note how Madison's realistic acceptance of the intractable shortcomings of human beings and human life is at the very heart of his thinking on the structure of government in *Federalist* 41:

> ... but cool and candid people will at once reflect that the purest of human blessings must have a portion of alloy in them; that the choice must always be made, if not of the lesser evil, at least of the GEATER, not the PERFECT, good; and that in every political institution, a power to advance the public happiness involves a discretion which may be misapplied and abused. They will see, therefore, that in all cases where power is to be conferred, the point first to be decided is whether such a power be necessary to the public good; as the next will be, in case of an affirmative decision, to guard as effectually as possible against a perversion of the power to the public detriment.[5]

The separation of powers and the checks and balances provided in the U.S. Constitution were necessary not because a government so structured would bring about a transformative liberation of the human spirit, but because, just as the passions of the ruled must be constrained, so the ruler would abuse his powers if he were not subject to outside constraints: "The accumulation of all powers, legislative, executive, and judiciary, in the same hands, whether of one, a few, or many, and whether hereditary, self-appointed, or elective, may justly be pronounced the very definition of tyranny."[6]

The anthropology of *The Federalist Papers* was deeply indebted to Christianity, regardless of whether the authors were themselves believing Christians or not. Hamilton, Madison and Jay accepted that there was an objective truth about human nature, and that human beings were subject to the truth about reality. They accepted that human beings, while capable of great good, were flawed and limited, and that they could not overcome their fallibility. They could only do their best within the possibilities given them in this world.

And the views on human nature and reality that informed *The Federalist Papers* are still the prevailing, instinctive views of

Americans today, regardless of whether most Americans are believing Christians or not. Culturally, America is still Judeo-Christian.

"GOVERNANCE" AND HUMAN NATURE

It has become a stretch to claim that Europe is culturally religious at all, and that is the most profound reason why the gulf between the *Federalist Papers'* anthropology and that of the EU project and the global governance ideology is so great. The EU's pronouncements on the UN's Post-2015 Development Agenda, quoted in Chapter 10, reveal a belief that human nature is so malleable that by political effort it can burst the bonds of tradition and truth. As explained earlier, the post-2015 agenda picks up from the UN's Millennium Development Goals, the core of a grandiose project launched in 2000 and aimed at transforming the developing world by 2015. Now that 2015 has arrived, the UN, refusing to be chastened by its failure to achieve utopia, says on its website that "efforts to achieve a world of prosperity, equity, freedom, dignity and peace will continue unabated."[7]

The post-2015 agenda goes to the heart of the EU's reason for being: building the structures of global governance in order to create a world better than most dare to imagine. Thus the European Commission, in a document from which I have quoted earlier titled "A Decent Life for All," extravagantly declares:

> Eradicating poverty and achieving sustainable development are fundamental global challenges affecting the lives of current and future generations and the future of the entire planet. These challenges are universal and interrelated and need a global response. Addressing them requires strong political commitment and determined action at all levels and by all stakeholders.

> This agenda needs to be fit to address our globalized and inter-linked world, since business as usual is no longer an option whether in terms of human dignity, equity, equality or sustainability. The EU and its Member States have emphasized their commitment to work inclusively with all

partners and stakeholders to build consensus for a new
transformative post-2015 agenda.[8]

Not to be outdone, the Council of Ministers (one wonders which of the *ten* configurations of the supposedly *one* Council) declares itself up to the challenge of saving the world:

> The post-2015 agenda should therefore integrate the three dimensions of sustainable development in a balanced way across the agenda; ensure coherence and synergies; and address inter-linkages throughout the goals and targets. It is also crucial to ensure that the agenda has a rights-based approach encompassing all human rights and that it respects, supports, and builds on existing multilateral agreements, conventions, commitments, and processes....
>
> The agenda should leave no one behind. In particular, it must address, without any discrimination, the needs of the most disadvantaged and vulnerable, including children, the elderly and persons with disabilities, as well as of marginalised groups and indigenous peoples; and it must respond to the aspirations of young people. We should ensure that no person – wherever they live and regardless of ethnicity, gender, age, disability, religion or belief, race, or other status is denied universal human rights and basic economic opportunities. We emphasise the critical importance of quality education, universal health coverage, and social protection for all, which are central for the achievement of sustainable development.[9]

Here, politics, or "governance," is universal, global, all-encompassing, comprehensive. There are no constraints, no limits, neither geographical nor aspirational. There are no checks or balances to stand in the way of the good that can be accomplished by the global elite. The post-2015 agenda should leave no one behind, no one in the entire world; all "stakeholders" at all levels should show strong political commitment and undertake determined action; and so on. There is no end to the coherence, synergies, inter-linkages, universality and inclusiveness – all dry, bureaucratic, sterile, bloodless words like those of the new global ethic described earlier by Marguerite Peeters (sustainable development, multistakeholder consensus, transparency, inclusion, indicators of progress, etc.), in contrast with words of traditional faith such as "truth, morality, conscience, reason, heart, chastity, service, faith, charity, hope, suffering, sin, friend."[10]

THE HUMAN NEED FOR FAITH

I do not believe that those EU statements are intentionally bombastic. I have no doubt that the European Union has set these goals in good faith, hoping sincerely to build a better world. But it is amazing how irrepressible is the human desire for deliverance from this vale of tears. The difference between the American and European responses to this desire – and therefore the difference between the American and European views of government – is *religious*. The EU's post-2015 statements echo earlier statements of faith in the European idea, ranging from the Schuman Declaration, to the Rome Treaty's ever closer union, to the Convention on the Future of Europe called to draft a constitution for a nonexistent nation. As secular as Europe is and as cynical as many Europeans are about their political leaders and the European Union, the politics of the EU are marked by a quasi-religious fervor unmatched in the United States.

Global governance is a faith. It does not center on belief in God or in objective truth. Instead, it calls for a veneration of politics and "governance" as if they had a salvific power. The EU pronouncements on the Post-2015 Development Agenda are messages of hope for redemption, expressed in a heightened language that reads like the dying remnants of some Christian liturgy not yet lost to the continent's collective memory. Faith in global governance aspires to fill the dark void of hopelessness left by postmodern Europe's godlessness.

At its core, the EU's utopian vision, like that of every modern political utopia, is a faith commitment. In a post-Christian Europe, it is an attempt to salvage the hope of redemption without resorting to God. Enlightenment modernity may have been the beginning of the end of traditional Christian faith in Europe, but it could not extinguish the need for hope, the longing for a world better than this world could ever be. Thus, out of the Enlightenment, the political utopia of Marxism was born. Out of a Nietzschean revolt against modernity, fascism and Nazism were born. And out of the great wars of the twentieth century and the hideous crimes of Nazism and communism, the EU was born – animated by a new type of utopian ideology, a soft utopian creed that exalts a new dogma of human rights and seeks to build a global regime that would never repeat the crimes of communism and fascism. For reasons that are both historical and, in a profound sense, *religious*, the belief in global governance is what motivates the European Union at its deepest level. It is impossible to understand the EU without understanding this vision and recognizing it as the essence – the heart and soul and mind – of the entire European project.

PART SIX

SOFT UTOPIA AT A CROSSROADS

CHAPTER 17:
THE PRICE OF THE EURO:
UNPRECEDENTED INTEGRATION OR EU BREAKUP?

The eurozone crisis has brought the EU into a conundrum that will be hard to untangle. The policy response to the crisis points toward the member states relinquishing an unprecedented amount of power over economic policy and banking regulation to the EU. The Frankfurt-based European Central Bank, an appointed body officially independent of governments and unaccountable to voters, has amassed a tremendous amount of power over the fate of the euro and the taxpayer money that is spent to save it. On the ground in the member states, the questions posed by the eurozone crisis center on Britain's place in the EU, German commitment to the European idea, and the dire economic situation in the weaker countries.

Sovereigntist Great Britain is pushing to renegotiate its relationship with the EU, aiming to repatriate powers that have been ceded to the EU and safeguard its national sovereignty. Soon, the UK will hold an in-out referendum on EU membership that could result in its leaving the EU. Germans have been the most reliable supranationalists among the populaces of the large member states, but the cost to German taxpayers of the eurozone crisis could change that. Opposition to the euro and a more reserved attitude toward further European integration are gaining ground. Germany's dedication to the European idea is still alive, but it is no longer unquestioned, and the eurozone cannot survive without the German economic powerhouse. Elsewhere in the EU, the economic situation is dire, leading to increased political and social instability.

EU acolytes are hoping the EU will be able to muddle through with the supranationalist dream not only intact but progressing. They hope that the consolidation of economic "governance" at EU level will both save the eurozone and bring the EU closer to political union. But will that happen? And will the German commitment to the European idea survive? Will Britain ultimately stay in the EU and acquiesce, as it always has before, to the status quo in exchange for a few opt-outs? Will the economic situation improve enough in the weaker eurozone economies to stem growing anti-EU sentiment? These are the questions posed by the eurozone crisis.

AN EU WITHOUT BRITAIN?

In a major speech on Britain's future in the European Union in January 2013, Prime Minister David Cameron predicted that "the European Union that emerges from the Eurozone crisis is going to be a very different body. It will be transformed perhaps beyond recognition by the measures needed to save the Eurozone."[1] In that context, he called for a "new settlement" between the UK and the EU, one that would be "subject to the democratic legitimacy and accountability of national parliaments where Member States combine in flexible cooperation, respecting national differences,"[2] as opposed to an EU in which member states relinquish more and more national sovereignty in pursuit of an ever closer political union. Cameron has promised that there will be an in-out referendum on British EU membership by the end of 2017 at the latest, based on the results of that new settlement.

Euroskeptics have gained a voice that cannot be ignored in Britain, and many of them are vocally advocating an exit from the EU regardless of what the results of a "new settlement" would be. One Conservative member of Parliament, Laurence Robertson, puts his case for leaving the EU as follows:

> My bottom line is that the UK Parliament, acting on behalf of the people who vote for it, should make all the laws for

this country and should control the borders of the UK.... [G]iven that such fundamental renegotiation isn't even being considered, I feel safe in stating my case for leaving the EU.... I do want to cooperate with countries in the EU, on matters such as trade, security, the environment and so much more. But I don't want to make the laws which control the Italians, the Spaniards or the Poles, and I don't want them to make the laws which control me.[3]

Meanwhile, the pro-EU side generally focuses on the economy. Speaking to the British Chambers of Commerce on February 10, 2015, Ed Balls, a Labour politician who was serving as shadow chancellor (treasury secretary), said, "I fear that Britain walking out of the EU is the biggest risk to our economy in the next decade. EU exit risks British jobs, trade and investment and the future prosperity of the UK."[4]

The instinctively cautious British electorate is ambivalent about EU membership, wavering between concerns about being subject to the regulatory zeal of the Brussels technocracy and a desire to have a seat at the table in EU councils and full access to the EU-wide single market. Either way, Britain has its work cut out for it if serious negotiations for a new settlement come to pass. The unprecedented attempt to carve out a unique niche for Britain within the EU will be tantamount to unraveling and then reweaving sixty-five years' worth of treaties, agreements, precedent and practice. As the European Council president Donald Tusk said, renegotiating the EU treaties for Britain's sake would be "close to mission impossible."[5]

The pervasive EU penetration into every aspect of life in every EU member state, including Britain, and the vast and unpredictable implications of leaving the EU – not to mention decades of habit and pure inertia – all militate against Britain's leaving the EU. But it could happen. An EU without Britain is a distinct possibility. A Brexit – British EU exit – would probably be good for democracy in Britain. But it would not be good for U.S.-EU relations. It would mean an EU without our closest European ally and cultural cousin, without our Anglophone bridge to the continent.

Unlike the UK, Germany has always believed in European political union. While Britain retains it own currency, the pound sterling, Germany is a member of the eurozone. It is the EU's chief economic engine and its most populous member state. Without Germany's largesse the eurozone would probably not have survived the financial crisis intact. All of this puts Chancellor Angela Merkel, arguably the most powerful person in Europe, in a position very different from David Cameron's. For much of the last six years, Merkel has been walking the tightrope between her constitutional responsibility for Germany and her assumed responsibility for Europe with persistence and determination, but also more than a bit of trepidation.

Merkel's tightrope walk mirrors uncannily the continent's decades-long balancing act between reality and the European dream of global governance. Sixty-five years of checkered history is brought into focus in one person dealing with a single crisis in a relatively short period of time. Pulling Merkel on one side is German reality: the chancellor must protect German taxpayers from endless bailouts of hapless eurozone members, especially Greece. On the other side is the European dream: Merkel is shouldering what she sees as the world-historical responsibility of keeping the dream alive. Time and again, she has reluctantly decided that doing so requires placing Germans' hard-earned tax revenues at the disposal of "Europe," regardless of the fairness or the cost. Like Mario Draghi, president of the European Central Bank, she believes that she has to "do whatever it takes" to save the euro.

Torn between the forces of reality and the forces of utopia, Merkel has reached for the tried-and-true "Monnet method." As Jean Monnet would have done in her place, she has been moving gradually, as much as possible under the radar, and cloaked by rhetorical obfuscation, so that German voters don't understand how much she has been risking German prosperity in order to keep the eurozone intact. For half a decade, Merkel has vacillated between demanding full compliance of bailout recipients with strict economic reforms and repayment conditions, and then agreeing to spend millions to save the eurozone even though there are no guarantees that the bailouts will ever be enough or ever be paid back. She projects a tough image for strategic reasons: she wants

to appear a defender of German taxpayers even though she is ultimately agreeing to give their money away.

Her sporadic calls for "more Europe" exemplify the Merkel
update of the Monnet method. In appealing without elaboration
to a German European patriotism that German leaders have been
trying to foster ever since Adenauer in the late 1940s, Merkel is
taking the position that pursuing the utopian dream of European
integration is a higher interest to Germans than keeping their own
money in their own pockets. But of course she doesn't dare say it
openly and subject the proposition to real debate.

Merkel's commitment to saving the euro at all costs has
opened a rift with a significant number of prominent business
people, economists and bankers. Hans-Olaf Henkel, a former German Federation of Industry president whose book *Die Euro-
Lügner* (The Euro-Liars) is one basis for my analysis of Merkel's
actions, believes the euro is doomed to failure because the economies and cultures of the south are too different from those of the
north. Attempting to save the euro by transferring money and
resources from the frugal north to the profligate south is a cure
worse than the disease, bankrupting the north without motivating
the needed structural reforms in the south. In the "European Solidarity Manifesto," Henkel and eighteen other economists and
business people call for the "controlled segmentation of the Eurozone via a jointly agreed exit of the most competitive countries," in
which the prosperous northern EU states drop the euro and the
poorer southern states keep it, but "ultimately... return to the
national currencies or to different currencies serving groups of
homogeneous countries."[6]

Although Henkel has gone further than most in proposing
the breakup of the euro, he is not alone in his decisive break with
the government over Germany's role as the savior of the eurozone.
Axel Weber, former president of the German Bundesbank, and
Jürgen Stark, former chief economist of the European Central
Bank, both resigned because they disagreed with the "easy money"
bailout policy favored by most members of the ECB Governing
Council and the German government's uneasy acquiescence in it.
According to Henkel, even the early resignations of the last two
German presidents, Horst Köhler and Christian Wulff, had to do
with their opposition to misguided attempts to save the euro. Hen-
kel maintains that one of the reasons for Köhler's resignation was

his having been pressured by Angela Merkel to sign the law allowing the first Greek bailout immediately, without the time to consider all of its ramifications.[7] Wulff was hounded out of office on bogus corruption allegations, which Henkel theorizes were motivated by a speech in which Wulff said the ECB's bond-buying program violated EU law; the Wulff-hunt began soon afterward.[8]

The German Federal Constitutional Court (Bundesverfassungsgericht – BVG) apparently agrees with Christian Wulff. On January 14, 2014, the BVG punted a decision on the legality of the ECB's bond-buying program (called OMT, for outright monetary transactions) to the European Court of Justice (ECJ). But it punted with a stern demeanor. The BVG found the OMT decision to be in violation of EU law, and it "offered a clutch of conditions on how the EU court would have to interpret OMT in order for the German court to find it acceptable."[9] The justification for the BVG's referring the matter to the ECJ, rather than issuing a final ruling itself on OMT's legality, was that the question before it was a matter of EU law, and thus fell within the jurisdiction of the EU court.

This was consistent with the BVG's actions in a long line of cases involving the issue of whether the EU's claim of the precedence of EU over national law violates the German constitution. In a way typical of the postmodern "bothness" of the EU, the BVG and the ECJ have long been in a standoff that defies resolution: the BVG rightly claims the last word on the constitutionality of legislation in Germany, and the ECJ rightly claims the last word on the constitutionality of legislation in the EU. Unfortunately for democracy in Germany, the ECJ has consistently been the de facto winner of this standoff. In its rulings in conflict situations the BVG has typically managed to combine a stern assertion of the BVG's right to have the final word on law in Germany with an acceptance of whatever has been decided on the EU level, no matter how questionable its effects on German sovereignty. Not wanting to be a brake on European integration in a country whose wish to overcome its history has resulted in a deeply felt moral commitment to the European idea, the BVG has waffled and equivocated.[10]

Hans-Werner Sinn, the president of the Ifo Institute, one of the leading economic research organizations in Germany, believes the deferral to the European court on OMT is different from past decisions involving EU law. He believes that this time the BVG has lived up to its responsibility as the highest court in Germany, in

effect calling a stop to the OMT program and ushering in a new
era in which Germany will no longer allow the EU to overrun German national sovereignty:

> In reality, the constitutional court has only asked the ECJ for an opinion. The BVG remains the master of the proceedings. Since it has come to the view that the mere announcement of the intention to buy unlimited quantities of government securities violates the EU treaties, it did not ask whether the ECJ shares the same view, but rather only how one, in the view of the ECJ, could modify and limit the bond-buying program so that it would comply with EU law.[11]

From this, Sinn concludes that the German government's "eye-winking acquiescence" in the ECB's undemocratic "usurpation of power" will soon come to an end:

> Either way the official finding that this arrogation of power of the ECB – the court speaks of a "usurpation of power" – is a violation of the treaties has brought us to a point of historic significance in the development of the Federal Republic of Germany. For the first time the German constitutional court will stop the chosen course of [European] integration and force a change of direction. Whatever the details of the final result of this judicial process will be, it is already clear that the European policy of the German government, as it has been practiced until now, has come to its end.[12]

Unfortunately, there is reason to doubt Sinn's optimistic prediction. In June 2015 the ECJ ruled that the OMT program is compatible with EU law, thus in effect defying the BVG. Now it is up to the BVG to decide whether to forbid German participation in OMT. Most observers expect the German court to follow past practice and equivocate again, issuing a decision that basically says, as one ECJ judge has characterized previous BVG decisions on EU law, "not guilty, but don't do it again!"[13] So far, the ECJ has kept doing it again. Regardless of how it ends, this whole affair is but another illustration of how deeply the eurozone crisis has become a crisis of legitimacy for the EU.

The crisis has clearly weakened the German commitment to

supranational European integration, both in the business world and in the judiciary. A new party, the anti-euro Alternative für Deutschland (AFD), illustrates how the reevaluation of the European idea in Germany is occurring on the political front as well. Again, the concern is partly economic and partly one of democratic accountability. The AFD arose not only because of the costs of maintaining the euro, but also because of the palpable sense among Germans that their elected leaders are acting in the interests of Greece and the EU rather than in the interest of German citizens. In a development that would have been unimaginable before the eurozone crisis, this anti-euro party, little more than one year after its founding in February 2013, won seven seats in the May 2014 European Parliament elections. Since then, the AFD has won parliamentary seats in all five German state parliament elections in 2014–2015. As of summer 2015, the AFD's future was in question because of the ascension of far-right elements in the party. Hans-Olaf Henkel entered the EP in 2014 as a member of the AFD but has now left the party, saying it was becoming "a neo-Nazi party in sheep's clothing."[14] With the chaotic results of Merkel's late-summer announcement that Germany would accept up to 800,000 refugees from Syria, the AFD's fortunes revived and its poll numbers rose to around 10%.

The 2014 European elections will be discussed in greater detail in Chapter 19. For now, suffice it to say that the success of the AFD, along with declining poll numbers for the euro and the EU in Germany,[15] is another sign that the question is very much open: will Germany, until now an indispensable motor of the drive for supranational integration, pull back from the dream of European political union? And if so, will the dream survive?

... WHILE ATHENS (AND MADRID, AND LISBON, AND ROME) BURNS

As the UK plunges into a raucous debate about how and whether to stay in the EU, and as the German pro-EU consensus weakens, much of the rest of the EU is suffering immensely, with increasing political and social tensions as a consequence.

In the EU as a whole, the unemployment rate in the second quarter of 2014 was 10.3%. Overall youth unemployment was a mortifying 22%. Greece, the country hardest hit by the financial crisis, has seen widespread, sometimes violent unrest, anti-German animus, social breakdown and political radicalization. Unemployment in Greece in the second quarter of 2014 was 26.9%. Among youth, it was a whopping 52.2%. The Greek economy has contracted by 25% and public debt stands at a crushing 175% of GDP.[16] In January 2015 elections, the Greeks went radical in their desperation to regain control over their own fate, electing a far-left party, Syriza. Now, that very party – with the support of the majority of the Greek electorate – has largely agreed to the austerity measures it was elected to oppose. Fear of catastrophic consequences of a "Grexit," a Greek exit from the eurozone, changed the minds of many Greek voters and the majority of Syriza officials, led by the prime minister, Alexis Tsipras. It remains doubtful, however, that Syriza will actually impose those austerity measures to the satisfaction of its creditors.

Meanwhile, Spain's misery was comparable to Greece's, with 24.7% overall unemployment and 53.2% youth unemployment. In the remaining three bailout beneficiaries, the figures were also appalling. Portugal had 14.4% overall and 37.2% youth unemployment. The statistics for Cyprus were 15.9% and 37% respectively. Even in Ireland, the rescue-package recipient whose economic comeback has repeatedly been highlighted as a success story, the figures were 11.7% and 25.1%. Only in comparison with the Greek and Spanish basket cases could those statistics be touted as positive.

In Italy, with an economy similar to the bailout recipients but probably too big to bail out, the situation is no better. As of February 2015, Italy's overall unemployment rate was 12.7%, with youth unemployment rivaling all comers at 42.6%.[17] Italy's debt is second only to Greece among eurozone countries, at 132% of GDP.[18] In France also, unemployment and debt are high, overregulation stifles innovation, and social division and discontent are widespread. As we will see in more detail in Chapter 19, the economic dislocation caused or exacerbated by the eurozone crisis – along with people's awakening sense that the lack of democratic accountability in the EU hurts their pocketbooks – is having political ramifications throughout the EU. From north to south, anti-EU protest parties are experiencing a breathtaking ascent while the established parties are hemorrhaging support.

Could the situation be worse? At the height of the Great Depression, an experience that shaped the worldview of an entire generation in America, the estimated U.S. unemployment rate climbed to 24.75% at its very highest.[19] The most elevated rate of youth unemployment in the United States during the Great Depression was 23.6%, according to one estimate. As one analyst puts it, "For much of the Eurozone, the current crisis would be more accurately referred to as 'The Second Great Depression.'"[20]

Certainly, the euro is not solely to blame for this catastrophe. But it has played a central role. The introduction of a common currency for economies at completely different levels of development and productivity flooded the weaker countries with cheap money, creating the incentive to overspend on imports, overpay employees, incur unsustainable debt and ignore low productivity. All this created bubbles in bond and real estate markets that were bound to burst. When they did burst, the weaker economies faced bankruptcy. The necessary ratcheting down of spending exacerbated unemployment, dried up opportunity and spread misery and discontent. If economists such as Hans-Werner Sinn are correct, the outlook remains bleak. As we will see below, continuing to prop up the euro is leading to an EU economic governance that is even more supranational and less accountable to voters, and that strongly resembles a planned economy, diverting huge amounts of resources to the troubled economies of the eurozone and thereby robbing the productive economies of resources they could otherwise put to good use.

ECONOMIC GOVERNANCE AND THE "BANKERS' COUP"

There are three main areas of response to the eurozone crisis: economic policy coordination or "economic governance," banking regulation, and bailout mechanisms. The changes in "economic governance" subsequent to the eurozone crisis were all aimed at increasing the role of the European Union in economic policy making and decreasing the power of the member states to step out of the bounds put in place by the Brussels policy framework. This is easier said than done, of course. Member states, especially the larger member states, have a history of ignoring EU rules with impunity.[21]

That said, the main policy-coordination changes involved

increasing harmonization of economic and fiscal policy, and monitoring of member states' adherence to the agreed policies, especially the strengthening of the Stability and Growth Pact (SGP). Introduced along with the euro itself in 2002, the SGP mandates that all eurozone countries keep their budget deficit below 3% of gross domestic product and their public debt below 60% of GDP. The SGP has long been flouted with relative ease, but eurozone members have now attempted to give it real teeth in response to the crisis. These measures are designed to increase EU leverage over core economic and fiscal policy making in the member states. The European Commission now assesses member states' annual budget proposals, which must be submitted to the Commission before being adopted by a national parliament. A country must either keep its deficit and debt level under the SGP limits or agree to a plan to bring them back within those limits. Otherwise, the EU can impose sanctions and place the offending member state under the "enhanced surveillance" of the European Commission.

Connected with all of this is the Fiscal Compact. A serious encroachment on national sovereignty, it requires "euro area member states to implement uniform and permanently binding budgetary rules in their national legislation, preferably in their constitution."[22] The desired "budgetary rules" basically come down to a commitment to a balanced budget, enshrined if possible in the constitution, the supreme law of each member state. The fiscal compact has been ratified by all nineteen eurozone countries and by six EU members that are not in the eurozone. The Czech Republic and Croatia are still considering the treaty. The UK is the only member state that has unequivocally refused to join the Fiscal Compact.

Another part of the economic governance mix is the "European Semester," under which the European Commission analyzes "the economic situation in the EU" and sets policy priorities for the upcoming year. On this basis, the member states agree on general "policy orientations" and submit "medium-term" budget and economic plans to the Commission.[23] The Commission then prepares "country-specific recommendations" for each country, advising them on what economic and fiscal policies they should pursue. The member states are expected to take the recommendations into account in adopting their final budgets (which, again, must be submitted to the Commission for approval).

Finally, the European Commission annually assesses each member state in other key categories, such as "unemployment rates, labor costs, difference between imports and exports, and housing price trends." There are agreed limits for each of these indicators, and if any of the values goes beyond the limit, an early warning mechanism is triggered to prevent possible macroeconomic imbalances. The European Commission issues recommendations based on this assessment, and member states may suffer sanctions if they consistently fail to comply.[24]

All of these measures together represent a radical circumscription of national sovereignty in crucial policy areas. The mixed record so far in enforcing these rules is an indication of how difficult it is to impose a utopian scheme of supranational governance on the real world. Nevertheless, the fact that almost all of these rules have been agreed to – at least in principle – by almost all EU member states is an indication of how successfully the EU integrationists have used the eurozone crisis to institute "more Europe."

The policy response with respect to regulation of the banking sector portends a similarly radical move toward supranational governance. The banking union, as it is called, involves the establishment of new EU-wide "supervisory authorities for financial institutions," a "single rule book" on capital requirements, harmonized deposit guarantee schemes, and other measures. In the eurozone, the ECB, rather than national supervisory authorities, will now oversee the larger banks.[25] Complicated, specialized and difficult for nonexperts to understand, the banking union is, in essence, nothing less than a transfer of the supervision and regulation of the larger banks from the national to the EU level. It is a major step for supranationalism. Its legal basis is questionable, causing many ripples among German observers especially. Markus Kerber, a finance professor at Berlin Technical University, characterized the banking union as the "pinnacle of Brussels power-grabbing to date," noting that it has "no legal basis in the EU treaties and so represents a breach of constitutional rights."[26]

The third area of the policy response to the crisis was the eurozone bailouts, beginning in 2010 through a succession of temporary mechanisms, the most prominent of which was the European Financial Stability Facility. (Leave it to the EU to give it a name that rhymes.) Much of the support for Greece, Portugal and Ireland came through the EFSF. Then, in October 2012, a permanent mechanism, called the European Stability Mechanism (ESM), replaced the EFSF. The ESM can lend up to 500 billion euros, of which up to 60 billion "can be used to recapitalize banks directly."[27] ESM funds are supporting Cyprus.

The bailout loans are subject to strict fiscal, economic and financial conditions that are in reality also supremely political. And it cannot be emphasized too much that the governing is truly happening undemocratically. In the economically stronger north, governments are using taxpayers' money in ways they are not expressly authorized to do. In the economically weaker south, the makeup of nothing less than national governments has been determined over the heads of voters. The democratically elected leaders of Italy and Greece were ousted in late 2011 and new leaders were installed, basically at the behest of what the *New York Times* columnist Ross Douthat called the Brussels-Berlin-Paris axis. As Douthat observed, "Democracy may be nice in theory, but in a time of crisis it's the technocrats who really get to call the shots. National sovereignty is a pretty concept, but the survival of the European common currency comes first." The ousters of the Italian and Greek prime ministers, he wrote, "open a troubling window on what a true European state would look like. Stability would be achieved at the expense of democracy."[28]

In the January 2015 snap elections, the Greeks tried to take democracy back. They chose the radical left-wing party Syriza over the EU-favored center-right incumbent government. Syriza won on its pledge to restore Greece's sovereignty over its own affairs and terminate the austerity program required by Greece's EU and international creditors. As mentioned before, however, Syriza as of late 2015 has agreed to a new package of austerity measures in order to receive a third bailout. It is, at the very least, difficult to say whether the Greeks govern themselves or are governed by their creditors. Greece's primary leverage with its creditors to extract any concessions at all on the bailout requirements has been the widespread conviction that, in the words of Angela Merkel, "if the euro fails, Europe fails."[29] That leverage has lessened considerably now that most observers agree that a Grexit would not mean the failure of the euro.

In the midst of the eurozone's troubles, one observer noted that "the voice of the people isn't something that markets seem to want to hear these days."[30] And this is the general upshot of the policy response to the eurozone crisis: it has proved to be the technocrats' finest hour. It has all been one giant leap for EU supranationalism, over the heads of the voters. And the institution to gain far more *political* power than any gains made by the other EU institutions is the European Central Bank, which was expressly conceived to be independent and sealed off from political considerations in order to fulfill its mandate to set monetary policy with the goal of avoiding inflation.

What is generally credited with bringing the euro crisis under control is the statement by the ECB president Mario Draghi on July 26, 2012 that the ECB would "do whatever it takes" to save the euro.[31] Given the fragility of the eurozone economy, no elected government or national parliament dared contradict him. But what did Draghi mean by doing "whatever it takes"? He meant outright monetary transactions (OMT): he was asserting the ECB's right to pump staggering quantities of cash into the economy by buying government bonds on a massive scale from eurozone member states, purchasing other securities, and lending money to banks throughout the eurozone. The problem is that the ECB's trillions-of-euros lending power comes from the ability to print money out of thin air, thus transferring the cost to taxpayers in the stronger economies in the form of a loss of value of their savings and retirement benefits.

In effect, a supranational, unelected group of bankers from all over Europe, gathered together in the Governing Council of the ECB, has taken the situation into its own hands, stretching beyond recognition the ECB's mandate in the EU treaty. No one – not EU member-state governments (at least not officially), not the EU institutions, and certainly not the voters – had any say in the matter. Unlike the Federal Reserve in the United States, the ECB is not subject to the legislative powers of any unitary government. Furthermore, according to the EU treaty no EU member-state national government may exert influence on it. And with the ECJ's aforementioned rejection of the German Constitutional Court's finding that OMT ("doing whatever it takes") is illegal under the EU treaty, a group of judges in Luxembourg has now officially sanctioned the ECB as the ultimate arbiter of the eurozone's fate. The ECB has become "the true hegemon of Europe," as Hans-Werner Sinn remarks. It "can do what it chooses, in full independence, with a substantial share of Europeans' wealth."[32] It has authorized itself "to take actions that go far beyond its monetary policy mandate and will decisively change the real structure of Europe."[33] Could any other development have been more postdemocratic?

THE SOFT UTOPIA AT THE CROSSROADS

The eurozone crisis will in fact change the EU. More importantly, it has *already* changed the EU. An EU without Great Britain is now conceivable, however unlikely it may be. Also unlikely but now possible is a Germany that has been forced by pocketbook reality to abandon the commitment, shared by every postwar German generation, to a unified Europe that will never again suffer war on European soil. And a breakup of the eurozone – the abandonment of Greece to its own third-world-style devices – is still possible too.

On the other hand, the dream is not dead. There is no justification for the pragmatists to indulge, as usual, in underestimating the power of the European idea, however much the eurozone fiasco has exposed its inherent folly. The economic arguments of the pro-EU side in Britain evidence both the cleverness of Jean Monnet's strategy to advance political integration under cover of economic integration, and the unremitting tendency of economic elites to assume that supranational integration brings markets and buyers closer to them, a consideration that trumps national patriotism and democratic sovereignty. Also, if there is a Brexit, the project of supranational governance could actually benefit from the withdrawal of the EU's largest sovereigntist member state. The German political class remains overwhelmingly in favor of the European dream, and the majority of the German populace is, at the very least, acquiescent. The majority of Greeks, to say nothing of all the other weak economies, want to stay in the euro. And the EU elites appear to have taken advantage of the eurozone crisis to transfer unprecedented powers to the EU institutions.

The game is not over. The question "what is the EU and what do we want it to become" is still unanswered. In the remaining chapters, we will see how the EU has already changed, in interrelated ways. In Chapter 19 we will examine in more detail the crisis of democracy in the EU as it has been exacerbated by the eurozone crisis. But before that, in Chapter 18, we will examine demographic developments of great portent for the EU's future that have already changed the EU of today: the growth of Islam in Europe, now magnified by the migrant crisis of 2015, and the persistent infertility of native Europeans, which challenges the sustainability of the social-democratic welfare state.

CHAPTER 18:
DEMOGRAPHICS AND ISLAM:
THE CHALLENGES FOR EUROPE'S FUTURE

In a very real sense, even as the EU enlarges, the EU is shrinking. According to the CIA's *World Factbook,* there are no European countries in which the estimated total fertility rate (TFR) for 2014 is at or above the replacement rate of 2.1 children per woman of childbearing age, the average number of babies per woman that is generally necessary in the industrialized world in order to sustain population levels. Among EU member states, only France at 2.08 and Ireland at 2.0 have TFRs that come close to the replacement rate. Next come the United Kingdom at 1.90 and Sweden at 1.88. Seventeen of the twenty-eight EU member states have estimated 2014 TFRs below 1.6. The lowest are Poland and Slovenia at 1.33, Romania at 1.32 and Lithuania at rock bottom with 1.29.[1]

Although low birthrates may take awhile to result in the decline of overall population, some of the largest EU member states are already beginning to shrink. Germany, the most populous EU member state, had approximately 80.62 million inhabitants when its latest census was completed (in 2011), but that figure is 1.5 million lower than had been suggested by official intercensal updates, and demographers said that the total population could shrink to about 66 million by 2060.[2] The second most populous EU country,

France, is expected to hold its own, with the highest estimated TFR in the EU. Now at 64.59 million, it is expected to grow to 70.13 million by 2060.[3] The UK, the third largest EU member state, now at about 64 million inhabitants, is expected to count 72.16 million by 2060.[4] The fourth in line is Italy, now at 60.95 million and expected to decline to 52.49 million.[5]

The EU statistics agency Eurostat predicts that the total population of the EU (excluding Croatia, which joined in 2013) will increase to 521 million by 2035, and "thereafter gradually decline to 506 million in 2060." In its press release, the European Commission goes on to say that as of 2015, "deaths would outnumber births, and hence population growth due to natural increase would cease. From this point onwards, positive net migration would be the only population growth factor."[6]

A GROWING MUSLIM POPULATION

While the European population overall is stagnant or declining, the picture is quite different for one particular demographic group. The Muslim population in Europe is growing, both through higher birthrates and by immigration that has recently reached explosive proportions. And unlike the "native" European population, Muslims in Europe are not losing their religion. Today, Islam is the only dynamically growing, vital religious faith in Europe.

Even with the statistics available before the 2015 migration crisis, the numbers speak eloquently. According to "The Future of the Global Muslim Population," a 2011 study by the Pew Research Center's Religion and Public Life forum, "The number of Muslims in Europe has grown from 29.6 million in 1990 to 44.1 million in 2010. Europe's Muslim population is projected to exceed 58 million by 2030. Muslims today account for about 6% of Europe's total population, up from 4.1% in 1990. By 2030, Muslims are expected to make up 8% of Europe's population."[7] The growth is steady and impressive. Also, Muslims are heavily concentrated in many major urban areas, such as Brussels, where they now make up approximately 25% of the population.[8] Others among the cities with a high concentration of Muslims are Amsterdam, 24%; Stockholm, 20%; Cologne, 12%; Marseilles, 25%; and those of the Île-de-

France (the region surrounding Paris, including the notorious suburbs or *banlieues*), 10–15%.[9]

These numbers have already grown beyond all expectations. In 2015, close to a million immigrants mostly from Muslim countries – not only war-torn Syria but also Iraq, Iran, Pakistan, Afghanistan and elsewhere – will have poured into the EU. Chancellor Angela Merkel compounded the crisis immeasurably in August 2015 when she announced, in a fit of well-meaning sentimentality, that Germany's doors were open to Syrian refugees and that Germany would accept up to 800,000 Syrians in 2015. (That is approximately 1% of the entire population of Germany.) Because of the generally open borders within the EU, Merkel's announcement sparked an influx of unmanageable magnitude into EU countries on the southeast flank of the EU – such as Greece, Bulgaria, and Hungary – with most of them planning to move on to Germany or Sweden, another country with generous welfare benefits and open policies toward asylum seekers. In the meantime, though, the capacity of Greece and the other southeastern countries to house and feed the newcomers was overwhelmed, provoking not only political and social tensions but also a genuine humanitarian crisis. Soon, the intake capacities of even the wealthier countries such as Austria, Sweden and Germany itself came close to the breaking point. As at least one of the Paris terrorists of November 2015 appears to have entered the EU posing as a Syrian refugee, no one can guarantee that there are no terrorists among the hundreds of thousands more who are pouring in.

But this is far from the end of the story. The great majority of the immigrants are young men. As the journalist Christopher Caldwell points out, "When migrant families follow, as they inevitably do, the effect will be multiplied. Donald Tusk, the Polish president of the European Council, warns that the biggest tide of migrants 'is yet to come.'"[10]

And Muslims, unlike their post-Christian counterparts, are having children. This is a factor every bit as important as immigration. According to Caldwell, in his book *Reflections on the Revolution in Europe: Immigration, Islam, and the West* (2009), "the gap in fertility between immigrants and natives is at its widest for Muslim immigrants."[11] Fertility rates in Austria around the time that Caldwell wrote his book were 1.32 children per woman for

Catholics, 1.21 for Protestants, 0.86 for the nonreligious and 2.34 for Muslims. These rates mean that "Islam could be the majority religion among Austrians under fifteen" by 2050.[12] In 2008, Mohammed was the most popular name for newborn boys in the four biggest cities of the Netherlands – Amsterdam, Rotterdam, The Hague and Utrecht.[13] Mohammed was also the most common newborn boy's name in England and Wales in 2009, even though the British Office of National Statistics kept that fact half-hidden by not counting the twelve different spellings of the name together.[14] "In Belgium," writes Caldwell, "the relatively well-established Moroccan-Belgian community has a birthrate two and a half times higher than the native Belgian one. In Brussels... more than half of the children (57 percent) born in 2006 were born to Muslims, [and] the seven most common given boys' names were Mohamed, Adam, Rayan, Ayoub, Mehdi, Amine, and Hamza."[15] In the future, although fertility rates of Muslims in Europe are expected to fall, they are likely to remain higher than native European fertility rates.

Furthermore, unlike the great majority of European Christians, Muslims in Europe are highly religious, as a Pew Research Center report affirms:

> A 2001 poll published by the French newspaper *Le Monde*, for instance, found that Muslims were attending mosque and praying more frequently than they had been in 1994, when a similar survey was conducted. And in London a recent survey found that 80 percent of Muslims said they attend mosque regularly. Indeed, another survey in Britain found that even though Muslims make up about 3 percent of the largely Christian country's population, there are now more people attending mosque regularly than going to church.... Surveys show that many Muslims in Europe, especially the young, now identify with Islam more than either the country of their heritage or the country of their birth. Not feeling entirely accepted in either place, they look to Islam to help define themselves.[16]

This Islam, to a large extent, remains distinctly non-Western, and frequently anti-Western. There have been many attempts to domesticate Islam by both European governments and European Muslims themselves, such as the founding of the French Council of the Muslim Faith (CFCM) with encouragement from Nicolas Sarkozy, then the interior minister and later president. The CFCM is meant to be the more-or-less official representative of French Muslims to the French government, but it does not and cannot speak for individual Muslims. Certainly, it does not represent the radical and disaffected Muslims who are at the root of the French government's concerns. Largely the same can be said of similar organizations in other countries, such as the Muslim Council of Britain, the Muslim Council of Sweden and the Central Council of Muslims in Germany. Although they all offer a forum for exchange with their respective governments and citizenries, they have all failed to Europeanize Islam in any meaningful way. Average Muslims do not acknowledge their authority to speak for them, and many European Muslims sense that Europeanizing Islam would mean, in effect, to secularize it, to sap it of its vitality.

Reflecting this concern, Muslims also remain largely separatist, living apart from native Europeans. As Christopher Caldwell points out, it can be hard to tell whether immigrants desire to live separately or government policies make segregation inevitable. Throughout Europe in the 1950s and 1960s, he explains, gigantic housing projects were built for the poor. Immigrants ended up living there, often far away from jobs. While some projects were built near large employers, those jobs sometimes dried up. When that happened, native workers moved out and immigrants moved in, because governments often house immigrant newcomers, logically, in apartments that are empty. A prominent Swedish welfare-state economist pointed out that those apartments are "by definition in an area of high unemployment."[17]

And then there is the problem of criminality. Like so many housing projects in the United States, many areas in which Muslims live have become havens for criminals. The French *banlieues*, often characterized as virtual no-go zones for non-Muslims, are known in France as *zones de non-droit* – lawless zones. Not all of the criminality in these areas comes from Muslim inhabitants, but a great amount of it does. In fact, Muslim criminality is a huge problem in Europe, especially in France. Caldwell notes that "although precise numbers are hard to come by, Muslims make up 50 percent of the population in many French jails, and up to 80 percent in certain prisons near the banlieues."[18]

Also, the separatism of Muslims in Europe has made more

possible the widespread transplantation of Muslim cultural practices to Europe, and the de facto supremacy of sharia law in many
Muslim communities in Europe. "In Britain," Caldwell reports, "37
percent of Muslims between sixteen and twenty-four want the
introduction of sharia law, and 37 percent favor executing Muslims
who renounce Islam. In Ireland, a majority of Muslims (57 percent)
wish for Ireland to become an Islamic state."[19] One commonplace
aspect of this cultural transplantation is "marriage migration." These
are often arranged marriages, in which brides are brought from the
home country to marry young men in Europe, although the bride and
groom may have never met each other. Polygamy has also inserted
itself into public debate, in various places. In fact, the British Department for Work and Pensions in 2008 issued guidelines for paying
state benefits to multiple spouses.[20] Many Muslim communities in
Europe reportedly regulate divorce under sharia law, which discrim-
inates against women in ways that European divorce law forbids.

A visible reminder of the stark differences between Muslim
and European views of women is the increasingly common sight of
Islamic coverings for females, from the headscarf to the niqab or the
burka that covers the entire face and body. Not surprisingly in a continent where people are losing the ability to understand religion,
these trends have led to uncertainty regarding where to draw the
line between religious freedom and the common good. France has
made it illegal to wear a face-covering veil or any other "ostenta-
tious religious symbol" in public. In Germany there have been
numerous court cases over whether female teachers may wear veils
in public schools, culminating in a controversial March 2015 ruling
by the constitutional court that "a complete ban on teachers wear-
ing headscarves is not compatible with religious freedom."[21]

Finally, as the heinous attack on Paris in November 2015
unmistakably demonstrated, jihadist terrorism, often committed
by Muslims born and raised in Europe, has become a scourge on
the continent. The Madrid train bombings in 2004 took the lives
of 191 innocent people, wounded 1,800 and led to a change in government in Spain and the withdrawal of Spanish support for the
war in Iraq. Four suicide bombers in the London Underground
and on a London bus in July 2005 killed 52 people. After the Danish newspaper *Jyllands-Posten* published a dozen editorial cartoons depicting Mohammed in September 2005, violent protests

erupted around the world, including attacks on Danish and other Western embassies, and resulting in over 200 deaths. The cartoonist who created the famous "turban bomb" image has been the target of numerous planned or actual attacks, necessitating special police protection. In January 2015, jihadists murdered twelve journalists and staffers of the Paris satirical weekly *Charlie Hebdo*, which had published cartoons of Mohammed a number of times. In 2014 and 2015, an estimated several thousand European-born Muslims have gone to Syria to fight for the vicious terrorist group ISIS. And the ISIS-inspired atrocity in Paris in November 2015 left no doubt of the mortal danger that terrorism poses to innocent Europeans. As a German politician is reported to have said, Paris changes everything. After Paris, only sustained, willful blindness could deny the danger of jihadism in Europe.

ISLAMOPHOBIA VS. ISLAMOPHILIA

The increasing influence of Islam in Europe is also evident in the many examples of a backlash against the phenomenon, as well as in the widespread suppression of free speech critical of Islam. In late 2014 and throughout 2015, a relatively spontaneous protest movement made the news in Germany. A group calling itself Pegida, the German acronym for "Patriotic Europeans Against the Islamization of the West," organized demonstrations to decry Muslim influence on European culture and call for restriction of Muslim immigration. These attracted thousands of participants and, according to polls, the passive sympathy of a great many mainstream German citizens. Later, Pegida appeared to be fading fast, on account of growing counterprotests, threats of violence against Pegida, and the Pegida founder's foolish posting on Facebook of a joke picture of himself posing as Hitler. With the intensification of the migrant crisis and the Paris attack, however, Pegida reappeared on the scene in full force.

In the Netherlands, two charismatic politicians have brought the topic of Islam to the center of public debate in the past decade and a half. Both have paid dearly for it. Pim Fortuyn, the first of the two, believed as a gay man that Islam and Muslim immigration in combination with the Dutch elites' multiculturalist ideology were a threat to the Dutch tradition of tolerance and openness. Eventually, Fortuyn founded his own party, the Pim Fortuyn List (LPF). A few months later, only nine days before national elections in 2002, Fortuyn was assassinated. His murderer was a self-proclaimed environmental and animal-rights activist who wanted to stop Fortuyn from scapegoating Muslims and immigrants. Despite – or maybe because of – Fortuyn's death, the upstart LPF won 26 of 150 seats in the Dutch parliament and entered the government as a coalition partner. Soon thereafter, though, the LPF, rudderless and beset by infighting, disappeared from the scene.

Fortuyn's and the LPF's de facto successors are Geert Wilders and the Party for Freedom (PVV). Despite his being maligned nearly unanimously by the political and media establishment as a radical right-wing racist, Wilders and his PVV were immediately successful in gaining votes. At present, the PVV occupies a firm place among the six major parties in the splintered political landscape of the Netherlands. It is not unusual for the PVV to win first or second place among the parties in opinion polls. Wilders himself has received numerous death threats, and for more than a decade he has been under police protection, accompanied constantly by a security detail and living in a state-owned safe house.

The legal pursuit of Wilders for alleged hate speech is perhaps the most illustrative example of how European culture has become so tired and self-doubting that it often seems to know only appeasement. In Europe, the vociferous condemnation of "Islamophobia" has grown strong enough that it now represents a real threat to freedom of speech, particularly in combination with laws against "hate speech" (as discussed in Chapter 12). Even as a member of parliament backed by impressive numbers of voters, Wilders could have faced up to sixteen months in prison or a fine of almost 10,000 euros for exercising his freedom of speech. And this in a country in which criminal justice has become so lax that the most serious crimes are met with amazing leniency – for example, Pim Fortuyn's assassin has already been released.

From 2009 until his acquittal in 2011, Wilders faced prosecution for inciting hatred against Muslims with his many blunt and sometimes inflammatory statements about Islam. Wilders has said many questionable things about Islam. His suggestion that the Koran should be banned, for example, shows a seriously narrow view of religious freedom. Nevertheless, he expresses what many

Dutch voters think but dare not say regarding the influence of Islam in their country. Wilders denies he is far-right and claims a place within the legitimate democratic spectrum. What he says about Islam is hard-hitting and blunt, certainly offensive to Muslims, but not in any way close to anything that should be forbidden in a society that truly respects freedom of opinion.

In his closing remarks at his trial, Wilders declared his moral right – indeed, he claimed a moral responsibility – to speak as he did:

> I stand here because of my words. I stand here because I spoke. I spoke, I speak and I will continue to speak. Many have seen and have remained silent, but not Pim Fortuyn, not Theo Van Gogh.* I must speak. Because Netherlands is under threat from Islam. Islam is, as I have argued many times, an ideology above all. It is an ideology of hate, of destruction, of conquest. Islam – this is my certain conviction – threatens Western norms and values, freedom of speech, the equality of men and women, of heterosexuals and gays, of believers and unbelievers.[22]

Wilders was a bit self-glorifying in his comparison of himself to Martin Luther in the famous (although possibly misquoted) "Here I stand; I can do no other" speech before the Diet of Worms. But he had a point in underlining the irony that *he* was the one on trial, rather than those who threatened his life for stating his views:

> Freedom and truth. I pay the price for freedom and truth every day. Day and night I must be protected against people who want to kill me. I'm not complaining about that; it is my own decision to speak. But it isn't those who threaten me and other critics of Islam who are being held accountable here today. Instead, I stand accused. And that I do lament before this court.[23]

Wilders concluded: "I am not inciting hatred. I am not inciting discrimination. I am defending the uniqueness, the identity, the

---

* Theo Van Gogh was a Dutch filmmaker who was murdered by a young Dutch-Moroccan Muslim in retribution for a movie he made criticizing Islam.

culture, yes, the freedom of the Netherlands. *That* is the truth. That is why I stand here. That is why I speak."[24]

It is a telling comment on the state of free speech in Europe that a figure of questionable democratic credentials such as Geert Wilders has made arguably the most ringing defense of freedom of speech in recent memory in Europe.

It must be said that the success of parties such as Wilders' PVV is also largely due to the established parties' extreme slowness in speaking to Europeans' concerns about Islam. The power of political correctness is in large part the origin of the establishment's reticence. No one wants to be accused of the latest commonly imagined bigotry known as "Islamophobia." And this is understandable – Wilders is not the only person who has been threatened with legal sanction for the high crime of Islamophobia. The governing authorities' appeasement of Muslim sensitivities in the hope of keeping the peace at all costs can go to absurd lengths. In a case that particularly strains credulity, a retiree in Austria was charged in 2010 with "disparagement of religious symbols" for doing what Austrians do: he was yodeling in his backyard. His Muslim neighbors filed a complaint because they thought he was mockingly imitating the Muslim call to prayer, and the Austrian authorities brought criminal charges against him. Rather than endure a long court case, the man paid a 700-euro fine.[25]

SUSTAINING THE WELFARE STATE – AND THE EU'S LEGITIMACY

Europe has not only a growing Muslim population but also a shrinking native European population, and this has serious implications for the sustainability of the European welfare states. Fewer and fewer working-age people are around to pay the taxes to provide retirement income and expensive health care for more and more old people. In 2008, Eurostat projected that the share of the EU population age 65 and over would climb from 17.1% to 30.0% by 2060. That would mean a dramatic increase in the old-age dependency ratio – the number of people age 65 and older divided by the number who are of working age – from 25% to 53%. "In other words, there would be only two persons of working age for every person aged 65 or more in 2060, compared with four persons to one today."[26]

This situation has been a topic of general discussion particularly since the eurozone crisis. In fact, Randall Hansen and Joshua C. Gordon make the convincing argument that the EU is facing three great crises that will exacerbate each other, namely the deficit, democracy and demographic crises:

> [T]he EU and, above all, the eurozone are facing not one crisis – an economic and fiscal one – but three: an economic crisis, a crisis of institutions, and a crisis of demography. These crises are not simultaneous; they are overlapping and self-reinforcing, and there is a high degree of feedback across all three crises. Economically, the euro inflated economic growth and government revenue in the peripheral economies, giving those member states a false sense of their economic prospects. Institutionally, mechanisms were too weak at the EU level to prevent a dangerous escalation of asset (above all house) prices and too fragmented to confront the crisis through an immediate and decisive plan that would provide calm to the markets. Demographically, Europe's economic and fiscal problems are and will increasingly be exacerbated by the continent's demographic situation and its projected development, especially in southern Europe.[27]

It's all connected. The euro caused disastrous economic imbalances in the EU; the EU's lack of democratic legitimacy helped keep it from averting the economic crisis that ensued; and the aging and shrinking of the native population further complicate both the economic and the political quandaries.

In the Netherlands, formerly the paragon of the extensive and generous welfare state, the new king, Willem-Alexander, chose his first annual Speech from the Throne, in September 2013, to augur the end of the "classical welfare state" in the Netherlands. "Everyone who is able will be asked to take responsibility for their own lives and immediate surroundings," he said, explaining that, "As a consequence of social trends like demographic ageing and internationalisation, our labour market and system of public services no longer fully meet the demands of the 21st century.... [W]e must recognise that public services and schemes have to be adjusted."[28]

Germany's chancellor Angela Merkel also famously remarked, in an interview with the *Financial Times*, that "Europe today constitutes a little more than 7% of the world's population and generates 25% of global GDP, but it needs to finance 50% of all global social spending, so it is obvious that it will have to work very hard to maintain its prosperity and its style of life."[29]

Merkel knows what she's talking about. According to the Social Expenditure Database (SOCX) of the Organization for Economic Cooperation and Development (OECD), the European social model is in fact expensive. The SOCX measures social expenditure in thirty-four OECD countries from 1980 to 2014, covering spending on "old age, incapacity-related benefits, health, family, active labor market programmes, unemployment, housing, and other social policy areas." As a percentage of GDP, social spending in most of the measured EU member states has been consistently higher than elsewhere for the last thirty-five years. In 2013, the latest year for which all figures are available, the highest-spending EU member state, France, outspent the highest-spending non-EU country, Norway, by ten percentage points, 32% to 22%. Four EU countries, France, Belgium, Finland and Denmark, came in over the 30% mark, and five came in between 25% and 30%. By comparison, U.S. social expenditures in 2013 are listed as 18.6% of GDP. Of the measured EU member states, only Estonia, at 16.1%, spent less as a percentage of GDP than the United States.[30]

As one might conclude from the figures above, the guarantee of relative economic security has always been an important source of EU legitimacy in the eyes of average citizens. In fact, the EU has directly promised prosperity for all, as a right of citizenship. The Treaty of Rome establishing the EEC in 1957, as Chriss Street points out, "set standardized social objectives across the continent for 'promotion of employment, improved living and working conditions... proper social protection, dialogue between management and labor, the development of human resources with a view to lasting high employment and the combating of exclusion.'" The Maastricht Treaty of 1993 "legally required European states to provide high living standards and good working conditions."[31] The European social model is what "binds Europe together," according to the British historian and essayist Tony Judt.[32] Elaborating on this idea, Samuel Gregg explains that "many West Europeans associate concern for those in need almost exclusively with extensive and ongoing government economic intervention and large welfare states. This is key to grasping many of the policies associated with modern Europe's own grand experiment, the European Union...."[33]

Demographic decline is thus not only an economic and budgetary problem for the EU. It is also a legitimacy problem. The inability to deliver prosperity and economic security was one of the main reasons for the rise of Euroskepticism during the eurozone crisis, and avoiding a further loss of legitimacy will be one of the greatest challenges for the global governancers if population decline and aging in fact do make it necessary to rethink the European social model.

SOME SILVER LININGS?

No one can predict the future, of course. Despite the prevalence of doomsayers, the geopolitical analyst George Friedman argues that population decline may *not* result in economic decline. If population drops steadily and predictably, he writes, there is no reason to think that GDP would decline. Even if *total* GDP does fall, the *per capita* GDP – and thus individual prosperity – could still rise.[34]

Right now, though, the costs of the welfare state in the EU are stoking calls for less state intervention in the economy and a freer market. In fact, there have been significant free-market reforms in many countries of Europe, starting arguably with the Thatcher government in the UK from 1979 to 1990, and increasing since then.[35] Germany, Denmark, Sweden and others are now reaping the benefits from reforms made in the late 1990s and early 2000s.[36] Since the eurozone crisis, the bailout recipients have been forced to reform and are benefiting from it to various degrees. Even Greece has made reforms that could potentially result in more sustainable growth in the long run.

From the beginning, the European project has had a free-market side as well as a "social Europe" side. In the European Commission there has always been an uneasy coexistence of the two sides: one pushing to bring down trade barriers and encourage deregulation at the national level in order to promote the free movement of people, goods, services and capital and to create the single market; and the other insisting that "economic governance" is needed to force integration where it doesn't seem to be happening at the pace the supranationalists would prefer.

No one knows what will come of all this in the long term. But one thing is certain: just as the eurozone crisis has already changed

Europe in ways that go beyond the economic realm, the combination of declining population growth and increasing Muslim immigration have also already changed Europe. They will undoubtedly bring further, even more profound change in the medium to long term. A vital, youthful and energetic worldview is asserting itself in a tired, post-Christian culture, and that culture does not seem to have much with which to oppose it. Predictably, many EU elites insist that "more Europe" is the way both to get immigration under control and to assimilate hundreds of thousands of additional Muslim immigrants. But Europe's godlessness can match Islam only if young Muslims choose comfort and affluence over the purpose-driven life of faith. That would depend on Muslims' gaining more access to jobs, education and upward mobility, and finding a way to enjoy upward mobility as *European* Muslims rather than as a rejectionist outpost of a foreign value system.

The subject of comfort and affluence brings us back to the implications of demographic decline for affluent Europe. Many European economists maintain that the welfare state can be reformed to accommodate the demographic trends. In any case, though, the welfare state will certainly be forced to save money, and citizens' economic well-being will have to depend more on self-reliance and less on government expenditure. This reality seems to point to smaller government and more freedom. Maybe, just maybe, this unavoidable shrinking of the welfare state – along with a voter backlash against the now evident consequences of open internal borders and EU-led relocation of unwanted migrants from other EU member states to their countries – will result in a smaller EU and the emergence of a more realistic, limited form of the European idea characterized by more democratic sovereignty and less global governance.

But if anything has become clear, it is that global governancers believe in their cause. They will resist giving up their dream. Muslims believe in their faith, too, and there are few signs so far that either postmodern European relativism or the lingering remnants of Judeo-Christian tradition are exerting the attraction that would motivate adherents of that faith to assimilate into Europe as we know it.

CHAPTER 19:
THE CRISIS OF DEMOCRACY IN EUROPE

The May 2014 European elections, the EU-wide ballot to choose members of the European Parliament, were nothing short of explosive. In country after country, the established, pro-EU parties suffered devastating losses since the 2009 elections, while anti-EU parties made tremendous gains, sometimes winning outright victories. The triumphant anti-EU and Euroskeptic parties were not only far right or far left, as many pundits would have us believe, but covered virtually every point on the political spectrum.[1]

Notably, many of these parties were recently established protest parties. They were not experienced in electoral politics nor historically familiar to voters. Given that fact, their huge gains were even more telling. When the dust settled, the three traditionally dominant, pro-EU political groups (in which national parties join forces) occupied 63.8% of the seats in the European Parliament, down from 72.2% in the previous parliament. The three parliamentary groups that comprise most of the Euroskeptic parties held 22.6% of the seats, as opposed to 15.8% in the preceding term.

It's important to note at the outset that these results would have been even more stark if not for the fact that party-based Euroskepticism is less of a factor in the eleven EU member states from the former Eastern Bloc, with the exception of Poland and

Hungary. For countries still emerging from their communist past, EU membership understandably remains a powerful symbol of their turn to freedom, democracy and prosperity. Even in the East, though, apathy toward the EU expressed itself unmistakably at election time. Voter turnout in six of the eleven Eastern member states was below 30%, and only two countries posted a rate above 40%. Lithuania had the highest turnout, at 47.3% (more than double the rate of 2009), and was one of only two Eastern member states in which voter participation increased over the previous election. The explanation for this is simple: the Lithuanian presidential election was held at the same time as the European election. The lowest turnout was a basement-level 13% in Slovakia. Overall, less than three in ten eligible voters in Eastern Europe even bothered to go to the polls. Total EU-wide turnout, by the way, was 42.6%, also very low by European standards.[2]

THE WINNERS AND THE LOSERS

Who were the winners in the 2014 elections? In Great Britain, the United Kingdom Independence Party (UKIP), which advocates British withdrawal from the EU, came in first, beating both the Conservative Party and the Labour Party. This was unprecedented in the UK; it was the first time in modern history that a party other than the Conservatives or Labour won a national vote, and only the second time since 1918 that those two parties did not take first and second place.[3] (The first time was in the 2009 European elections, in which UKIP came in second, behind the Conservatives but ahead of Labour.)

In France, the right-wing Euroskeptic Front National clobbered the established parties, coming in first with 24.9% of the votes, approximately four times the percentage it had received in the 2009 European elections. Both the center-right UMP and the governing Socialists lost significant vote share compared with 2009. In Denmark, the right-wing Euroskeptic Danish People's Party won, almost doubling its vote percentage over the previous election and handily defeating the traditionally dominant parties. In Spain, a brand-new Euroskeptic leftist party, Podemos (We Can), received 8% of votes only four months after being established. The two parties otherwise unrivaled as the top parties in Spain, the center-right Popular Party and the center-left Spanish Socialist Workers' Party, were decimated, receiving an aggregate total of less than half of the vote, 49.1%, down from 80.7% in 2009. In Greece, the winner was the far-left party Syriza, which ran against the austerity program imposed by the European Union and garnered 26.6% of the vote. The governing center-right party, New Democracy, came in second with 22.8%, far less than the 32.3% received in 2009. The establishment center-left PASOK, running as the Olive Tree Democratic Alignment, almost fell off the map, dropping from 36.6% in 2009 to a paltry 8% in 2014. Golden Dawn, a far-right Euroskeptic party, beat PASOK with 9.4% of the vote, after receiving only 0.5% in 2009.

In Sweden, while the Social Democrats performed just as well in 2014 as in 2009, winning around 24% in both elections, the center and center-right pro-EU parties lost significant vote share to the right-wing Euroskeptic Sweden Democrats, who received 9.7% in 2014, almost tripling their 2009 vote of 3.3%. As described in Chapter 17, even in Germany – where everyone wants to be a good European – the anti-euro Alternative für Deutschland (AFD), still new and inexperienced after being founded in 2013, made waves by winning 7.1%, an unprecedented performance for a party perceived to be anti-EU.

And who were the losers of the 2014 European elections? Clearly, it was the EU establishment. If you were to name an established, pro-EU party anywhere in Western Europe, you would likely hit upon a party that suffered severe losses in the May 2014 European elections. To give some further examples: the UK Liberal Democrats, the only unabashedly pro-EU party in the UK, suffered a crippling blow in the European elections, going from 13.4% of the vote in 2009 to 6.7% in 2014. In the Netherlands, the two traditionally dominant parties continued their slide: the center-right Christian Democratic Appeal took 15.2% in 2014, compared with 20% in 2009; and the center-left Labor Party got 9.4%, down from 12%. The Dutch anti-EU Party for Freedom received only 13.3%, compared with 17% in 2009, probably in large part because of a gaffe by its charismatic leader Geert Wilders. At a campaign event in March 2014, Wilders, like some sort of xenophobic cheerleader at a high-school pep rally, led a question-and-answer chant for "few-er, few-er, few-er" Moroccans in the Netherlands.[4] Because of that incident, Wilders is now being charged again with incitement to discrimination and hatred. On the left, though, the Euroskeptic Socialist Party tallied 9.6% of the vote, a notable gain over its 2009 result of 7.1%, and just enough to beat the establishment Labor Party, its closest rival.

The exceptions to the losing trend that battered pro-EU establishment parties in Western Europe were few and far between. In fact, they were rare enough to prove the rule and were almost always offset by large votes for Euroskeptic rivals.

The pro-EU German CDU (together with its sister party, the Bavarian CSU), arguably the most powerful party in Europe, maintained its top spot among German parties with 35.3% of the vote, decidedly more than any rival and down only about 2% from 2009. The political skill and reliable image of Chancellor Angela Merkel, along with Germany's persistently pro-EU culture, were central to this success. The center-left, pro-EU Social Democrats also did well, increasing their vote to 27.3%, from 20.8% in 2009. Meanwhile, though, the centrist Free Democrats, fielding a pro-EU slate, almost disappeared from the scene, in contrast with the AFD's impressive showing.

In Italy, the establishment center-left Democratic Party scored a smashing success, with 40.8% of the vote, on the coattails of a popular and dynamic party leader, Matteo Renzi, who had been elevated to prime minister three months before. At the same time, though, the anti-establishment, anti-EU party, the Five Star Movement, came in second with 21.1% of the vote, a very strong showing for a party founded in late 2009 and distinguished by an unusually high level of turmoil. The Five Star Movement came out well ahead of Forza Italia, the principal establishment party on the center-right, founded by the longtime prime minister Silvio Berlusconi. In Ireland, the three established pro-EU parties did about as well in aggregate as they did in 2009, but the Euroskeptic Sinn Fein (known as the political arm of the IRA during the Northern Ireland conflict) received 19.52%, nearly doubling its vote percentage over 2009 and coming within less than 2% of the top two parties in the Irish landscape.

In a small number of the Western European member states, Euroskeptic forces either posted only modest gains or were not a significant factor. In Belgium and Luxembourg, probably the two most Europhile member states and the hosts of most of the principal EU institutions, Euroskepticism did not have a noticeable effect on the vote. Neither did Euroskepticism show a discernible effect in Portugal or Malta. In Finland, the established pro-EU parties received in 2014 a proportion of the vote comparable to 2009. The Euroskeptic Finns Party (formerly the True Finns Party) got 12.9% of the vote, a respectable gain over the 9.8% received in 2009. Nevertheless, this result was the third disappointment in a row for the Finns Party after garnering 19% in the 2011 national parliamentary elections.[5] In Austria, the right-wing, soft-Euroskeptic Freedom Party gained vote share in 2014, but it was unclear how much its Euroskepticism contributed to the result. The established, pro-EU center-right and center-left parties performed virtually the same in Austria as they had in 2009.

THE DESTABILIZATION OF POLITICS IN EUROPE

As of late 2015, it is becoming more implausible – with each opinion poll, with each local, provincial and national election – to write off May 2014 as a one-time protest vote. The Euroskeptic anti-establishment wave is not subsiding. As mentioned above, the left-wing Syriza won two Greek elections in 2015. In Germany, the AFD has established itself as an electoral force, gaining state parliament seats in Saxony, Brandenburg, Thuringia, Hamburg, and Bremen, the five states that have held elections since the European elections. According to polls, people voted AFD for good reason – because of agreement with the AFD platform and because they felt unrepresented by the mainstream parties. In France, more than one poll has suggested that Marine Le Pen, the leader of the far-right Front National, could beat President François Hollande in a two-way contest. Front National outdid the Socialists in nationwide local elections in March 2015, winning representation in somewhere between 43 and 57 municipal councils according to preliminary results. In Spain, one poll showed 20% of voters backing Podemos. The new party garnered 14.8% in the March 2015 regional ballot in Andalusia. In polls in the Netherlands, Geert Wilders' PVV continues to jockey for the top position in a close contest among the top three parties. The Sweden Democrats came in third in the September 2014 national elections, with 12.9%, and now "hold the balance of power" in the Swedish parliament.

In Britain, UKIP won two of four by-elections since May 2014 to fill vacant House of Commons seats, and placed second in the two it didn't win. In the May 7, 2015 national elections, UKIP received 12.9% of the vote. Although UKIP won only one seat in the House of Commons because of Britain's first-past-the-post electoral system, 12.9% was a respectable result.

On top of all this, the migrant crisis and the attack on Paris have resulted in a renewed upsurge for anti-EU protest parties and Euroskeptic politicians throughout Europe, making outright electoral victories for parties such as the Front National and Wilders's Party for Freedom – an unconscionable thought to EU elites – even more plausible than previously imagined.

European voters are not happy with the pro-EU establishment, and they are shaking up the political landscape. But this didn't all appear out of nothing in May 2014, and there is little reason to believe it will die down if the migrant crisis ever subsides. This is a decades-long trend.

For years, the destabilization of established politics has become steadily more apparent throughout Europe. The rise of anti-EU parties is one side of that phenomenon. The other side, perhaps even more significant, is the weakening of long-dominant parties and the splintering of political affiliations. In Germany, the center-right CDU and the center-left SPD have been the two major parties – roughly equivalent to the Republicans and the Democrats in the United States – since the Federal Republic was founded in 1949. Now, beset by other parties from both left and right, the CDU and the SPD are often receiving a significantly smaller vote proportion in national and state elections than they always had for several decades. Twice in the last ten years they have been forced to govern together in a "grand coalition," a problematic state of affairs in which the two major parties that are meant to oppose each other as representatives of the two sides of the mainstream democratic political spectrum instead govern together, as if center-right and center-left, conservative and liberal no longer mean anything.

The situation is similar in the Netherlands, where the political landscape has been undergoing what might prove to be a lasting and radical transformation. Traditionally, a center-right party and a center-left party have vied for dominance and then formed coalitions with smaller parties, but now there are six parties that claim substantial constituencies, all fighting against and forming coalitions with each other. The rise of Euroskeptic parties on the right and the left has been a principal cause of this development. British politics, because of UKIP and Scottish separatism, may have come to a point at which a British version of a grand coalition is thinkable. In other countries too – including France, Italy, Denmark and Sweden – the shakeup of the political landscape was intensified by the May 2014 elections, but it began before that. An ironic twist is that the EU's *supranational* erosion of national loyalties has promoted a *subnational* weakening of those same loyalties, and thus a new fragmentation beneath the superstructure of union. The Scottish National Party in the UK, the Catalonian separatist movement in Spain, and the New Flemish Alliance in Belgium could also transform the political landscapes – not to mention redraw the borders – in their respective countries.

Not only at the European level but also at the national and even the regional level, fewer and fewer people are willing to accept the elite-driven consensus represented by the established parties or their unresponsiveness to average voters. It is becoming ever harder to distinguish between the mainstream center-left and the mainstream center-right, so more and more people are no longer trying. The pernicious effects of the EU democratic deficit are degrading the national politics of the member states.

FOR LACK OF A BETTER IDEA: BUSINESS AS USUAL

Back to Brussels for a moment, in late May 2014. Battered and bloodied – or least you'd think they'd have been battered and bloodied – the EU prime ministers and presidents got together for a postmortem discussion of the European elections. Afterward, the European Council president, Herman van Rompuy, had this to say:

> We discussed the results of the European elections. Of course the situation differs in every country, with a mix of continuity and change. Overall, voters sent a strong message, and this message was at the heart of our discussions tonight. In terms of the way ahead, the European Council as the EU's strategic agenda-setting body has a key role to play and must give clear guidance.... All the leaders agree that a key issue at hand is to set these priorities and the strategic agenda for the crucial years ahead.[6]

Would you vote for this man? Would you want to vote for *anyone* who, after the message that voters throughout Europe had sent, would engage in a discussion that could be described as van Rompuy described it?

The unelected president of the European Council, and through him all the gathered leaders of the EU, had their own clear message: They didn't get it. And if they did, they weren't going to admit it. They might try to appear more responsive to voters' concerns in talks with them at home, but as for their discussions in Brussels, the voters would never find out what they *really* talked about.

And what has the EU done since then? Not much has changed. The machinery of European supranational governance grinds on. Shortly after the elections, EU leaders installed Jean-Claude Juncker, former prime minister of Luxembourg and far more of an EU establishment apparatchik than Herman van Rompuy, as the new European Commission president. He quickly announced that the Commission – the unelected "guardian of the Treaties" that is charged with representing "the interests of the Union as a whole" – was going to become more "political." In EU-Speak, the Commission's becoming more "political" does not mean its becoming less technocratic/bureaucratic and more responsive to the citizenry; it means asserting the EU's unearned political authority over the member states and the voters, and implying that this authority has somehow become more legitimate because now it is deemed "political" rather than "bureaucratic."

Unfortunately, few among the established elite seem to have drawn the real conclusion: after sixty-five years, the EU has conclusively shown itself to be inherently undemocratic, unaccountable and unresponsive to voters, and the voters want political power transferred back to their national governments, the ones they vote in and vote out and thus the ones that are, or at least should be, accountable to them, the people they claim to serve. The first "final straw" was the eurozone crisis and the severe economic hardship engendered by the politically motivated decision to establish a common currency for hugely differing economies. The latest final straw is the 2015 immigration crisis and all of the disruption it is causing and the dangers it could bring. How many more final straws can the EU take?

In reporting and analysis of the ongoing shakeup of the political landscape, the press and pundits repeatedly talk of a populist surge. "Populist" is a dirty word in the EU lexicon. After all, as the *Washington Post* told us years ago, average people are largely poor (or at least poorly dressed), undereducated and easily led. And again, the elites – with our own best interest in mind, of course – are undaunted in their determination to make the world safe for global governance.

But the Euroskeptic parties are changing. They are becoming more mainstream. With increasing electoral success, many parties that were originally far right – along with parties that were never far right but were tarred by the establishment as such – are sparing no effort to broaden their appeal. Among others, UKIP, the AfD, the Dutch PVV, the Sweden Democrats, the Danish People's Party and even the Front National are all eager to show they are respectable conservative parties, and they seem to be largely succeeding. A similar phenomenon is occurring on the Euroskeptic left wing. As a result, the political spectrum in Europe might be broadening again to accommodate legitimate views that do not conform to EU-style political correctness.

In the long run, like the possible silver lining to Europe's demographic winter and its migrant spring, the destabilization of the established political landscape in Europe may augur the revival of responsive democracy in Europe, the victory of a more sober, realistic idea of European integration, and the realization of a more modest EU of closely cooperating sovereign democracies. Sometimes it takes crisis to elicit a revival. And certainly, it is hard to deny the crisis of democracy in Europe.

EPILOGUE:
WILL AMERICA FOLLOW THE EU
INTO THE SOFT UTOPIA?

Much of what has been said about Europe in this book also applies to the United States. It is not a coincidence that the question whether Americans want their country to become more like Europe has become a recurring theme in U.S. politics in recent years. The issue flared up especially when the eurozone crisis was at its height. During the 2012 presidential campaign, for example, Newt Gingrich, a Republican candidate and former Speaker of the House, said with reference to Obama, "I am for the Constitution; he is for European socialism." Piling on, another Republican presidential hopeful, the former Pennsylvania senator Rick Santorum, suggested, "If you want to see America after the Obama administration is through, just travel around, just read up on Greece. Read up on Portugal. Read up on France."[1] In the New Hampshire primary debate, Mitt Romney said, "We are increasingly becoming like Europe. Europe is not working in Europe. It will never work here."[2] The EU-oriented website *Nouvelle Europe*, taking note of Romney's claim that "the Obama administration was the 'worst of what Europe has become,'" was moved to comment, "it seems that Romney is running as much against Europe – or American perceptions of the Old Continent – as he is against Obama."[3]

What does it mean to become like Europe? The candidates quoted above were referring principally to the eurozone crisis and Europe's large welfare states and unsustainable sovereign debt. But the theme of Europeanization struck a chord in the United States because it encompassed much more than just the economy. As Samuel Gregg puts it in *Becoming Europe: Economic Decline, Culture, and How America Can Avoid a European Future,* by becoming like Europe, people mean taking on a Europeanized "culture of expectations, beliefs, values and institutions that themselves are embedded in a history that is economic, but also more than economic."[4] The 2012 campaign debate was about the sense that America might be weakening its own cultural identity because it was coming to value that which is distinctive to Europe's cultural identity. As Gregg writes, "the intentions, principles, ideas and beliefs to which a given society ascribes high value" are the heart of a culture's identity.[5] Romney, along with many others, was fretting that European values might one day – given continued growth of the American welfare state and overregulation of the economy – overtake American values.

NEOPROGRESSIVISM AND THE EXPANDING STATE

William B. Allen describes this Europeanization process in a talk titled "Moral Frontiers: American National Character and the Future of Liberty." Reflecting on the growing uncertainty in the United States about what it means to be an American, Allen asks whether we have "a national character," and if so, "is it a lover of liberty?"[6] To answer these questions, he casts a critical eye upon the neoprogressive view of liberty and human rights, a view shared broadly among Americans of the center-left, as outlined in the "Progressive Tradition Series" of the Center for American Progress.[7] CAP is a left-of-center think tank that, according to its website, is "dedicated to improving the lives of Americans through progressive ideas and action."[8]

In his analysis of the CAP document, Allen deftly traces a development in the American center-left that is uncannily reminiscent of the EU. Starting from the founding American principle that governments derive "their just powers from the consent of the governed," he argues that the source of the neoprogressive detour from the original American principle of liberty is "the abandonment of the idea of consent as fundamental to political legitimacy and the substitution in the place of consent of a welfare or enjoyment model of political legitimacy."[9] Neoprogressivism, he explains, "is formulated specifically to replace consent… with the welfare model, which holds that states are legitimate to the degree that governments extend enjoyments rather than to the extent that they are obedient to the commands of citizens."[10]

This trajectory mirrors that of the EU to a remarkable extent, and in both the EU and the U.S. the abandonment of the principle of legitimacy by consent is linked to relativism. If there is no such thing as objective truth or unchanging human nature, then, in principle, citizens cannot claim truly inalienable rights – rights that are rooted in human nature and objective truth, and that pre-exist government. In the absence of these rights, the human person is not the shaper of his own destiny, with government as his servant. Instead, it is the state – the government – that shapes the individual. The source of political legitimacy is thus not the consent of the governed, expressing their immutable dignity by their agency in their own governance, but rather the government's success in providing its citizens with the good things in life. In a meaningless world, there can be nothing more than comfort and entertainment – eat, drink and be merry, for tomorrow we die.

Allen goes on to state two corollaries of this profoundly relativistic view: (1) that essentially "unlimited government power is required to effectuate… civil rights"; and (2) that "human rights are to be protected, not for this or that particular people, but… for people globally."[11]

Why do these two principles arise from the relativistic foundation of neoprogressivism? Because once objective truth has been jettisoned and the government as provider of enjoyments becomes the accepted model, then those enjoyments become entitlements and the entitlements become rights, and the rights inflate until they become *human* rights. And with no authoritative narrative to fall back on, the standard for determining what human rights *are* is up for grabs. Human rights must be, and will be, determined by an elite – none other than those who hold political power. Once one has given up the idea of objective truth to embrace relativism, power can be attained and held only by coercion, since there is no generally acknowledged objective basis for persuasion. In principle, no relativist is far from Mao Zedong's famous dictum, "Political power grows out of the barrel of a gun."[12] Just as ominously, there is no authoritatively objective basis for limiting political power once attained. There is no truth above and independent of the political authority that could limit it.

So government as provider expands, as if by sleight of hand, to government as master. And with the global reach of communications, travel, commerce and ideas, government as master expands geographically as well. Just as government power to determine what human rights *are* is in principle unlimited, so also it becomes impossible to limit the power of government – or *governance* – to a certain geographical area or people. National sovereignty becomes – again, in principle – an impermissible limit on the elites' power to decide *for everyone everywhere* what is just and true. In Europe, the migrant crisis is merely the latest illustration of this: the national sovereignty of EU member states and the misgivings of everyday people about accepting unprecedented numbers of immigrants who hold a very different worldview cannot be allowed to stand in the way of welcoming Middle Easterners into the brave new EU world of tolerance, diversity and human rights. Global governance thus unmasks itself not as a benign desire to improve the lot of humanity, but instead as an unlimited power grab to define truth and justice, under the banner of "universal human rights."

It is important to emphasize that I am talking here about the "in principle," the logical ramifications of what Allen's neoprogressives and the global governancers believe. Most neoprogressives and global governancers are sincerely convinced that they are for human freedom and democracy. And we might have the good fortune never to see the destructive potential of the logical ramifications play out to its full extent. Nevertheless, although the "in principle" may never fully be translated into reality, it manifests symptoms in the real world that help us recognize it for what it is. The symptoms we can see in the U.S. are similar to those in the EU.

First, we have in the United States a growing affinity for a European-style social democracy of sorts, with a large welfare state, and an increasing distaste for the free market. There is a growing belief that government can and should make life pleasant, provide comfort, even foster a feeling of community and give us a sense of purpose. And the more that government attempts to provide all this, the more that people demand as a matter of entitlement. If Mitt Romney's famous gaffe about 47% of Americans receiving more in welfare and government services than they pay in taxes is anywhere near true, then the oversized welfare state has already done severe damage to the American ideal of the free citizen fulfilling his responsibility to provide for himself.[13]

And, as Charles Murray's book *Coming Apart* amply documents, it all goes much further than just the extent of government intervention in the free market, or the balance between individual freedom and government power. It has to do with the entire culture. Just as Gregg and Allen do, Murray homes in on the centrality of freedom. He illuminates the connection between personal freedom and personal responsibility as the basis of a fulfilled life, and thus highlights the destructive moral and cultural consequences that follow from the loss of freedom: "All of these good things in life – self-respect, intimate relationships, and self-actualization – require freedom in the only way that freedom is meaningful: freedom to act in all arenas of life coupled with responsibility for the consequences of those actions. The underlying meaning of that coupling – freedom *and* responsibility – is crucial."[14]

On the basis of this key connection between freedom and responsibility, Murray then analyzes how excessive government intervention in people's lives, *à la* Europe, has contributed to the devastating social breakdown that he describes among what he dubs America's "new lower class":

> When the government intervenes to help, whether in the European welfare state or in America's more diluted version, it not only diminishes our responsibility for the desired outcome, it enfeebles the institutions through which people live satisfying lives.... When the government says it will take some of the trouble out of doing the things that families and communities evolved to do, it inevitably takes some of the action away from families and communities. The web frays, and eventually disintegrates.[15]

This, he believes, is the danger to the United States of a process of Europeanization that is already well underway.

Murray allows that "Europe has proved that countries with

enfeebled family, vocation, community, and faith can still be pleasant places to live," but he decries the meaninglessness of what he characterizes as the "view of life" of many Europeans. Echoing Allen, he locates the roots of this view of life in the pursuit of pleasurable ease and the shriveling of freedom and responsibility that has resulted from the interventionist welfare state. Murray calls it the Europe Syndrome: "The purpose of life is to while away the time between birth and death as pleasantly as possible, and the purpose of government is to make it as easy as possible to while away the time as pleasantly as possible – the Europe Syndrome."[16] Is America beginning to suffer from the Europe Syndrome? As Allen, Murray and Gregg show, the signs are abundant.

THE LOSS OF FAITH AND CIVILIZATIONAL EXHAUSTION

More basic than the abdication of personal responsibility is the loss of religion and tradition that is occurring in America, even though it is still much more religious than Europe. Over the past generation, the percentage of "nones," Americans who describe themselves as unaffiliated with any religion, has grown tremendously. According to a survey by the Pew Research Center's Forum on Religion and Public Life, 19.6% of Americans were "nones" in 2012 – up from 15.3% only five years before.[17] If one goes back a bit further, the contrast is even sharper. In 1972 the General Social Survey, one of the most frequently used sources of social science information, reported that 5% of Americans gave their religious preference as "none." By 1990, that figure had almost doubled, reaching 9%. By 2012, fully 20% of Americans said they preferred no religion.[18]

And of course, the void left by the loss of religion must inevitably be filled by a post-Christian moral paradigm. In Europe and increasingly in the United States, this is seen perhaps most clearly in the transformative and liberationist human rights paradigm, analyzed in Part Four, with its rejection of the constraints imposed by religion and tradition. On both sides of the Atlantic, this bursting of Judeo-Christian moral boundaries has been most evident in the area of sexuality. The Supreme Court has now mandated the acceptance of gay marriage throughout the United States. More and more, in the name of nondiscrimination, freedom of conscience is being denied to those – usually traditional Christians – who do not wish to participate in the culture's fawning embrace of LGBT rights.

Meanwhile, the United States under President Obama, consistent with William B. Allen's analysis of the progressive dynamic, is "protecting the new human rights globally." In a truly astounding manner, the U.S. has raised LGBT rights to a place of utmost honor worldwide, hoisting the rainbow flag, the symbol of the gay rights movement, alongside the U.S. flag at several U.S. missions overseas. According to press reports, the rainbow flag appeared directly below the American flag at the embassies in Madrid and Tallinn, Estonia, in May 2014, in recognition of the UNESCO-endorsed International Day Against Homophobia and Transphobia (May 17).[19] In June of that year, the U.S. embassy in Tel Aviv displayed the rainbow flag below the U.S. flag in recognition of the city's Gay Pride week. "Proudly flying the colors!" announced the Facebook page of the ambassador's office. "For the first time in history, the U.S. Embassy in Tel Aviv has raised the Pride flag together with our American flag. We are proud to join with the municipality of Tel Aviv–Yafo and its residents in celebrating LGBT Pride Week."[20] According to various press reports, the rainbow flag has also been hoisted at U.S. embassies and consulates in Bratislava, Stockholm and Shenyang, and draped over the entrance of the embassy in London.[21] Symbols are powerful. How much further can one go than to associate the symbol of gay pride with the enduring symbol of the American nation?

The display of the rainbow flag at U.S. embassies was only part of a larger campaign.[22] In a major policy speech in Geneva in December 2011, Secretary of State Hillary Clinton declared that "gay rights are human rights, and human rights are gay rights."[23] She promised, among other things, that a "toolkit" would be provided to all U.S. embassies to help them defend the "human rights of LGBT people" and that the U.S. government would "ensure that our foreign assistance promotes the protection of LGBT rights."[24] Clinton's speech coincided with President Obama's release of a presidential memorandum on the same day declaring that "the struggle to end discrimination against lesbian, gay, bisexual, and transgender persons is a global challenge, and one that is central to the United States' commitment to promoting human rights." The president directed "all federal agencies engaged abroad to ensure that U.S. diplomacy and foreign assistance promote and protect the human rights of LGBT persons."[25] In effect, Obama and Clinton – as well as Clinton's successor, John Kerry – have made the protection of LGBT rights a central U.S. foreign policy concern.

This has all come about in large measure because the loss of religious faith leaves a vacuum that human nature abhors. Fading religious hope must be replaced by some kind of secular hope. And thus, political utopianism is almost inevitable.

In the United States as in Europe, the utopia that entices is a soft utopia. It emerges out of the overriding desire for ease and comfort. It is not a revolutionary utopia of the disenfranchised and discontented, burning with indignation at the injustice that they believe they are suffering. Rather, it is a utopia of the comfortable, whose primary interest is health and wealth, and who seek a government that will take care of everything for them in return for substantial tax payments. It is the utopia of civilizational exhaustion.

And no temporary comforts can compensate for the weariness. An exhausted civilization, sapped of its clarity of conviction, loses its resolve as well. Without a binding idea of truth to hold a civilization together, the will to defend that civilization and its way of life quickly weakens.

As Mark Steyn argues in *America Alone*, Europe has long exhibited that loss of resolve, and so America has been left alone to defend the Western heritage. In his bracing jeremiad, Steyn laments "the larger forces at play in the developed world that have left Europe too enfeebled to resist its remorseless transformation into Eurabia," in particular: "(1) demographic decline; (2) the unsustainability of the advanced Western social-democratic state; and (3) civilizational exhaustion."[26] Like Allen, Murray and Gregg, Steyn ties cultural exhaustion – recognizable primarily by moral and philosophical relativism and a rejection of the concept of objective truth – to the interventionist welfare state whose main function is to increase the comfort and ease of its citizens. In Steyn's analysis, "the enervated state of the Western world, the sense of civilizational ennui, of nations too mired in cultural relativism to understand what's at stake," is closely related to the loss of freedom and responsibility in the modern welfare state, which "has gradually annexed all the responsibilities of adulthood – health care, child care, care of the elderly – to the point where it's effectively severed its citizens from humanity's primal instincts, not least the survival instinct."[27]

Taking this line of argument to the geopolitical level, Steyn explains Europe's lack of resolve to defend itself as a consequence of being able to rely on America as "a kind of geopolitical sugar daddy." The United States, by paying for the defense of Europe, sought to prevent a reemergence of the traditional rivalries for power among European nations. "Nice idea," Steyn remarks. "But it also absolved them of the traditional responsibilities of nationhood, turning the alliance into a dysfunctional sitcom family, with one grown-up presiding over a brood of whiny teenagers – albeit (demographically) the world's wrinkliest teenagers."[28] Now, Steyn's "wrinkly teenagers" are risking what might turn out with time to be something close to cultural suicide by accepting hundreds of thousands of mostly Muslim immigrants and doing their best to ignore the fact that jihadism in Europe might thereby be greatly strengthened. It is a tragic revelation of the true face of soft utopianism: while EU elites are laudibly seeking to be charitable, the European supranational dream turns out to be little more than a symptom of cultural exhaustion and a self-destructive lack of resolve.

With a similar abdication of personal responsibility to a nanny state taking place in America, as cultural relativism grows apace, there may soon be no one left with the resolve to defend the West and the way of life we have attained. The world as we know it, Steyn observes, depends on "whether America can summon the will to shape at least part of the emerging world. If not, then it's also the end of the American moment, and the dawn of the new Dark Ages…."[29]

From the Schuman Declaration's agenda of "world peace" that lies at the heart of the European project, to Obama's irresolution as the Middle East descends into terrorist chaos and Iran receives U.S. permission to become a nuclear power, what has emerged is not peace, but the delusional soft utopia of civilizational exhaustion. "'Peace, peace,' they say, when there is no peace." Meanwhile, Paris buries its dead.

SELF-GOVERNMENT AND THE SPLENDOR OF OBJECTIVE TRUTH

What is the remedy for civilizational exhaustion? It is not to be found in reducing the size of government or taking a more belligerent stance against jihadism or other international threats. The issue – what is at stake – is much larger than that. As I have argued throughout this book, the struggle between liberal democracy and global governance is, at the deepest level, a struggle to define the human person and the purpose of human life. Most fundamentally, it is a struggle between the belief in and the denial of objective truth. In broad terms, the advocates of robust liberal democracy in the West come down on the side of objective truth and of the Judeo-Christian view of an unchanging human nature embedded in tradition, religion and family. The partisans of global governance come down on the side of a radically secularist, postmodern commitment to the radical autonomy of the individual and the virtually unlimited malleability of human nature according to each person's choice, independent of traditional institutions and social connections. But this radical autonomy depends on the rejection of objective truth in favor of the individual will.

Ironically, the elevation of individual choice over objective truth ends up destroying the freedom to choose of everyone except those who manage to position themselves as the gatekeepers who decide what the truth is. And even that ideological hegemony would most likely be temporary. In a relativist world of constant change, there is no reason to think that those on top at one moment could not find themselves underfoot with merciless suddenness. Once objective truth has been abandoned, the state becomes the ultimate arbiter of which version of truth is to be enforced. If there is no objective truth about human freedom that limits and binds the state, there is nothing left to protect the individual – or the mediating institutions of civil society in which individuals gather together of their own volition – from the encroachments of the state, or of the global networks of governance.[30] Neither is there any reason to put geographical limits on the power of the state, or of the global networks of governance. In Europe, a growing and vital Islam could plausibly change the game completely, eclipsing the EU's current infatuation with individual autonomy and global governance by positing an alternative that demands a response much more real and resolute than the reimagining of the world as a supranational utopia of peace and harmony.

There is another irony: An ideology based on the revolt against truth is philosophically weak, because it is so patently out of line with reality. It lacks credibility and cannot argue its own case, and thus it does not willingly tolerate any ideological rivals. If it is to survive, it must be imposed universally – not just in one nation or another, not just in the United States or Europe, but globally.

While the idea of global governance is utopian and unrealistic, and ultimately will not work, we have already traveled a considerable distance along the globalist route. As the assault on objective truth and the hollowing out of liberal democracy continue, who among the heirs of the West is most likely to win the power to harness the state – or the "global networks of governance" – to their own version of truth? Again, it is the elite opinion makers and power brokers, who to a large extent are already committed to the rejection of objective truth in favor of the glorification of individual choice.

In his book on the ideology of global governance, *Sovereignty or Submission,* John Fonte identifies the American elite as the channel through which global governance could wreak its havoc in the United States. The danger, Fonte argues, is that "the transnational progressive ideology of global governance ... might attain a considerable degree of influence among a critical mass of opinion makers and statesmen in Western democracies," and in this way it could attain what the Italian Marxist thinker Antonio Gramsci called "ideological hegemony."[31] Fonte continues:

> It is unlikely that American submission to global authority could be imposed by outside forces at the UN, EU, IMF, WTO, ICC, and elsewhere. American submission would have to be voluntary, led by American elites. The actual process of subordination would unfold only gradually, over a long period. It would involve the type of supranational legalism and transnational politics ... in which "disaggregated" elites ... join with their political allies outside America's constitutional system to subordinate our democratic sovereignty.[32]

WHAT IS TO BE DONE?

I borrow this very practical question from the unrivaled pioneer of really existing totalitarian utopianism, Vladimir Ilyich Lenin.[33] As Fonte shows, the global governance ideology can subvert American democracy only if we let it. The same goes for the Europeans. As I said on the very first page, I write this book out of admiration for Europe. Europe is America's most important ally. And those who think it absurd to suggest that America might be following Europe into the soft utopia are laboring under a very shortsighted historical perspective. America has always been and remains as much a follower of Europe as vice versa. Nearly everything that America built was built upon the European heritage. American democracy, prosperity and the human flourishing that our society makes possible are to a great extent due to our application of the achievements of Europe to our American context. America owes an immeasurable debt to Europe.

And it is not too late. Europe is still a wonderful place. With its established democracies, with the prosperity and well-being enjoyed by the great majority of everyday Europeans in the freedom to live dignified and beneficent lives, with its majestic architecture and its spectacular achievements in the arts, science and technology, the continent still lives and breathes the unrivaled heritage of Athens, Rome and Jerusalem. The good Europe, the old and distinguished Europe that birthed Western civilization, is still alive and kicking. And this despite the increasingly uneasy coexistence with the new Europe, with its post-Christian bipolarity that mixes despair and exhaustion with a thinly messianic utopianism.

What is needed – in Europe and increasingly in the United States – is a reformation, a return to a humble respect for the truths and traditions at the root of Western culture, to the indispensable foundations of self-government. This does not entail the end of the EU. The EU exists, and it could be a force for much greater good in the world. A reformed EU of sovereign nation-states could build on the tremendous accomplishments for which the European idea deserves a share of the credit, especially the achievement of an unprecedentedly close and amicable cooperation among European nations. The EU, along with NATO and other factors, shares responsibility for a continental peace so stable that it is almost impossible to imagine another war among the nations that fought each other so savagely in the first half of the twentieth century. But democratic sovereignty is the only basis for realizing the positive potential of the European idea. Neither the Europeans nor we Americans can build justice, peace and prosperity upon a deception. Global governance is a lie, and it will turn on those who succumb to its spell.

We have a choice between self-government and the slow suicide of liberal democracy.[34] We can either continue the advance toward the hubristic, postdemocratic soft utopia of global governance, or reclaim and strengthen the democratically accountable self-government of the free peoples of the West. And if we choose self-government, we can sustain it only within the bounds of the truth about human nature, the manifold but limited possibilities of politics, and a sober recognition of what is evil and what is good.

ACKNOWLEDGMENTS

I am grateful for the helpful efforts and support of friends and colleagues who have contributed greatly to this book. Frank Holub was a reliable, intelligent and insightful research assistant from the very beginning. He checked every fact, noted every source and helped give shape to the book at each stage of its development. Carol Staswick was a tremendous editor. She improved the manuscript immensely, increased its readability and sharpened my arguments. Richard Gaffin III, my friend and former Foreign Service colleague, carefully read the chapters for which I needed his expertise. His suggestions not only saved me from several errors but also made those chapters much better. Wallace Bratt, Steve Vanderwey, Linda Gaffin and Steve Gaffin took the time to read the manuscript or portions of it, encouraged me and provided several needed reality checks.

Roger Kimball and the team at Encounter believed in this project, gave me essential advice and guidance, and showed me the ropes. Thank you to Lauren Miklos, Heather Ohle, Sam Schneider, Nola Tully and Katherine Wong.

I benefited from countless shared experiences, conversations and debates with many former State Department colleagues, especially those from USEU Brussels and the State Department Office of European Union and Regional Affairs. Most of them will probably disagree with most of this book, but they taught me much about the European Union. I immensely respect the dedication of my former colleagues from Europe who are devoted to the European idea out of a deep patriotism and commitment to their fellow Europeans. Needless to say, all of the opinions in this book are my own and reflect neither the positions and policies of the U.S. government nor the views of my former colleagues.

A big thank you to my dear friends from Brussels: Heidi Führmann, Jones Hayden, Regine Kramer, John and Carolyn Stanton, and Graham Ziegner. You are salt and light to me, and not only regarding all matters European. I owe much also to Henk Jan van Schothorst, my friend and cofounder of the Transatlantic Christian Council, and to Miriam Lexmann, TCC board member and friend.

I appreciate my colleagues at the Acton Institute and at the Paul B. Henry Institute for the Study of Christianity and Politics for stimulating conversations and help with the manuscript, and for cheering me on in multiple ways: Jordan Ballor, Mike Cook, John Couretas, Kevin den Dulk, Brett Elder, Stephen Grabill, Sam Gregg, Kishore Jayabalan, Ken Marotte, Kris Alan Mauren, Michael Miller and Father Robert A. Sirico.

I am especially indebted to David Aikman, John Fonte and Os Guinness. David encouraged me to write the book, helped me with the book proposal, and provided perceptive insights throughout the process. John's brilliant writing on global governance was the principal intellectual inspiration for the book. John connected me with Encounter Books and supported the project in innumerable ways. Os read the book proposal and the manuscript, gave invaluable advice and encouraged me to keep at it.

For their love and selflessness throughout the years, I thank my parents, Marvin and Carolynn Huizinga, and my brother, David. My lifelong friends Ron Villerius and Doug Boone have my deep appreciation as well.

Above all, I thank my precious wife, Vici, my beloved sons, Philip and Nicholas, and my cherished daughter, Sarah. This book is dedicated to them.

NOTES

INTRODUCTION – UNDERSTANDING THE EU

1   Treaty Establishing the European Economic Community (Rome, March 25, 1957), Preamble, 3, CVCE, http://www.cvce.eu/en/obj/treaty_establishing_the_european_economic_community_rome_25_march_1957-en-cca6ba28-0bf3-4ce6-8a76-6b0b3252696e.html (accessed May 14, 2015).

CHAPTER 1 – SOMETHING COMPLETELY DIFFERENT

1   Council of Europe, Joint Declaration by the Signatory Ministers, April 18, 1951, CVCE, http://www.cvce.eu/obj/joint_declaration_by_the_signatory_ministers_18_april_1951-en-a5bee6ca-6506-48bb-9bd5-c1aa8487bdfd.html.

2   "The American States establish by this Charter the international organization that they have developed to achieve an order of peace and justice, to promote their solidarity, to strengthen their collaboration, and to defend their sovereignty, their territorial integrity, and their independence. Within the United Nations, the Organization of American States is a regional agency. The Organization of American States has no powers other than those expressly conferred upon it by this Charter, none of whose provisions authorizes it to intervene in matters that are within the internal jurisdiction of the Member States." Charter of the Organization of American States (signed on February 27, 1967), 3, http://www.oas.org/dil/treaties_A-41_Charter_of_the_Organization_of_American_States.pdf.

3   See Paul Coleman, Elyssa Koren and Laura Miranda-Flefil, *The Global Human Rights Landscape: A Short Guide to Understanding the International Organizations and the Opportunities for Engagement* (Vienna: Kairos Publications, 2014), 99–113.

4   Daniel Hannan, "The EU Is Not a Free Trade Area but a Customs Union," *Telegraph*, October 23, 2012, http://blogs.telegraph.co.uk/news/daniel

hannan/100186074/the-eu-is-not-a-free-trade-area-but-a-customs-union-until-we-understand-the-difference-the-debate-about-our-membership-is-meaningless/.

5   Luuk van Middelaar, *De passage naar Europa: Geschiedenis van een begin* (Groningen: Historische Uitgeverij, 2011), 248–53.

6   Ibid., 250.

7   Ibid.

8   The Court of Justice interprets EU law to make sure it is applied in the same way in all EU countries. It also settles legal disputes between EU governments and EU institutions. Individuals, companies or organizations can also bring cases before the Court if they feel their rights have been infringed by an EU institution. European Union, Institutions and Bodies, "Court of Justice of the European Union," http://europa.eu/about-eu/institutions-bodies/court-justice/index_en.htm (accessed May 11, 2015).

9   Open Europe website, http://openeurope.org.uk/Content/Documents/PDFs/acquis.pdf (accessed December 14, 2014).

10 European Commission, *Special Eurobarometer 415: Europeans in 2014* (July 2014), 103, http://ec.europa.eu/public_opinion/archives/ebs/ebs_415_en.pdf.

CHAPTER 2 – POSTMODERN: THE EU AS AN UNANSWERED QUESTION

1   Alcide De Gasperi, "Aims and Prospects of European Policy," speech at the Consultative Assembly of the Council of Europe, Strasbourg, France, December 10, 1951, 23, http://www.epp-ed.eu/Activities/docs/cd-rom/degasperi-en.pdf.

2   "Charles de Gaulle: A Life of Political Influence," France 24, November 9, 2010, http://www.france24.com/en/20101109-charles-de-gaulle-life-political-influence-timeline-france/.

3   Margaret Thatcher, "Speech to the College of Europe," Bruges, Belgium, September 20, 1988, http://www.margaretthatcher.org/document/107332.

4   Helmut Kohl, quoted in Viviane Reding, "Why We Need a United States of Europe Now," speech at the Centrum für Europarecht, University of Passau, Germany, November 8, 2012, European Commission Press Release Database, http://europa.eu/rapid/press-release_SPEECH-12-796-en.htm.

5   José Manuel Durão Barroso, "On Europe: Considerations on the Present and Future of the European Union," speech at Humboldt University of Berlin, May 8, 2014, European Commission Press Release Database, http://europa.eu/rapid/press-release_SPEECH-14-355-en.htm.

6   Patrick Wintour, "Tony Blair 'Not Seeking European Leadership Role,'" *Guardian*, June 2, 2014, http://www.theguardian.com/politics/2014/jun/02/uk-create-manifesto-change-europe-commission-tony-blair. This relatively sovereigntist statement must be understood in the Euroskeptical context of British politics. Compared with many of his fellow political leaders in the UK, and certainly compared with the opposition Tories, Blair was very pro-EU. The above statement was primarily an attempt, not to beat back the encroachments of Brussels on national sovereignty, but to

chart a way forward for the EU that would be acceptable to British public opinion and undercut the Euroskepticism of Blair's political rivals.

7   De Gasperi, "Aims and Prospects of European Policy," 23.

8   "Technisch beschrieben, wäre Europa so etwas wie eine „Mehr-Ebenen-Demokratie": kein Bundesstaat, dessen Schwergewicht im Zentrum eines quasinationalstaatlichen Gemeinwesens läge. Aber zugleich viel mehr als ein Staatenbund, dessen verbindendes Element dürftig und schwach legitimiert bliebe. Sondern Europa wäre ein sich ergänzendes, ineinandergreifendes System von Demokratien verschiedener Reichweite und Zuständigkeiten: eine national-europäische Doppeldemokratie." Wolfgang Schäuble, "Die neue europäische Ernsthaftigkeit," *Frankfurter Allgemeine Zeitung*, May 21, 2014, http://www.faz.net/aktuell/feuilleton/debatten/europas-zukunft/wolfgang-schaeuble-ueber-die-zukunft-der-eu-die-neue-europaeische-ernsthaftigkeit-12949008.html?printPagedArticle=true#pageIndex_2. Translated from the German by Todd Huizinga.

9   "Wir beschliessen etwas, stellen das dann in den Raum und warten einige Zeit ab, was passiert. Wenn es dann kein großes Geschrei gibt und keine Aufstände, weil die meisten gar nicht begreifen, was da beschlossen wurde, dann machen wir weiter – Schritt für Schritt, bis es kein Zurück mehr gibt." Hans-Olaf Henkel, *Die Euro-Lügner: Unsinnige Rettungspakete, vertuschte Risiken – So werden wir getäuscht* (Munich: Wilhelm Heyne Verlag, 2013), 32–33. Translated from the German by Todd Huizinga.

CHAPTER 3 – THE UTOPIAN DREAM OF WORLD PEACE

1   The Schuman Declaration (May 9, 1950), http://europa.eu/about-eu/basic-information/symbols/europe-day/schuman-declaration/index_en.htm (accessed May 13, 2015).

2   Quoted by Pascal Lamy, "Global Governance: Lessons from Europe," speech at Bocconi University, Milan, Italy, November 9, 2009, https://www.wto.org/english/news_e/sppl_e/sppl142_e.htm.

3   Ibid.

4   Jürgen Habermas, *The Divided West*, trans. Ciaran Cronin (Cambridge: Polity Press, 2006), 175–76.

5   Ibid., 43.

6   Lamy, "Global Governance."

7   "Hier mit einer national-europäischen Doppeldemokratie der Welt ein Modell für globales Regieren im 21. Jahrhundert anzubieten könnte nicht nur Inspiration für andere, sondern auch eine neue Quelle von Identifikation und Freude der Europäer an ihrem Europa sein." Wolfgang Schäuble, "Die neue europäische Ernsthaftigkeit," *Frankfurter Allgemeine Zeitung*, May 21, 2014. Translated from the German by Todd Huizinga.

8   Saba Riazati, "A Closer Look: Professor Seeks Stronger U.N.," *Daily Bruin*, October 17, 2006, http://dailybruin.com/2006/10/17/a-closer-look-professor-seeks/.

9   Thomas G. Weiss and Ramesh Thakur, *Global Governance and the UN: An Unfinished Journey* (Bloomington: Indiana University Press, 2010), 6.

10   Thomas G. Weiss and Ramesh Thakur, *The UN and Global Governance: An Idea and Its Prospects* (Bloomington: Indiana University Press, 2006).

11   Cram101 Textbook Reviews, Just the Facts101 e-Study Guide for Alan Sitkin, *International Business*, 2nd ed. (Content Technologies Inc., 2015), chap. 4, "Global Frameworks."

12   Habermas, *The Divided West*, 134.

13   Ibid., 135.

14   Ibid., 135–36. Emphasis in the original.

15   Ibid.

16   John Fonte, *Sovereignty or Submission: Will Americans Rule Themselves or Be Ruled by Others?* (New York: Encounter Books, 2011), 343.

17   Ibid., 342.

18   Ibid., 366.

19   Ibid., 183.

20   Ibid., 359.

21   Ibid., 365.

22   Ibid., 344.

23   Ibid., 358. Emphasis added.

24   Ibid., xx.

25   Habermas, *The Divided West*, 48. Emphasis in the original.

26   Fonte, *Sovereignty or Submission*, xx.

27   Lamy, "Global Governance."

CHAPTER 4 – OUT OF THE ASHES

1   The Schuman Declaration (May 9, 1950), http://europa.eu/about-eu/basic-information/symbols/europe-day/schuman-declaration/index_en.htm (accessed May 13, 2015).

2   Ibid.

3   Treaty Establishing the European Coal and Steel Community (Paris, April 18, 1951), Preamble, 3, CVCE, http://www.cvce.eu/en/obj/treaty_establishing_the_european_coal_and_steel_community_paris_18_april_1951-en-11a21305-941e-49d7-a171-ed5be548cd58.html (accessed May 13, 2015).

4   Jean Monnet, *Mémoirs* (Garden City, N.Y.: Doubleday, 1978), 316. To be found also at "9th May 1950: The Schuman Declaration," 11 and 23, http://arc.eppgroup.eu/Activities/docs/divers/infodoc-schuman-en.doc.

5   "Treaty Establishing the European Coal and Steel Community," Preamble, 3.

6   Immanuel Kant, *Perpetual Peace: A Philosophical Sketch* (1795), https://www.mtholyoke.edu/acad/intrel/kant/kant1.htm (accessed January 17, 2015).

7   "President Woodrow Wilson's Fourteen Points," Avalon Project, Yale Law School, http://avalon.law.yale.edu/20th_century/wilson14.asp (accessed May 13, 2015).

8   See Joschka Fischer, *Scheitert Europa?* (Cologne: Kiepenheuer & Witsch, 2014), 153.

"Jean Monnet," *New World Encyclopedia*, http://www.newworldencyclo **217**
pedia.org/entry/Jean_Monnet (accessed October 23, 2015).

10 The Schuman Declaration.

CHAPTER 5 – THE TRANSFORMATION OF EUROPE

1 Article 2, Treaty Establishing the European Economic Community (Rome, March 25, 1957), 4, CVCE, http://www.cvce.eu/en/obj/treaty_establishing_the_european_economic_community_rome_25_march_1957-en-cca6ba28-0bf3-4ce6-8a76-6b0b3252696e.html (accessed May 14, 2015).

2 Dick Leonard, *Guide to the European Union* (New York: Wiley, 2002), 319.

3 Summary of the Treaty Establishing the European Economic Community, EEC Treaty – original text (non-consolidated version, 1957), http://europa.eu/legislation_summaries/institutional_affairs/treaties/treaties_eec_en.htm (accessed May 14, 2015).

4 Single European Act (February 1986), Article 13, *Official Journal of the European Communities* L 169/7 (June 29, 1987), http://eur-lex.europa.eu/legal-content/EN/TXT/?uri=OJ:L:1987:169:TOC (accessed October 2015).

5 Treaty on European Union (February 7, 1992), http://europa.eu/eu-law/decision-making/treaties/pdf/treaty_on_european_union/treaty_on_european_union_en.pdf.

6 Desmond Dinan, *Ever Closer Union: An Introduction to European Integration*, 2nd ed. (Boulder: Lynne Rienner, 1999), 182.

7 Treaty of Nice Amending the Treaty on European Union, the Treaties Establishing the European Communities and Certain Related Acts (March 10, 2001), http://eur-lex.europa.eu/legal-content/EN/TXT/PDF/?uri=CELEX:12001C/TXT&from=EN (accessed May 14, 2015).

8 Treaty of Lisbon: Introduction (last updated July 14, 2010), http://europa.eu/legislation_summaries/institutional_affairs/treaties/lisbon_treaty/ai0033_en.htm.

9 Jens-Peter Bonde, *From EU Constitution to the Irish Referendums on the Lisbon Treaty* (Foundation for EU Democracy, 2009), http://en.euabc.com/upload/from_eu_constitution.pdf.

10 Ibid., 54.

11 Ibid., 58.

12 Ibid., 59.

CHAPTER 6 – THE CLOAK OF CONSTRUCTIVE AMBIGUITY

1 "As regular readers will know, the Open Europe team has gone to hell and back trying to answer this question, and our conclusion is that it's virtually impossible to determine with any degree of certainty what the share of EU-derived laws is. It all depends on what you count, how you define an EU-derived law and what the counter-factual is.... Now, a new Swedish study has thrown in another number to debate. The Riksdag & Departement – the Swedish Parliament's in-house magazine – has reviewed 1,300 Swedish legislative proposals, dating back to 2005. It found that the share of

legislative proposals in 2012 originating in the EU stands at 43% – a dramatic increase compared to 2010 when the share was 28%. Of the 104 laws that so far have been proposed by the Riksdag this year, about a third originate in the EU.... A 2010 report by the Swedish Association of Local Authorities and Regions – who should know a thing or two about local decision-making – does address this very question. It says this:

> 'The report shows that, on average, the EU affects 60 percent of items on municipal council agendas. The number is slightly lower for county councils and regions, where the EU influences around 50 percent of agenda items.... A few conclusions:
>
> · Viviane Reding really must be on the UKIP payroll
>
> · It remains incredibly difficult to nail down exactly how many laws originate in the EU
>
> · The share of EU laws is best measured in terms of domestic legislation "influenced by" or "linked to" EU decisions, ideally in combination with the measurable impact of these laws (our preferred way) to get a sense of the relative impact
>
> · Any EU law count must also look at the local or regional level
>
> · Still, a h*** of a lot of domestic laws stem from the EU."

"9%, 43%, 50%, 60%, 84%: How Many Domestic Laws Are Linked to EU Law? The Case of Sweden," Open Europe, November 4, 2013, http://open europeblog.blogspot.com/2013/11/9-43-50-60-84-how-many-domestic-laws.html.

2   Treaty Establishing the European Economic Community (Rome, March 25, 1957), Preamble, 3, CVCE, http://www.cvce.eu/en/obj/treaty_establishing_ the_european_economic_community_rome_25_march_1957-en-cca6ba28-0bf3-4ce6-8a76-6b0b3252696e.html (accessed May 14, 2015).

3   Luuk van Middelaar, *De passage naar Europa: Geschiedenis van een begin* (Groningen: Historische Uitgeverij, 2011), 70–77.

4   Joseph H. H. Weiler, *The Constitution of Europe: "Do the New Clothes Have An Emperor?" and Other Essays on European Integration* (Cambridge: Cambridge University Press, 1999), 327.

5   Cris Shore, "'In uno plures'(?): EU Cultural Policy and the Governance of Europe," *Cultural Analysis* 5 (2006), 7–26, http://socrates.berkeley.edu/~caforum/volume5/pdf/shore.pdf.

6   Mr. Willy De Clercq et al., *Reflection on Information and Communication Policy of the European Community*, Commission of the European Communities (March 1993), 3, http://aei.pitt.edu/29870/1/DE_CLERCQ_REPORT_INFO._COMM._POLICY.pdf.

7   Shore, "'In uno plures,'" 6.

8   Ibid., 7.

9   Government of the Netherlands, "European Where Necessary, National Where Possible," June 21, 2013, http://www.government.nl/news/2013/06/21/european-where-necessary-national-where-possible.html.

1   "Jean Monnet," *New World Encyclopedia*, http://www.newworldencyclo pedia.org/entry/Jean_Monnet (accessed October 23, 2015).

2   "Statement by Mr Delors on Behalf of the Commission after the Danish Referendum," June 3, 1992, European Commission Press Release Database, http://europa.eu/rapid/press-release_IP-92-456_en.htm.

3   "Mr Major's Commons Statement on the Maastricht Treaty (Danish Referendum)," June 3, 1992, http://www.johnmajor.co.uk/page1180.html.

4   "Mr Major's Joint Doorstep Interview with Poul Schluter," December 2, 1992, http://www.johnmajor.co.uk/page1449.html.

5   "Denmark and the Treaty on European Union," *Official Journal of the European Communities* C 348/1 (December 31, 1992), http://eur-lex.europa.eu/ legal-content/EN/TXT/HTML/?uri=CELEX:41992X1231&from=EN.

6   Christopher Follett and Lars Foyen, "Path Looks Smoother for Denmark as Three Key Parties Approve Agreement," *Herald Scotland*, December 14, 1992, http://www.heraldscotland.com/spl/aberdeen/path-looks-smoother-for-denmark-as-three-key-parties-approve-agreement-1.780754.

7   Council of the European Union, *Seville European Council, 21 and 22 June 2002, Presidency Conclusions* (October 24, 2002), 27–30, http://www.con silium.europa.eu/uedocs/cms_data/docs/pressdata/en/ec/72638.pdf.

8   Ian Traynor, Nicholas Watt and Jenny Percival, "No EU Lisbon Treaty without Irish People's Approval, Says Miliband," *Guardian*, June 20, 2008, http://www.theguardian.com/world/2008/jun/20/eu.foreignpolicy.

9   Ian Traynor and Nicholas Watt, "Lisbon Treaty: Pressure on Ireland for Second Vote," *Guardian*, June 19, 2008, http://www.theguardian.com/ world/2008/jun/19/lisbon.ireland.

10 Guy Verhofstadt, *The United States of Europe* (London: The Federal Trust, 2006).

11 European Union, "The Outcome of the European Convention," http:// europa.eu/scadplus/european_convention/introduction_en.htm.

CHAPTER 8 – *ÉCRASEZ L'INFÂME*: RELIGION AND THE EU CONSTITUTION

1   The Constitution of the United States, U.S. National Archives, http://www. archives.gov/exhibits/charters/constitution_transcript.html.

2   Basic Law for the Federal Republic of Germany, trans. Christian Tomuschat and David P. Currie, Bundesministerium der Justiz und für Verbraucherschutz (2014), http://www.gesetze-im-internet.de/englisch_gg/ englisch_gg.html#p0012.

3   The Constitution of the Republic of Poland of 2nd April 1997, Sejm of the Republic of Poland, http://www.sejm.gov.pl/prawo/konst/angielski/kon1. htm.

4   Treaty Establishing a Constitution for Europe (October 29, 2004), http:// europa.eu/eu-law/decision-making/treaties/pdf/treaty_establishing_a_ constitution_for_europe/treaty_establishing_a_constitution_for_europe_ en.pdf.

5   Andrew Smith, "Divisions over the Place of Religion in the Treaty Estab-

lishing a Constitution for Europe," Lancaster University, http://www.lancaster.ac.uk/staff/kallis/EURO100/page4/files/Seminar%204%20article.pdf.

6 "Europa hingegen muss seit dem 19. Jahrhundert mit einem doppelten Erbe leben, einem spirituellen, religiösen Erbe und einem rein weltlichen politischen System, in dem die Religion keine Rolle spielt." Valéry Giscard d'Estaing, interviewed by Susanne Fuehrer, "Zum Erfolg verdammt: Vom Kontinent zur Föderation – ein ZEIT-Gespräch mit Valéry Giscard d'Estaing, dem Präsidenten des EU-Konvents, über Europas wachsendes Selbstbewußtsein," *Zeit Online*, January 30, 2003, http://www.zeit.de/2003/06/Zum_Erfolg_verdammt. Translated from the German by Todd Huizinga.

7 "Mir persönlich erscheint ein Bezug auf Gott nicht angebracht. Andere denken da anders: Ich komme gerade aus Polen zurück. Für einen Polen heißt 'Gott' einfach Christus. Denn die allermeisten dort sind Katholiken. In Frankreich liest sich das anders. Dort gibt es Protestanten, Juden, Muslime. 'Gott' hat nicht mehr denselben Inhalt." Ibid. Translated from the German by Todd Huizinga.

8 European Convention, "Draft Text of the Articles of the Treaty Establishing a Constitution for Europe," Articles 1–16 (February 6, 2003), 2, http://european-convention.europa.eu/pdf/reg/en/03/cv00/cv00528.en03.pdf.

9 Gareth Harding, "God Splits EU Blueprint-Drafters," *Ecclesia Report*, Church of Greece, Communication and Cultural Service, March 4, 2003, http://www.ecclesia.gr/English/EnPressOffice/report/04-03-2003.html.

10 Ibid.

11 Smith, "Divisions over the Place of Religion." I am indebted to Andrew Smith for this chronological summary of the debate.

12 Honor Mahony, "Giscard against Religious Interference in Constitution," *EU Observer*, January 30, 2003, https://euobserver.com/institutional/9192.

13 Harding, "God Splits EU Blueprint-Drafters."

14 Pope John Paul II, "Post-Synodal Apostolic Exhortation *Ecclesia in Europa* of His Holiness Pope John Paul to the Bishops, Men and Women in the Consecrated Life and All the Lay Faithful on Jesus Christ Alive in His Church the Source of Hope for Europe," Libreria Editrice Vaticana, June 28, 2003, 108, http://w2.vatican.va/content/john-paul-ii/en/apost_exhortations/documents/hf_jp-ii_exh_20030628_ecclesia-in-europa.html.

15 Ibid., 114.

16 Costas Kydoniatis, "International Press Welcomes Archbishop Christodoulos' Letter to Valery Giscard D'Estaing Concerning a Reference to Religion in the Future EU Constitution," *Ecclesia Report*, Church of Greece, Communication and Cultural Service, March 4, 2003, http://www.ecclesia.gr/English/EnPressOffice/report/04-03-2003.html.

17 Harding, "God Splits EU Blueprint-Drafters."

18 Smith, "Divisions over the Place of Religion."

19 Ian Black, "Christianity Bedevils Talks on EU Treaty," *Guardian*, May 24, 2004, http://www.theguardian.com/world/2004/may/25/eu.religion.

20 Ibid.

21 Lucia Kubosova, "EU Needs Constitution with Christian Reference, Merkel Says," *EU Observer*, August 29, 2006, https://euobserver.com/institutional/22280.

22 Treaty Establishing a Constitution for Europe.

CHAPTER 9 – THE EUROZONE CRISIS AND THE POLITICS BEHIND THE MONEY

1 Herman van Rompuy, President of the European Council, "Speech on the Occasion of the Departure of the President of the ECB," October 19, 2011, European Commission Press Release Database, http://europa.eu/rapid/press-release_PRES-11-379_en.htm.

2 John Peet and Anton La Guardia, *Unhappy Union: How the Euro Crisis – and Europe – Can Be Fixed* (London: The Economist, 2014), 31.

3 Committee for the Study of Economic and Monetary Union, *Report on Economic and Monetary Union in the European Community* (April 17, 1989), http://aei.pitt.edu/1007/1/monetary_delors.pdf.

4 Ibid.

5 Intervention by Henning Christophersen at Deutschen Raiffeisentag 1994, "Standort Europa im Blick auf das Jahr 2000," Hannover, September 15, 1994, European Commission Press Release Database, http://europa.eu/rapid/press-release_SPEECH-94-93_en.htm.

6 Council of the European Union, *The Economic and Monetary Union: Stronger Economies for a Stronger Union* (2014), 8, http://www.consilium.europa.eu/en/workarea/downloadasset.aspx?id=40802190815.

7 ECB website, https://www.ecb.europa.eu (accessed January 15, 2015).

8 Valentina Pop, "Kohl Confesses to Euro's Undemocratic Beginnings," *EU Observer*, April 8, 2013, https://euobserver.com/political/119735.

9 European Commission, Economic and Financial Affairs, "A Symbol of European Identity," http://ec.europa.eu/economy_finance/euro/why/identity/index_en.htm (accessed October 23, 2015).

10 Michael Sauga, Stefan Simons and Klaus Wiegrefe, "You Get Unification, We Get the Euro," *Der Spiegel*, as published at *VoxEurop*, October 1, 2010, http://www.voxeurop.eu/en/content/article/351531-you-get-unification-we-get-euro.

11 Ibid.

12 European Commission, *Eurobarometer: Public Opinion in the European Community* 38 (December 1992), 34, http://ec.europa.eu/public_opinion/archives/eb/eb38/eb38_en.pdf.

13 Ibid.

14 Greg Ip, "Benefit of ECB's Bond Buying: Fiscal Breathing Room: Countries, Such as Spain and Italy, Gain Leeway to Stabilize Their Debt Ratios," *Wall Street Journal*, February 11, 2015, http://www.wsj.com/articles/benefit-of-ecbs-bond-buying-fiscal-breathing-room-1423700220.

15 Roger Bootle, *The Trouble with Europe: Why the EU Isn't Working, How It Can Be Reformed, What Could Take Its Place* (Boston: Nicholas Brealey Publishing, 2014), 93.

16 Hans-Olaf Henkel, *Die Euro-Lügner: Unsinnige Rettungspakete, vertuschte Risiken – So werden wir getäuscht* (Munich: Wilhelm Heyne Verlag, 2013), 40–41.

17 Bootle, *The Trouble with Europe*, 89.

18 "Wir haben ein zentralplanerisches System geschaffen, in dem das Kapital durch zwei Organisationen, die EZB und den ESM, und unter Bedingungen, die im politischen Prozess festgelegt werden, nach Südeuropa gelenkt wird. Wohlgemerkt: im politischen Prozess, nicht im Marktprozess.... Was in der Eurozone derzeit geschieht, unterhöhlt die Grundregel der Marktwirtschaft... dass hinter jedem Kapitaleinsatz auch ein Vermögen und ein Eigentümer steht, der... versucht, sein Geld in möglichst sichere und ertragreiche Investitionen zu lenken. Diese aus der Eigenverantwortung entstehende Sorgfalt ist das Lebenselixier der kapitalistischen Marktwirtschaft.... Mit dem, was wir in Europa derzeit machen... opfern wir dieses Lebenselixier und ersetzen es durch Zentralplanungsbehörden.... Mit den Beschlüssen der Euroländer wird es immer mehr öffentlich gesicherte und gelenkte Kapitalflüsse in politisch gewünschte, aber ineffiziente Investitionsprojekte geben, die die Wachstumskräfte Europas weiter aushöhlen." Hans-Werner Sinn, *Gefangen im Euro* (Munich: Redline Verlag, 2014), 106–7. Translated from the German by Todd Huizinga.

19 "Spätestens in 15 bis 20 Jahren wird es uns also hinten und vorne kneifen." Ibid., 122. Translated from the German by Todd Huizinga.

20 "Viele Bürger scheinen zu denken, die Finanzkrise sei nun überstanden und alles werde wieder gut. Politik und Medien tun das Ihrige, dass die Bürger in falscher Sicherheit gewiegt werden. Die meisten Menschen übersehen aber, dass die Märkte nur deshalb beruhigt wurden, weil sie als Steuerzahler und Rentner die Schulden der Südländer mit neuen Krediten ausgelöst haben und dafür später einmal die Zeche werden zahlen müssen." Ibid., 113–14. Translated from the German by Todd Huizinga.

21 "Das wird die Völker Europas gegeneinander aufbringen." Ibid., 108.

22 Hans-Werner Sinn, "Rescuing Europe from the Ground Up," Project Syndicate, December 21, 2013, http://www.project-syndicate.org/commentary/hans-werner-sinn-argues-that-reconstructing-the-euro-is-the-only-way-to-save-the-european-integration-project#1j7jqV8s2EUbRSGJ.99.

23 "Irgendwann werden die Bürger auch merken, dass ein Teil ihres Vermögens schon verloren ist, dass der Lebensstandard, den man sich mit seiner Ersparnis für das Alter sichern wollte, durch die von der Politik verursachten Vermögenseinbussen nicht mehr zu halten ist. Auch wenn man dann vielleicht immer noch nicht versteht, wie das alles gekommen ist, und wenn es auch zu spät ist, an dem Vermögensverlust noch etwas zu ändern, werden die Menschen mit der Ablehnung des Staates reagieren.... Die Politik... riskiert die Flucht der Bürger aus den traditionellen Parteien und Institutionen." Hans-Werner Sinn, *Gefangen im Euro* (Munich, Redline Verlag, 2014), 117–18. Translated from the German by Todd Huizinga.

24 "Wenn sich die Dinge in der gleichen Logik weiterentwickeln wie bisher,

vermute ich, dass es in einigen Jahren größere soziale Verwerfungen in der deutschen Gesellschaft geben wird, die an den ökonomischen und politischen Grundfesten unseres Staates rütteln warden.... Mit nur 8,1 Kindern pro 1000 Einwohner... werden die Rettungsaktionen der Staatengemeinschaft und der EZB die Staatsbudgets der noch gesunden Länder in hohem Maße belasten.... Die vermeintlichen Ersparnisse der Deutschen werden sich teilweise in Luft auflösen." Ibid., 120–21. Translated from the German by Todd Huizinga.

25 "Wir sind gefangen im Euro. Nun müssen wir raus aus diesem Gefängnis." Ibid., 127. Translated from the German by Todd Huizinga.

CHAPTER 10 – ABSOLUTE AUTONOMY: THE GLOBAL ETHIC OF WOMEN'S RIGHTS

1 The Declaration of Independence, U.S. National Archives, http://www. archives.gov/exhibits/charters/declaration_transcript.html.

2 European Union, "Regulation (EC) No 1905/2006 of the European Parliament and of the Council of 18 December 2006 Establishing a Financing Instrument for Development Cooperation," *Official Journal of the European Union* L 378/46 (2006), http://eur-lex.europa.eu/legal-content/EN/ TXT/PDF/?uri=CELEX:32006R1905&from=EN.

3 European Dignity Watch, *The Funding of Abortion through EU Development Aid: An Analysis of EU's Sexual and Reproductive Health Policy* (March 2012), 2–4, 8–9, http://www.europeandignitywatch.org/fileadmin/user_ upload/PDF/Day_to_Day_diverse/Funding_of_Abortion_Through_EU_ Development_Aid_full_version.pdf.

4 European Union Delegation to the United Nations, "EU Statement – United Nations Commission on Population and Development: General Debate," New York, April 7, 2014, http://eu-un.europa.eu/articles/en/ article_14875_en.htm.

5 European Dignity Watch, *The Funding of Abortion*, 15.

6 Ibid.

7 Poul Nielson, European Commissioner for Development and Humanitarian Aid, "European Responses to the HIV/AIDS Pandemic: Challenges Ahead and the Role of Foundations and Civil Society," speech at the European Policy Centre, Brussels, June 3, 2004, European Commission Press Release Database, http://europa.eu/rapid/press-release_SPEECH-04-296 _en.htm?locale=EN.

8 VoteWatch Europe, *The Votes That Shaped EU Global Health Policy: Analysis of European Parliament Voting Behaviour on Global Health R&D and SRHR 2009–2014*, research commissioned by DSW, IPPF EN, EPF and MSI, 5, http://www.dsw.org/uploads/tx_aedswpublication/VoteWatch_ EU_GH_Report.pdf (accessed June 17, 2015).

9 Ibid.

10 Heidi Hautala and Sophie in 't Veld, "Abortion: Choice Is a Human Right," EurActiv, December 9, 2014, http://www.euractiv.com/sections/develop ment-policy/abortion-choice-human-right-310689.

11 Edite Estrela, *Report on Sexual and Reproductive Health and Rights* (2013/2040(INI)), Committee on Women's Rights and Gender Equality, European Parliament (September 26, 2013), Minority Report, 27, http://www.europarl.europa.eu/sides/getDoc.do?pubRef=-//EP//NONSGML+REPORT+A7-2013-0306+0+DOC+PDF+V0//EN.

12 Asian-Pacific Resource and Research Centre for Women, *An Advocate's Guide: Strategic Indicators for Universal Access to Sexual and Reproductive Health and Rights* (2013), 21, http://www.arrow.org.my/publications/AdvocateGuide_Final_RN_Web.20131127.pdf.

13 Ibid., 19–20.

14 Ibid. I am indebted to Sharon Slater of Family Watch International for drawing my attention to this document.

15 European Commission, *A Decent Life for All: From Vision to Collective Action*, Communication from the Commission to the European Parliament, the Council, the European Economic and Social Committee and the Committee of the Regions (June 2, 2014), 6, http://eur-lex.europa.eu/resource.html?uri=cellar:441ba0c0-eb02-11e3-8cd4-01aa75ed71a1.0001.02/DOC_1&format=PDF.

16 European Parliament, "Resolution of 25 November 2014 on the EU and the Global Development Framework after 2015," http://www.europarl.europa.eu/sides/getDoc.do?pubRef=-//EP//TEXT+TA+P8-TA-2014-0059+0+DOC+XML+V0//EN.

17 Council of the European Union, *Council Conclusions on a Transformative Post-2015 Agenda* (December 16, 2014), 1, http://italia2014.eu/media/4287/council-conclusions-on-a-transformative-post-2015-agenda.pdf.

18 Ibid., 4.

19 Marguerite A. Peeters, "The New Global Ethic: Challenges for the Church," Pontifical Council for the Laity: Women: Philosophy, 6, http://www.laici.va/content/dam/laici/documenti/donna/filosofia/english/new-global-ethic-challenges-for-the-church.pdf (accessed June 17, 2015). For this section, I am deeply indebted to Peeters' monograph, which is the source of the quoted passages in the rest of this chapter. All emphasis in the original.

20 Ibid., 6.

CHAPTER 11 – THE DECONSTRUCTION OF HUMAN NATURE: LGBT RIGHTS

1 Gabriele Kuby, *Die globale sexuelle Revolution: Die Zerstörung der Freiheit im Namen der Freiheit*, 2nd ed. (fe-medienverlags GmbH, 2012), 134. Translated from the German by Todd Huizinga.

2 Ibid., 134.

3 European Commission, Directorates-General, Home Affairs and Justice, "Final Audit Report: On-the-Spot Check of the Expenditure under the Operating Grant VS/2010/158," July 31, 2012, http://www.asktheeu.org/en/request/621/response/2546/attach/html/4/Final%20Audit%20Report.pdf.html.

4 ILGA-Europe, "Vision, Mission, Core Values," http://www.ilga-europe.org/

who-we-are/what-ilga-europe/vision-mission-core-values (accessed June 18, 2015).

225

NOTES

5   Council of the European Union, *Guidelines to Promote and Protect the Enjoyment of All Human Rights by Lesbian, Gay, Bisexual, Transgender and Intersex (LGBTI) Persons* (June 24, 2013), 1, http://www.consilium.europa. eu/uedocs/cms_data/docs/pressdata/en/foraff/137584.pdf.

6   *The Yogyakarta Principles: Principles of the Application of International Human Rights Law in Relation to Sexual Orientation and Gender Identity* (March 2007), http://www.yogyakartaprinciples.org/principles_en.pdf.

7   Ibid., 7.

8   Ibid., 8.

9   Ibid., 11. Emphasis added.

10 Ibid., 12. Emphasis added.

11 EU Agency for Fundamental Rights (FRA), "About the FRA," http://fra. europa.eu/en/about-fra (accessed June 18, 2015).

12 Ibid.

13 EU Agency for Fundamental Rights (FRA), "Tackling Sexual Orientation and Gender Identity" Conference Conclusions, October 24, 2014, 3, http:// fra.europa.eu/sites/default/files/fra-it-presidency-conclusions-lgbti-con ference-28-10-2014.pdf.

14 Charter of Fundamental Rights of the European Union, *Official Journal of the European Union* C 364/1 (December 18, 2000), Article 9, http://www. europarl.europa.eu/charter/pdf/text_en.pdf.

15 European Convention on Human Rights (June 1, 2010), Article 12, https:// ec.europa.eu/digital-agenda/sites/digital-agenda/files/Convention_ENG. pdf.

16 European Court of Human Rights, "Case of Christine Goodwin v. The United Kingdom," July 11, 2002, 29, http://hudoc.echr.coe.int/sites/eng/ pages/search.aspx?i=001-60596#{"itemid":["001-60596"]}.

17 Jackie Jones, "Human Dignity in the EU Charter of Fundamental Rights and Its Interpretation before the European Court of Justice," *Liverpool Law Review* 33:281–300 (2012), 298.

18 Sherif Girgis, Ryan T. Anderson and Robert P. George, *What Is Marriage? Man and Woman: A Defense* (New York: Encounter Books, 2012), 6–7.

CHAPTER 12 – ANTIDISCRIMINATION AND RELIGIOUS FREEDOM

1   Definition of "hatred," *Merriam-Webster Dictionary*, http://www.merriam-webster.com/dictionary/hatred (accessed June 18, 2015).

2   The Legal Project, "European Hate Speech Laws" (last modified 2015), http://www.legal-project.org/issues/european-hate-speech-laws.

3   ILGA-Europe, "Hate Crime and Hate Speech" (last modified 2015), http:// www.ilga-europe.org/what-we-do/our-advocacy-work/hate-crime-hate-speech.

4   Ibid. Emphasis in the original.

5   "Homophobia," Wikipedia (last modified June 5, 2015), https://en. wikipedia.org/?title=Homophobia.

6 "Pastor Ake Green's Sermon," The Ake Green Case, July 2003, http://www.akegreen.org/.

7 Ibid., 8.

8 Paul Coleman, *Censored: How European "Hate Speech" Laws Are Threatening Freedom of Speech* (Vienna: Kairos Publications, 2012).

9 Ibid., 57.

10 Ibid., 58, quoting Gerard Alexander, "Illiberal Europe: The Long and Growing List of Things You Can't Legally Say," American Enterprise Institute, April 10, 2006, 3, emphasis added.

11 EU Agency for Fundamental Rights (FRA), *EU LGBT Survey Technical Report: Methodology, Online Survey, Questionnaire and Sample* (2013), http://fra.europa.eu/sites/default/files/eu-lgbt-survey-technical-report_en.pdf.

12 European Dignity Watch, "EU Fundamental Rights Agency Fabricates Victims of LGBT 'Discrimination' in a New Survey," April 4, 2012, http://europeandignitywatch.org/day-to-day/detail/article/eu-fundamental-rights-agency-fabricates-victims-of-lgbt-discrimination-in-a-new-survey.html.

13 FRA, *EU LGBT Survey Technical Report*, 57.

14 Ibid., 61–62.

15 Ibid., 64–65.

16 Ibid., 65–66.

17 Ibid., 69.

18 Ibid., 72.

19 Ibid., 103–4.

20 For the analysis of the EU LGBT survey, I am indebted to European Dignity Watch, "EU Fundamental Rights Agency Fabricates Victims."

21 European Parliament, "Hearing of Rocco Buttiglione (Justice, Freedom and Security)," October 5, 2010, http://www.europarl.europa.eu/press/audicom2004/resume/041005_BUTTIGLIONE_EN.pdf.

22 "Wie kann ich diesem Mann vertrauen, dass er Homosexuelle vor Diskriminierung schützt, wenn er Homosexualität für unmoralisch halt?" Kathalijne Buitenweg, quoted in "Homo-Ehe: Italiens EU-Kommissar in spe in Verteidigungshaltung," *Spiegel Online*, October 5, 2004, http://www.spiegel.de/politik/ausland/homo-ehe-italiens-eu-kommissar-in-spe-in-verteidigungshaltung-a-321622.html. Translated from the German by Todd Huizinga.

23 European Commission, "Proposal for a Council Directive on Implementing the Principle of Equal Treatment between Persons Irrespective of Religion or Belief, Disability, Age or Sexual Orientation," July 2, 2008, 2, http://eur-lex.europa.eu/legal-content/EN/TXT/PDF/?uri=CELEX:52008PC0426&from=en.

24 Sophia Kuby, "'Principle of Equality' to Overrule Fundamental Freedoms," European Dignity Watch, September 8, 2010, http://europeandignitywatch.org/reports/detail/article/principle-of-equality-to-overrule-fundamental-freedoms.html.

25 Ibid.

26 Paul Coleman and Roger Kiska, "The Proposed EU 'Equal Treatment' Directive: How the UK Gives Other EU Member States a Glimpse of the Future," *IJRF* 5:1 (2012), 113–28. Emphasis in the original.

27 Ibid.

28 Gudrun Kugler and Sophia Kuby, "The Principle of Equality Turned Upside Down," European Dignity Watch, July 19, 2014, http://www.europeandig nitywatch.org/day-to-day/detail/article/the-principle-of-equality-turned-upside-down.html.

29 Paul Moynan, "The Proposed Equal Treatment Directive: An Attack on Subsidiarity and Fundamental Freedoms," Care for Europe briefing, July 2014, www.careforeurope.org.

30 "ADF: Stop Parent's Second Prison Sentence for Keeping Children from German 'Sex Education' Programs," Alliance Defending Freedom, March 24, 2011, http://www.adfmedia.org/News/PRDetail/4691.

31 Gabriele Kuby, *Die globale sexuelle Revolution: Die Zerstörung der Freiheit im Namen der Freiheit*, 2nd ed. (fe-medienverlags GmbH, 2012), 299.

32 Ben Waldron, "Home Schooling German Family Allowed to Stay in US," ABC News, March 5, 2014, http://abcnews.go.com/US/home-schooling-german-family-allowed-stay-us/story?id=22788876.

33 Erin Kelly, "House Panel Approves Asylum Bill for Homeschoolers," *USA Today*, March 18, 2015, http://www.usatoday.com/story/news/politics/2015 /03/18/house-judiciary-committee-immigration-enforcement-bills/24960 965/.

34 "Desperate Homeschooling Parents Plead for Help – Hope Court Will Hear Case," HSLDA, April 16, 2013, http://www.hslda.org/hs/international/ sweden/201304160.asp.

35 Wikipedia, "Educación para la Ciudadanía en España," https://es.wiki pedia.org/wiki/Educación_para_la_Ciudadan%C3%ADa_en_España (accessed November 7, 2015).

36 Kuby, *Die globale sexuelle Revolution*, 309–10.

37 Ibid., 305.

38 Ibid., 317, quoting Dr. Karlheinz Valtl, *Sexualpädagogik in der Schule* (1998).

39 Ibid., 318. For a comprehensive review of sex education in German schools, see Kuby, *Die globale sexuelle Revolution*, chap. 12, "Sex-Erziehung in Schule und Kindergarten."

40 Luca Volonte, "Obligatory Deconstruction of 'Gender Stereotypes' and Violation of Parents' Rights," Council of Europe, June 4, 2013, http:// assembly.coe.int/nw/xml/XRef/Xref-XML2HTML-en.asp?fileid=19774& lang=EN. Parentheses and ellipses in source document.

41 Kiley Crossland, "French Conservatives Nix Gender Theory Education Program," *WORLD Magazine*, July 8, 2014, http://www.worldmag.com/ 2014/07/french_conservatives_nix_gender_theory_education_program.

42 Besorgte Eltern website, http://www.besorgte-eltern.net/ (accessed June 19, 2015).

43 The European Citizens' Initiative, Official Register, "FAQ on the EU

Competences and the European Commission Powers," European Commission (last modified July 28, 2015), http://ec.europa.eu/citizens-initiative/public/competences/faq.

44 Bruce C. Hafen, "Abandoning Children to Their Autonomy: Children's Needs and the Rights of Parents in the UN Convention on the Rights of the Child," speech at a UNHRC side event organized by the UN Family Rights Caucus and Family Watch International, inter alia, Geneva, Switzerland, September 12, 2014, 3–4.

45 Ibid., 2–3, quoting Mary Ann Glendon.

46 Mary Ann Glendon, "What Happened at Beijing," *First Things*, January 1996, http://www.firstthings.com/article/1996/01/005-what-happened-at-beijing. Glendon, who later served as U.S. ambassador to the UN in 2008–9, attended the Beijing conference as the head of the Vatican delegation.

47 European Commission, "Towards an EU Strategy on the Rights of the Child," Communication for the Commission, July 4, 2006, 7, http://eur-lex.europa.eu/LexUriServ/LexUriServ.do?uri=COM:2006:0367:FIN:en:PDF.

48 World Health Organization, *Standards for Sexuality Education in Europe* (2010), 27, available at http://www.bzga-whocc.de/?uid=20c71afcb419f260c6afd10b684768f5&id=home.

49 Ibid., 21.

50 Ibid., 29.

51 Ibid., 47.

52 Ibid., 48–49.

53 Ibid., 18.

54 Alasdair Glennie and Jennifer Newton, "Before She Had a Beard: See the amazing transformation of Conchita Wurst from male singer to Eurovision diva (and she's now going to rake in £25MILLION)," *Daily Mail*, May 12, 2014, http://www.dailymail.co.uk/tvshowbiz/article-2625866/Winner-whisker-Austrias-bearded-lady-conquers-Eurovision-Russias-rage.html.

CHAPTER 13 – GLOBAL GOVERNANCE AND NATIONAL SOVEREIGNTY

1 John Fonte, *Sovereignty or Submission: Will Americans Rule Themselves or Be Ruled by Others?* (New York: Encounter Books, 2011), 8.

2 Ibid., 36.

3 Ibid., 37.

4 The Declaration of Independence, U.S. National Archives, http://www.archives.gov/exhibits/charters/declaration_transcript.html.

5 United Nations, "We Can End Poverty: Millennium Development Goals and Beyond 2015," www.un.org/millenniumgoals/pdf/EN_MDG_backgrounder (accessed October 27, 2015).

6 Fonte, *Sovereignty or Submission*, 155.

7 Jürgen Habermas, *The Divided West*, trans. Ciaran Cronin (Cambridge: Polity Press, 2006), 179.

1   Lee A. Casey and David B. Rivkin, Jr., "The Dangerous Myth of Universal Jurisdiction," in *"A Country I Do Not Recognize": The Legal Assault on American Values*, ed. Robert H. Bork (Stanford, Calif.: Hoover Institution Press, 2005), 136, available at http://www.hoover.org/sites/default/files/uploads/documents/0817946020_135.pdf. I am indebted to Casey and Rivkin's work on both universal jurisdiction and the ICC.

2   Ibid., 142.

3   Ibid., 154.

4   Ibid., 153–56.

5   Ibid., 158.

6   Ian Black and Ewen MacAskill, "US Threatens Nato Boycott over Belgian War Crimes Law," *Guardian*, June 13, 2003, http://www.theguardian.com/world/2003/jun/13/nato.warcrimes.

7   See Thomas Sowell, *The Quest for Cosmic Justice* (New York: Touchstone, 1999).

8   Casey and Rivkin, "The Dangerous Myth of Universal Jurisdiction," 173.

9   For a full definition of "war crimes" see the Rome Statute of the International Criminal Court, Article 8, http://www.icc-cpi.int/nr/rdonlyres/ea9aeff7-5752-4f84-be94-0a655eb30e16/0/rome_statute_english.pdf.

10 Caroline Fehl, *Living with a Reluctant Hegemon: Explaining European Responses to US Unilateralism* (Oxford: Oxford University Press, 2012), 103.

11 "Statement by US President Bill Clinton, authorizing the US signing of the Rome Statute of the International Criminal Court," December 31, 2000, http://www.iccnow.org/documents/USClintonSigning31Dec00.pdf.

12 Fehl, *Living with a Reluctant Hegemon*, 102.

13 Ibid.

14 Dahr Jamail, "International Lawyers Seek Justice for Iraqis," Truthout, April 19, 2014, http://www.truth-out.org/news/item/23175-international-lawyers-seek-justice-for-iraqis.

15 Ibid.

16 ICC, "Prosecutor of the International Criminal Court, Fatou Bensouda, Re-opens the Preliminary Examination of the Situation in Iraq," May 13, 2014, http://www.icc-cpi.int/en_menus/icc/structure%20of%20the%20court/office%20of%20the%20prosecutor/reports%20and%20statements/statement/Pages/otp-statement-iraq-13-05-2014.aspx.

17 ICC, "The Prosecutor of the International Criminal Court, Fatou Bensouda, Opens a Preliminary Examination of the Situation in Palestine," January 16, 2015, http://www.icc-cpi.int/en_menus/icc/press%20and%20media/press%20releases/Pages/pr1083.aspx.

18 Thomas Escritt and Anthony Deutsch, "ICC Opens Investigation into Israeli-Palestinian Conflict," Reuters, January 16, 2015, http://www.reuters.com/article/2015/01/16/us-icc-palestinians-examination-idUSKBN0KP1PR20150116.

19 Casey and Rivkin, "The Dangerous Myth of Universal Jurisdiction," 178–79.

20 Ibid., 179.

21 Ibid., 182.

CHAPTER 15 – BINDING THE LEVIATHAN IN ITS WAR ON TERROR

1 Jean-Marie Colombani, "Nous sommes tous Américains," *Le Monde*, May 23,2007, http://www.lemonde.fr/idees/article/2007/05/23/nous-sommes-tous-americains_913706_3232.html#cMyxhomqdrP8BWCM.99.

2 U.S. Department of State, Office of the Coordinator for Counterterrorism, "Europe Overview: Patterns of Global Terrorism," May 21, 2002, http://www.state.gov/j/ct/rls/crt/2001/html/10240.htm.

3 Ibid.

4 European Council, *Conclusions and Plan of Action of the Extraordinary European Council Meeting on 21 September 2001*, https://www.consilium.europa.eu/uedocs/cms_data/docs/pressdata/en/ec/140.en.pdf.

5 The Patriot Resource, "Report on the Extraordinary European Council of September 21, 2001," October 3, 2001, http://www.patriotresource.com/wtc/intl/oct/0103/eu.html.

6 Nicole Fontaine, President of the European Parliament, speech at the opening session of the Laeken European Council, December 14, 2001, CVCE, http://www.cvce.eu/content/publication/2005/4/28/e8f4aa41-afe5-4f1d-9f49-99bd05111aef/publishable_en.pdf.

7 European Council, *Presidency Conclusions, European Council Meeting in Laeken, 14 and 15 December 2001*, Annexes, 19–26, https://www.consilium.europa.eu/uedocs/cms_data/docs/pressdata/en/ec/68827.pdf.

8 European Delegation to the United Nations, "EU Response to September 11," New York, June 3, 2002, http://eu-un.europa.eu/articles/en/article_1425_en.htm.

9 Ibid. Emphasis in the original.

10 Ibid.

11 David Miller, "World Opinion Opposes," Global Policy Forum, November 21, 2001, https://www.globalpolicy.org/component/content/article/154/26553.html.

12 See Kirsty Hughes, "After Iraq: Can Europe Overcome Its Divisions?" *Global Dialogue* 5:3 (2003), http://www.worlddialogue.org/content.php?id=268.

13 "Un cahier spécial sur l'Europe: Conférence de presse de M. Jacques Chirac," *Le Monde Diplomatique*, February 12, 2004, http://www.monde-diplomatique.fr/cahier/europe/conf-chirac.

14 Philip Gourevitch, "The Congo Test," *New Yorker*, June 2, 2003, http://www.newyorker.com/magazine/2003/06/02/the-congo-test.

15 "Retour sur: le discours de Dominique de Villepin, ONU 2003," *Perspectives Geopolitiques*, February 28, 2011, http://geopolitique.over-blog.fr/article-retour-sur-le-discours-de-dominique-de-villepin-onu-2003-68291445.html. Translated from the French by Todd Huizinga.

16 Jürgen Habermas, *The Divided West*, trans. Ciaran Cronin (Cambridge: Polity Press, 2006), 39.

17 Ibid., 42.

18 Ibid., 149.

19 Statement by President Bush to the United Nations General Assembly, New York, September 12, 2002, http://www.un.org/webcast/ga/57/statements/020912usaE.htm.

20 Habermas, *The Divided West*, 148.

21 "Transcript of President Bush's Remarks," NPR, September 6, 2006, http://www.npr.org/templates/story/story.php?storyId=5777480.

22 Dick Marty, "Alleged Secret Detentions and Unlawful Inter-State Transfers Involving Council of Europe Member States," Council of Europe, June 7, 2006, 4, http://assembly.coe.int/committeedocs/2006/20060606_ejdoc162006partii-final.pdf. Marty, a Swiss politician, is not a citizen of the EU. Also, as mentioned before, the Council of Europe is not a part of the EU. Nevertheless, Marty's views encapsulate very well the supranationalist view on Guantanamo that is widespread in the EU.

CHAPTER 16 – POST-CHRISTIAN EUROPE AND RELIGION IN AMERICA

1 Robert Manchin, "Religion in Europe: Trust Not Filling the Pews," Gallup, September 21, 2004, http://www.gallup.com/poll/13117/religion-europe-trust-filling-pews.aspx.

2 Frank Newport, "In U.S., Four in 10 Report Attending Church in Last Week," Gallup, December 24, 2013, http://www.gallup.com/poll/166613/four-report-attending-church-last-week.aspx.

3 Pew Research Center, Global Attitudes Survey, Topline 2011–2013 findings, "Q178 How important is religion in your life – very important, somewhat important, not too important, or not at all important?" http://www.pewglobal.org/files/2015/03/Religion-and-GDP-Topline.pdf.

4 Alexander Hamilton, *Federalist* 15, in *The Federalist Papers*, ed. Clinton Rossiter (New York: Penguin Putnam, 1961), 78.

5 James Madison, *Federalist* 41, in ibid., 223–24. Emphasis in the original.

6 Madison, *Federalist* 47, in ibid., 269.

7 United Nations, "We Can End Poverty: Millennium Development Goals and Beyond 2015," http://www.un.org/millenniumgoals/pdf/EN_MDG_backgrounder (accessed October 27, 2015).

8 European Commission, *A Decent Life for All: From Vision to Collective Action*, Communication from the Commission to the European Parliament, the Council, the European Economic and Social Committee and the Committee of the Regions (June 2, 2014), http://eur-lex.europa.eu/resource.html?uri=cellar:441ba0c0-eb02-11e3-8cd4-01aa75ed71a1.0001.02/DOC_1&format=PDF.

9 Council of the European Union, *Council Conclusions on a Transformative Post-2015 Agenda* (December 16, 2014), 2, http://italia2014.eu/media/4287/council-conclusions-on-a-transformative-post-2015-agenda.pdf.

10 Marguerite A. Peeters, "The New Global Ethic: Challenges for the Church,"

Pontifical Council for the Laity: Women: Philosophy, 84, http://www.laici.
va/content/dam/laici/documenti/donna/filosofia/english/new-global-
ethic-challenges-for-the-church.pdf (accessed June 17, 2015).

CHAPTER 17 – THE PRICE OF THE EURO

1   "David Cameron's EU Speech in Full," *Telegraph*, January 23, 2013, http://
www.telegraph.co.uk/news/worldnews/europe/eu/9820230/David-
Camerons-EU-speech-in-full.html.

2   Ibid.

3   Laurence Robertson, MP, "Why I'm Campaigning for an EU Referendum –
and to Come Out," http://www.laurencerobertsonmp.com/eureferendum.
html (accessed February 4, 2015).

4   Anoosh Chakellan, "Ed Balls: 'EU Exit Is the Biggest Risk to Our Economy
in the Next Decade,'" *New Statesman*, February 10, 2015, http://www.new
statesman.com/politics/2015/02/ed-balls-eu-exit-biggest-risk-our-economy-
next-decade.

5   Nikolaj Nielsen, "UK Demands for EU Treaty Change Are 'Mission Impossible,'" *EU Observer*, March 16, 2015, https://euobserver.com/political/
127997.

6   "European Solidarity Manifesto," January 24, 2013, http://www.european-
solidarity.eu/EuropeanSolidarityManifesto.pdf.

7   Hans-Olaf Henkel, *Die Euro-Lügner: Unsinnige Rettungspakete, vertuschte
Risiken – So werden wir getäuscht* (Munich: Wilhelm Heyne Verlag, 2013),
74–75.

8   Ibid., 116–29.

9   "That German Court Decision," *EU Observer*, February 14, 2014, https://
euobserver.com/news/123124.

10 Dr. Gunnar Beck, "The German Constitutional Court versus the EU: Self
Assertion in Theory and Submission in Practice – Euro Aid and Financial
Guarantees, Part 2," *EUtopia Law*, October 25, 2011, http://eutopialaw.com/
2011/10/25/the-german-constitutional-court-versus-the-eu-self-assertion-
in-theory-and-submission-in-practice-%E2%80%93-euro-aid-and-finan
cial-guarantees-part-2/.

11 "In Wahrheit hat das Verfassungsgericht den EuGH nur um eine
Meinungsäußerung gebeten und bleibt Herr des Verfahrens. Da es selbst
zu der Auffassung gekommen ist, dass schon die Ankündigung eines unbe-
grenzten Aufkaufs von Staatspapieren den Unionsverträgen widerspricht,
hat es nicht gefragt, ob der EuGH das genauso sieht, sondern nur, wie man
nach Meinung des EuGH das Aufkaufprogramm so modifizieren und
begrenzen könnte, dass es mit dem Unionsrecht kompatibel wird." Hans-
Werner Sinn, *Gefangen im Euro* (Munich: Redline Verlag, 2014), 82–83.
Translated from the German by Todd Huizinga.

12 "So oder so sind wir durch die nun offiziell festgestellte vertragswidrige
Machtanmaßung – das Gericht spricht von 'Machtusurpation' – der EZB
an einem Punkt von historischer Bedeutung für die Entwicklung der
Bundesrepublik Deutschand angekommen. Erstmals wird das deutsche

Verfassungsgericht den eingeschlagenen Integrationsweg stoppen und eine Richtungsänderung erzwingen." Ibid., 91. Translated from the German by Todd Huizinga.

13   Maximilian Steinbeis, "Nebeneinander statt gegeneinander: Das schwierige Verhältnis zwischen Europäischem Gerichtshof und Bundesverfassungsgericht," June 17, 2012, http://www.deutschlandfunk.de/nebeneinander-statt-gegeneinander.724.de.html?dram:article_id=209270 (accessed October 21, 2015).

14   "Ich bin aus der Partei AFD ausgetreten! Meine Presseerklärung: 'AFD wird mit Petry/Pretzell zu einer "NPD im Schafspelz"'!" Website of Hans-Olaf Henkel, www.hansolafhenkel.de. Translated from the German by Todd Huizinga.

15   "An den Euro glauben 2013 nur 38,4 Prozent." Henkel, *Die Euro-Lügner*, 198.

16   "Greek Elections: Outgoing Prime Minister Antonis Samaras Concedes Defeat," ABC, January 26, 2015, http://www.abc.net.au/news/2015-01-26/outgoing-greek-pm-concedes-defeat-in-elections-syriza/6045712.

17   For the statistics in this section, see Eurostat, "Unemployment Statistics: Main Statistical Findings: Recent developments in unemployment at a European and Member State level," http://ec.europa.eu/eurostat/statistics-explained/index.php/Unemployment_statistics#Recent_developments_in_unemployment_at_a_European_and_Member_State_level (accessed June 23, 2015).

18   "Italy's Debt Burden Now at Record High 132% of GDP," RT, March 13, 2015, http://rt.com/business/240497-italy-debt-GDP-ratio/.

19   Barry Eichengreen and Tim Hatton, "Interwar Unemployment in International Perspective," Institute for Research on Labor and Employment, University of California at Berkeley, January 4, 1988, 32, http://escholarship.org/uc/item/7bw188gk#page-1.

20   William K. Black, "Comparing Unemployment During the Great Depression and the Great Recession," *New Economic Perspectives*, April 5, 2013, http://neweconomicperspectives.org/2013/04/comparing-unemployment-during-the-great-depression-and-the-great-recession.html.

21   Christian Reiermann and Klaus Wiegrefe, "Chancellor Schroder's Legacy: Germany's Leading Role in Weakening the Euro," *Spiegel Online International*, July 16, 2012, http://www.spiegel.de/international/germany/chancellor-gerhard-schroeder-key-in-weakening-the-euro-stability-pact-a-844458.html; "European Union Grants France Two Year Deficit Extension," BBC, March 10, 2015, http://www.bbc.com/news/business-31815975; Jan Strupczewski and Ingrid Melander, "Update 1 – EU Gives France Third Extension to Cut Its Budget Deficit," Reuters, March 10, 2015, http://www.reuters.com/article/2015/03/10/eu-france-deficit-idUSL5N0WC2LY20150310.

22   Council of the European Union, *The Economic and Monetary Union: Stronger Economies for a Stronger Union* (2014), 12–13, http://www.consilium.europa.eu/en/workarea/downloadasset.aspx?id=40802190815.

23 Ibid., 14–15.

24 Ibid., 15.

25 Ibid., 17.

26 Honor Mahony, "Banking Union Faces Legal Challenge in Germany," *EU Observer*, July 28, 2014, https://euobserver.com/economic/125117.

27 Council of the European Union, *The Economic and Monetary Union*, 19.

28 Ross Douthat, "Conspiracies, Coups, and Currencies," *New York Times*, November 19, 2011, http://www.nytimes.com/2011/11/20/opinion/sunday/douthat-conspiracies-coups-and-currencies.html.

29 "'If the Euro Fails, Europe Fails': Merkel Says EU Must Be Bound Closer Together," *Spiegel Online International*, September 7, 2011, http://www.spiegel.de/international/germany/if-the-euro-fails-europe-fails-merkel-says-eu-must-be-bound-closer-together-a-784953.html.

30 Stephan Faris, "Regime Change in Europe: Do Greece and Italy Amount to a Bankers' Coup?" *Time*, November 11, 2011, http://content.time.com/time/printout/0,8816,2099350,00.html#.

31 Jeff Black and Jana Randow, "Draghi Says ECB Will Do What's Needed to Preserve Euro: Economy," *Bloomberg Business*, July 26, 2012, http://www.bloomberg.com/news/articles/2012-07-26/draghi-says-ecb-to-do-whatever-needed-as-yields-threaten-europe.

32 "Als viel problematischer für die Zukunft Europas könnte sich erweisen, daß sich der Rat der EZB, der ohne demokratische Kontrolle und in vollständiger Unabhängigkeit über erhebliche Teile des Vermögens der Europäer verfügen kann, in der Krise als der wahre Hegemon Europas etabliert hat." Hans-Werner Sinn, *Gefangen im Euro* (Munich: Redline Verlag, 2014), 107.

33 "Der Rat der EZB wurde zu Aktionen ermächtigt – oder hat sich selbst dazu ermächtigt – die weit über ein geldpolitisches Mandat hinausgehen und die reale Struktur Europas maßgeblich verändern werden." Ibid., 107.

CHAPTER 18 – DEMOGRAPHICS AND ISLAM: THE CHALLENGES FOR EUROPE'S FUTURE

1 The Eurasian "stans," Tajikistan, Kyrgyzstan, Kazakhstan and Turkmenistan, are the exceptions; they have 2014 estimated TFRs of 2.1 or above. Central Intelligence Agency, *The World Factbook*, Country Comparison: Total Fertility Rate, https://www.cia.gov/library/publications/the-world-factbook/rankorder/2127rank.html (accessed June 23, 2015).

2 Suzanne Daley and Nicholas Kulish, "Germany Fights Population Drop," *New York Times*, August 13, 2013, http://www.nytimes.com/2013/08/14/world/europe/germany-fights-population-drop.html?pagewanted=all&_r=1. The German census of 2011 was the first complete census since the reunification.

3 Pardee Center for International Futures, "Country Profile – France: Population Forecast for France," University of Denver, http://www.ifs.du.edu/ifs/frm_CountryProfile.aspx?Country=FR (accessed June 23, 2015).

4 Pardee Center for International Futures, "Country Profile – United

Kingdom: Population Forecast for the United Kingdom," University of Denver, http://www.ifs.du.edu/ifs/frm_CountryProfile.aspx?Country=GB (accessed June 23, 2015).

5   Pardee Center for International Futures, "Country Profile – Italy: Population Forecast for Italy," University of Denver, http://www.ifs.du.edu/ifs/frm_CountryProfile.aspx?Country=IT (accessed June 23, 2015).

6   Eurostat, "Population Projections 2008–2060: From 2015, Deaths Projected to Outnumber Births in the EU27," August 26, 2008, European Commission Press Release Database, http://europa.eu/rapid/press-release_STAT-08-119_en.htm.

7   Pew Research Center, "The Future of the Global Muslim Population – Region: Europe," January 27, 2011, http://www.pewforum.org/2011/01/27/future-of-the-global-muslim-population-regional-europe/.

8   Soeren Kern, "Brussels: The New Capital of Eurabia," Gatestone Institute, November 22, 2011, http://www.gatestoneinstitute.org/2602/brussels-eurabia.

9   Islam in Europe blog, "Muslim Population in European Cities," November 23, 2007, http://islamineurope.blogspot.com/2007/11/muslim-population-in-european-cities.html.

10 Christopher Caldwell, "The Rising Migrant Tide: What Merkel Wrought," *Weekly Standard*, October 26, 2015, 26.

11 Christopher Caldwell, *Reflections on the Revolution in Europe: Immigration, Islam and the West* (New York: Doubleday, 2009), 118.

12 Ibid., 119.

13 Bruno Waterfield, "Mohammed Is Most Popular Boy's Name in Four Biggest Dutch Cities," *Telegraph*, August 13, 2009, http://www.telegraph.co.uk/news/worldnews/europe/netherlands/6022588/Mohammed-is-most-popular-boys-name-in-four-biggest-Dutch-cities.html.

14 Soeren Kern, "Creeping Sharia Slides Over Britain," Gatestone Institute, November 11, 2010, http://www.gatestoneinstitute.org/1656/creeping-sharia-britain.

15 Caldwell, *Reflections on the Revolution in Europe*, 119.

16 Pew Research Center, "An Uncertain Road: Muslims and the Future of Europe," October 2005, 6, http://www.pewforum.org/files/2005/10/muslims-europe-2005.pdf.

17 Caldwell, *Reflections on the Revolution in Europe*, 122–24.

18 Ibid., 136.

19 Ibid., 222.

20 Ibid., 223.

21 Timothy Jones, "Constitutional Court Strikes Down Absolute Headscarf Ban," Deutsche Welle, March 13, 2015, http://www.dw.com/en/constitutional-court-strikes-down-absolute-headscarf-ban/a-18313377.

22 "Ik sta hier vanwege mijn woorden. Ik sta hier omdat ik sprak. Ik sprak, ik spreek en ik zal blijven spreken. Velen hebben gezien en gezwegen, maar niet Pim Fortuyn, niet Theo Van Gogh, niet ik. Ik moet spreken. Want Nederland wordt bedreigd door de islam. De islam is, zoals ik al vele

malen heb beargumenteerd, vooral een ideologie. Die ideologie is er een van haat, van vernietiging, van verovering. De islam – is mijn stellige overtuiging – bedreigt de Westerse normen en waarden, de vrijheid van meningsuiting, de gelijkheid van mannen en vrouwen, van hetero's en homo's, van gelovigen en ongelovigen.... De uitspraken die mij ten laste zijn gelegd, deed ik als politicus in het kader van het publieke maatschappelijke debat. Mijn uitspraken waren niet gericht tegen personen, maar tegen de islam en het proces van islamisering." "Laatste woord Geert Wilders, Proces Amsterdam, 1 juni 2011," Tweede Kamerfractie, June 1, 2011, http://www.pvv.nl/index.php/36-fj-related/geert-wilders/4375-laatste-woord-geert-wilders-proces-amsterdam-1-juni-2011.html. Translated from the Dutch by Todd Huizinga.

23 "Vrijheid en waarheid. Ik betaal er elke dag de prijs voor. Dag en nacht moet ik beschermd worden tegen mensen die mij willen doden. Ik klaag daar niet over; het is mijn eigen beslissing om te spreken. Maar niet diegenen die mij en andere critici van de islam bedreigen staan hier vandaag terecht. Ik sta hier terecht. En daar klaag ik wel over." Ibid. Translated from the Dutch by Todd Huizinga.

24 "Ik zet niet aan tot haat. Ik zet niet aan tot discriminatie. Maar ik verdedig de eigenheid, de identiteit, de cultuur en ja de vrijheid van Nederland. Dát is de waarheid. Daarom sta ik hier. Daarom spreek ik." Ibid. Emphasis in the original. Translated from the Dutch by Todd Huizinga.

25 Paul Coleman, *Censored: How European "Hate Speech" Laws Are Threatening Freedom of Speech* (Vienna: Kairos Publications, 2012), 55–56.

26 Eurostat, "Population Projections 2008–2060."

27 Randall Hansen and Joshua C. Gordon, "Deficits, Democracy, and Demographics: Europe's Three Crises," *West European Politics* 37:6 (2014), Abstract, http://www.tandfonline.com/doi/full/10.1080/01402382.2014.929336.

28 "Speech from the Throne 2013," Het Koninklijk Huis (Royal House of the Netherlands), September 17, 2013, http://www.koninklijkhuis.nl/globale-paginas/taalrubrieken/english/speeches/speeches-from-the-throne/speech-from-the-throne-2013/ (accessed February 16, 2015).

29 Wharton School, "Reforming the European Welfare State," University of Pennsylvania, March 6, 2013, http://knowledge.wharton.upenn.edu/article/reforming-the-european-welfare-state/.

30 OECD.Stat, "Social Expenditure – Aggregated Data," https://stats.oecd.org/Index.aspx?DataSetCode=SOCX_AGG (accessed October 2015).

31 Chriss Street, "Europe Declares the Welfare State Dead," *American Thinker*, September 24, 2013, http://www.americanthinker.com/articles/2013/09/europe_declares_the_welfare_state_dead.html.

32 Paul Laity, "Uncomfortable Truths," *Guardian*, May 17, 2008, http://www.theguardian.com/books/2008/may/17/politics1.

33 Samuel Gregg, *Becoming Europe: Economic Decline, Culture, and How America Can Avoid a European Future* (New York: Encounter Books, 2013), 92.

34 George Friedman, "Population Decline and the Great Economic Reversal,"

Geopolitical Weekly, February 17, 2015, https://www.stratfor.com/weekly/population-decline-and-great-economic-reversal?mc_cid=a0f058f040&mc_eid=52cd73ae36.

35 Roger Bootle, "Margaret Thatcher: The Economic Achievements and Legacy of Thatcherism," *Telegraph*, April 8, 2013, http://www.telegraph.co.uk/news/politics/margaret-thatcher/9979362/Margaret-Thatcher-the-economic-achievements-and-legacy-of-Thatcherism.html.

36 Johnny Munkhammar, "The Swedish Model," *Wall Street Journal*, January 26, 2011, http://www.wsj.com/articles/SB10001424052748704698004576104023432243468; Christian Dustmann, et al., "From Sick Man of Europe to Economic Superstar: Germany's Resurgent Economy," *Journal of Economic Perspectives* 28:1 (2014), 167–88, http://www.ucl.ac.uk/~uctpb21/Cpapers/jep_germany_competitiveness.pdf.

CHAPTER 19 – THE CRISIS OF DEMOCRACY IN EUROPE

1 European Parliament, "Results of the 2014 European Elections," July 1, 2014, http://www.europarl.europa.eu/elections2014-results/en/election-results-2014.html. Most of the results mentioned in this chapter come from this link.

2 This analysis does not include Croatia, the newest member state, which did not participate in the 2009 elections and joined the EU less than a year before the 2014 elections.

3 Feargal McGuinness et al., "UK Election Statistics: 1918–2012," House of Commons Library, August 7, 2012, http://researchbriefings.parliament.uk/ResearchBriefing/Summary/RP12-43.

4 Anna Holligan, "Dutch Politician Wilders Accused of Discrimination," BBC, March 20, 2014, http://www.bbc.com/news/world-europe-26667788.

5 Tuomas Iso-Markku, "Euroscepticism vs. Political Pragmatism: The Finns Party Tones Down Its Criticism of the EU," EPIN–European Policy Institutes Network, Commentary 19 (June 26, 2014), available at http://www.epin.org/new/pubs.

6 Remarks by President Herman Van Rompuy following the informal dinner of Heads of State or Government, European Council, May 27, 2014, http://www.consilium.europa.eu/en/press/press-releases/2014/05/pdf/remarks-by-president-herman-van-rompuy-following-the-informal-dinner-of-heads-of-state-or-government/.

EPILOGUE – WILL AMERICA FOLLOW THE EU INTO THE SOFT UTOPIA?

1 "How GOP Candidates Get Europe Wrong," CBS News, March 25, 2012, http://www.cbsnews.com/news/how-gop-candidates-get-europe-wrong/.

2 "2012 Presidential Elections: Is Mitt Romney's Europe-Bashing a Campaign Strategy?" *TransAtlantic Magazine*, June 26, 2012, http://transatlantic-magazine.com/2012-presidential-elections-america-and-europe-is-mitt-romneys-europe-bashing-a-campaign-strategy/.

3 Mathilde Bonneau, "The EU in the Republican Electoral Debate," *Nouvelle Europe*, March 23, 2012, http://www.nouvelle-europe.eu/node/1457.

4   Samuel Gregg, *Becoming Europe: Economic Decline, Culture, and How America Can Avoid a European Future* (New York: Encounter Books, 2013), 7.

5   Ibid., 8.

6   William B. Allen, "Moral Frontiers: American National Character and the Future of Liberty," speech at the Acton Institute, Grand Rapids, Michigan, December 2, 2014, https://www.youtube.com/watch?v=oBFoxDaMPSg.

7   Center for American Progress, "Progressive Traditions," https://www.americanprogress.org/series/progressive-traditions/view/ (accessed June 24, 2015).

8   "About the Center for American Progress: Our Mission," https://www.americanprogress.org/about/mission/ (accessed June 24, 2015).

9   Allen, "Moral Frontiers," unpublished manuscript of the Acton Institute speech, 6.

10 Ibid.

11 Ibid., 8–9.

12 Mao Zedong on "War and Peace," quoted at the Marxist Internet Archive, https://www.marxists.org/reference/archive/mao/works/red-book/ch05 .htm (accessed June 24, 2015).

13 Ryan Grim and Matt Sledge, "Mitt Romney Video: Barack Obama Voters 'Dependent on Government' (Updated)," *Huffington Post*, September 17, 2012, updated November 29, 2012, http://www.huffingtonpost.com/2012/ 09/17/mitt-romney-video_n_1829455.html.

14 Charles Murray, *Coming Apart: The State of White America, 1960–2010* (New York: Crown Forum, 2012), 281. Emphasis in the original.

15 Ibid., 282.

16 Ibid., 283–84.

17 Pew Research Center, Religion and Public Life "'Nones' on the Rise," October 9, 2012, http://www.pewforum.org/2012/10/09/nones-on-the-rise/.

18 Michael Hout, Claude S. Fischer and Mark A. Chaves, "More Americans Have No Religious Preference: Key Finding from the 2012 General Social Survey," Institute for the Study of Societal Issues, University of California at Berkeley, March 7, 2013, http://issi.berkeley.edu/sites/default/files/shared/ docs/Hout%20et%20al_No%20Relig%20Pref%202012_Release%20Mar%20 2013.pdf.

19 Cheryl K. Chumley, "U.S. Embassy in Madrid Flies Rainbow-Colored Flag in Honor of LGBT Day," *Washington Times*, May 22, 2014, http://www.washingtontimes.com/news/2014/may/22/us-embassy-madrid-flew-rain bow-colored-flag-honor-/#ixzz3RGlEoXWv.

20 Paul Alster, "Gay Pride Flag Hoisted above US Embassy in Israel," Fox News, June 14, 2014, http://www.foxnews.com/world/2014/06/14/gay-pride-flag-hoisted-above-us-embassy-in-israel/.

21 S. Noble, "Gay USA, Here Come the Flags," *Independent Sentinel*, June 18, 2014, http://www.independentsentinel.com/gay-usa-here-come-the-flags/.

22 "Obama Uses Embassies to Push for LGBT Rights Abroad," *Guardian*, June 28, 2014, http://www.theguardian.com/world/2014/jun/28/obama-gay-rights-abroad-embassies-activism.

23 Hillary Rodham Clinton, Secretary of State, "Remarks in Recognition of International Human Rights Day," U.S. Department of State, December 6, 2011, http://www.state.gov/secretary/20092013clinton/rm/2011/12/178368.htm.

24 Ibid.

25 The White House, Office of the Press Secretary, "Advancing Rights of LGBT People Globally," Fact Sheet, December 6, 2011, http://iipdigital.usembassy.gov/st/english/texttrans/2011/12/20111206171357su0.5089381.html#ixzz3RM1I8S7G.

26 Mark Steyn, *America Alone: The End of the World as We Know It* (Washington, D.C.: Regnery Publishing, 2006), xv–xvi.

27 Ibid., xx.

28 Ibid., xxiii.

29 Ibid., xiii.

30 See e.g. Anne-Marie Slaughter, *A New World Order* (Princeton, N.J.: Princeton University Press, 2004).

31 John Fonte, *Sovereignty or Submission: Will Americans Rule Themselves or Be Ruled by Others?* (New York: Encounter Books, 2011), 344–45.

32 Ibid., 346.

33 Vladimir Ilyich Lenin, "What Is to Be Done?" trans. Joe Fineberg and George Hanna (Moscow: Foreign Languages Publishing House, 1961), available at https://www.marxists.org/archive/lenin/works/1901/witbd/.

34 Fonte, *Sovereignty or Submission*, 345.

INDEX

First American edition published in 2016 by Encounter Books,
an activity of Encounter for Culture and Education, Inc.,
a nonprofit, tax exempt corporation.
Encounter Books website address: www.encounterbooks.com

Manufactured in the United States and printed on
acid-free paper. The paper used in this publication meets
the minimum requirements of ANSI/NISO Z39.48–1992
(R 1997) (*Permanence of Paper*).

FIRST AMERICAN EDITION

LIBRARY OF CONGRESS CATALOGING-IN-PUBLICATION DATA

Names: Huizinga, Todd, author.
Title: The new totalitarian temptation : global governance and the crisis of
democracy in Europe / by Todd Huizinga.
Description: New York : Encounter Books, [2016] | Includes bibliographical
references and index.
Identifiers: LCCN 2015020473| ISBN 9781594037894 (hardcover : alk. paper) |
ISBN 9781594037900 (ebook)
Subjects: LCSH: European Union. | Democracy – European Union coun-
tries. |Supranationalism – European Union countries.
Classification: LCC JN30 .H84 2016 | DDC 341.242/2 – dc23
LC record available at http://lccn.loc.gov/2015020473

A NOTE ON THE TYPE

THE NEW TOTALITARIAN TEMPTATION *has been set in Jonathan Hoefler's Mercury types. Originally created for the* New Times *newspaper chain and later adapted for general informational typography, the Mercury types were drawn in four grades intended to be used under variable printing conditions – that is, to compensate for less-than-optimal presswork or for regional differences in paper stock and plant conditions. The result was a family of types that were optimized to print well in a vast number of sizes and formats. In books, Mercury makes a no-nonsense impression, crisp and open, direct and highly readable, yet possessed of real style and personality.* ♦♦♦ *The display type is Joanna Sans Nova, Terrance Weinzier's contemporary synthesis of Eric Gill's typographic work and an outgrowth of his work in Monotype's recent reissue of Gill's original designs.*

DESIGN & COMPOSITION BY CARL W. SCARBROUGH